AF631355

SPORTS ADMINISTRATION

SPORTS ADMINISTRATION

Amitabh Suri

CRESCENT
PUBLISHING CORPORATION

[The responsibility for the facts stated, conclusions reached and plagiarism, if any, in this book is entirely that of the Author. And the Publisher bears no responsibility for them, whatsoever.]

Sports Administration

© Reserved

First Published : 2009

ISBN 978-81-8342-104-1

Published by :

CRESCENT PUBLISHING CORPORATION
4831/24, Prahlad Street,
Ansari Road, Darya Ganj,
New Delhi - 110002
Ph. : 23272541, 23257835
Fax : 91- 011- 23257835
e-mail : campusbooks@hotmail.com

Printed at :

Roshan Offset Printers
Delhi

Preface

Sports today are not just an effective medium of entertainment and recreation, but comprise a field which is a recognised profession, with its own rigmarole. They are no longer haphazardly organised activities which are restricted to the elite or for leisure, but are part of an enterprise which has its complex set of rules and measurements, scoring, training for the game, sports agents, coaches managers, and of course, the athletes. The stakes and expectations from a sporting game, be it local international are always high, and with extensive media coverage, these do not show any signs of relenting.

This book in the encylopaedia of sports has been designed to cater to the needs of those who already are or contemplating a career in the field of sports administration. With the kind and amount of financial aid that goes into the management of sporting events, the spectator and audience expectation, and the media and publicity coverage, a sports administrator needs to have an understanding of not just business, but has to combine his managerial acumen with the insight of a sportsperson. The book is a comprehensive manual which takes an in-depth look into the management of sport, right form individual athletes to teams, from sporting venues to media coverage, making an extensive exploration of the issues which comprise administration.

It takes a pragmatic approach to the topic, taking into account current practices, trends and developments in the field. Guiding readers on effective sports administration, it also gives experience-based insight, which can prove highly resourceful.

It is hoped that the erudition and insight of the book proves to be of great use to readers.

Amitabh Suri

Contents

1

Sports Motivation

There are two types of motivation: intrinsic and extrinsic. Intrinsic motivation is found in an individual who participates in an activity without any outside rewards. It usually leads to experiencing the most pleasure. External motivation relies on outside influences to persuade an individual to participate in an activity. When external motivation is removed, the individual often ceases participation in the activity. The level of happiness that is derived from extrinsic motivation is usually not as great as that from intrinsic motivation.

Motivational Climate, Need Satisfaction and Indices of Well-being in Team Sports

Perceived Motivational Climate, Need Satisfaction and Indices of Well-being in Team Sports: A Longitudinal Perspective, is a research study of Michael Reinboth (Telemark University College, Norway) and Joan L. Duba (The University of Birmingham, UK). The purpose of this stdy was to examine the relationship between changes in perceptions of the motivational climate to changes in athletes' need satisfaction and indices of psychological and physical well-being over the course of a competitive sport season.

Specifically, the motivational attributes of the sporting environment are presumed to play a vital role in influencing potential psychological, emotional, and physical effects (both positive and negative) of sport involvement. Although well-being has been conceptualised in different ways, most definitions emphasise positive psychological states as opposed to the absence of negative cognitions and feelings. Furthermore, according to Caspersen, Powell, and Merritt, well-being is one of the two elements of quality of life and is concerned with the subjective internal states of the individual, or the way in which the individual feels physically and mentally. In their definition of health, the World Health Organization recognises that mental well-being plays an all-important rote in health measurements as they state that health incorporates "a state of complete physical, mental, and social well-being not merely the absence of disease".

One theory well suited to study the potential implications of social environmental factors on wellbeing in sport is the recently formalized sub-theory of self-determination theory (SDT), termed basic needs theory (BNT). BNT assumes three needs to be fundamental for the nurturance and growth of the human psyche: namely the psychological needs for autonomy, competence, and relatedness. The satisfaction of the need for autonomy involves the experience of choice and the feeling that one is the initiator of one's own actions, but also that one's actions are in accordance with one's values as opposed to being controlled by external forces or internal pressures. The satisfaction of the need for competence is fulfilled by the experience that one can effectively bring about desired effects and outcomes. Satisfaction of the relatedness need pertains to feelings that one is securely connected to and understood by others. According to BNT, variations in need satisfaction will directly predict variations in indices of psychological and physical well-being.

Applied to the domain of sport, satisfaction of athletes' needs for autonomy, competence, and relatedness via their sport environment should lead to higher levels of well being. To the extent that the needs are suppressed in the sport setting, inverse relationships are hypothesised. What is particularly attractive about the concept of need satisfaction is that it allows researchers to identify the environmental conditions under which the three needs could be satisfied and, in turn, promote well being.

One important social environmental factor assumed to nurture the fundamental needs is the motivational climate created by the coach. Coaches design practice sessions, group athletes, give recognition, evaluate performance, share their authority and shape the sport setting. In doing so, they create a motivational climate which can have an important impact on an athlete's motivation. Indeed, past work has suggested that the coach has a major influence on athletes' stress responses, reported enjoyment and feelings of self-efficacy in sport settings.

Grounded in the achievement goal framework, more or less ego-involving (or performance) and/or task-involving (or mastery) climates are hypothesized to exist and sport research has supported this supposition. An ego-involving climate, is characterized by interpersonal competition, social comparison and public evaluation. In contrast, an emphasis placed on task mastery, learning, effort exertion and improvement distinguishes a task-involving climate.

The motivational climate is assumed to promote the differential occurrences of task or ego states of involvement within the person. When task-involved, a person is trying to demonstrate mastery of the task rather than being focused on showing normatively high ability.

In this case perceived ability is self-referenced and the person feels competent when realizing learning, personal improvement and mastering a skill with high effort expenditure. In contrast, when ego-involved, improvement, understanding and learning are seen more as a means to an end rather than outcomes in their own right.

The individual in a more ego-involving context will try to demonstrate superiority and is therefore concerned about how able she or he is compared to others. Recent work has given insight into the underlying dimensions comprising task- and ego-involving climates in sport. In the majority of this research, the Perceived Motivational Climate in Sport Questionnaire-2 (PMCSQ-2) has been used to assess athletes' perceptions of the goal perspective(s) emphasised by the coach.

In a perceived task-involving sport environment, achievement is viewed in a self-referenced manner, which is considered to be more within the individual's control. Being in control of one's actions also increases the chances of feeling like the originator of one's own behaviour and, thus, would be expected to foster athletes' satisfaction of the need for autonomy. In contrast, a strong ego-involving climate, is assumed to lead athletes to focus on outcomes more outside their personal control. Therefore, perceptions of an ego-involving climate are expected to thwart the satisfaction of the need for autonomy.

According to Duda and colleagues, a task-involving environmental focus should foster perceptions of competence, because the self-referenced criteria underlying competence judgments and ensuing feelings of success are more controllable and readily achievable compared to normative-based criteria (e.g. winning). Also, the emphasis in such environments is on developing competence rather than protecting one's ability. In contrast, in an ego involving climate, perceptions of competence are held to be more fragile because competence is construed on the basis of what others have done/are doing and there is greater preoccupation with the adequacy of one's ability.

With respect to the need for relatedness, the heightened inter-individual comparison and rivalry among athletes assumed to mark an ego-involving sporting atmosphere should undermine the sense that one is closely connected with others. In contrast, an emphasis on co-operation is fundamental to a taskinvolving environment. Thus, we would assume that a more task-involving climate should foster `feelings of belongingness' and promote the satisfaction of the need for relatedness. In support of these assumptions, a study by Chi and Lu among intercollegiate basketball teams, found a moderate positive link between perceptions of a task-involving climate and reported task cohesion. A negative relationship emerged between perceptions of an egoinvolving climate and task, as well as social cohesion.

Previous research in the physical domain has supported the aforementioned hypothesised assumptions, showing moderate to strong positive links between perceptions of a task-involving motivational climate and the satisfaction of the basic need for autonomy, competence, and relatedness. In contrast, a rather weak negative link has been found between perceptions of an ego-involving climate and the need for autonomy and relatedness.

Limited research has tested the relationship between need satisfaction and well-being in the physical domain. In a study by Ntoumanis in a PE setting, students' perceptions of competence and relatedness were positively related to intrinsic motivation which in turn was negatively related to boredom. Recently, a diary-based study by Gagne, Ryan, and Bargman found that daily need satisfaction predicted increases in daily well-being (e.g. subjective vitality and self-esteem) among young female gymnasts in the US. Similar results have also been found by Pensgaard and Duda among a sample of adolescent Norwegian elite athletes.

A cross-sectional study by Reinboth et al. involving British adolescent athletes found that features in the perceived coach-created sport environment (i.e. autonomy support, focus on improvement, and social support) were positively linked to the three basic needs (i.e. autonomy, competence, and relatedness, respectively), which in turn predicted indices of well/ill-being (e.g. subjective vitality and physical symptoms). Overall, there is a paucity of investigations that have examined the influence of perceptions of the motivational climate over time in the athletic setting. To the best of our knowledge, no study has attempted to test the theoretically assumed motivational sequence between the social environment, need satisfaction and well-being in a longitudinal design. Thus, it is not clear whether changes in coaching emphasis over time on ego-or task-involving structures may be linked to changes in athletes' reported satisfaction of the basic needs which in turn influences theirs well-being in sport. In the present study, they examined the links between perceptions of the motivational climate to need satisfaction and athletes' reported subjective vitality and physical symptoms over the course of a competitive season.

Despite the significance to the human experience and its prevalence in the literature, autonomy is a construct lacking theoretical homogeneity as well as a common operational definition. Even within the SDT framework, there are inconsistencies in its measurement. To date, research assessing the need for autonomy has measured this as a one-dimensional theoretical concept.

However, Reeve (2002)' argues that the experience of autonomy is mufti-faceted, and that it involves both the sense of realistic choice and decision-making, as well as the feeling of an internal perceived locus of causality (IPLOC) (e.g. feeling that one is the cause of ones' actions). In this study, they examined two aspects of the need `for autonomy (choice and IPLOC) to indices of well-being. In previous research, the need for relatedness in sport has only been assessed with regards to other members of the team. However, athletes also vary in the degree to which they feel connected to their coach and this relationship is meaningful to the quality of their sport experience. In the present study, relatedness was measured specific to the coach as well as with reference to one's team members.

In sum, the major purpose of the present study was to investigate whether changes in perceptions of the coach-created perceived motivational climate would be related to changes in athletes' satisfaction of the basic needs for autonomy (in terms of choice and IPLOC), competence and relatedness (with respect to team members and the coach) and indices of psychological and physical well-being over the course of 5 months during a competitive season. The researchers hypothesized that perceptions of a task-involving coaching emphasis over the course of the season would be a positive predictor of changes in the satisfaction of the athletes' needs for autonomy, competence and relatedness across the season.

In contrast, it was predicted that the more egoinvolving the climate was perceived to be, the less the needs would be satisfied. Need satisfaction in sport was, in turn, hypothesised to positively predict indices of well-being (i.e. subjective vitality) in sport and to negatively predict indices of physical ill-being (i.e. reported physical symptoms) over the course of the season. Based on the assumptions by Deci and Ryan that the IPLOC aspect of autonomy plays a more central role with regards to subjective well-being, the IPLOC aspect of autonomy to be a stronger predictor of indices of psychological well/ ill-being compared to the choice/ decision-making aspect. It was hypothesised that the two relatedness variables (e.g. coach or team-mates) would both emerge as positive predictors of indices of well-being and negative predictors of indices of physical ill-being. Based upon the predictions of SDT, there are three needs would emerge as mediators of the relationship between the perceived motivational climate engineered by the coach and indices of athletes' psychological and physical well-being.

Method

One hundred and twenty-eight (89 females, 39 males; M age = 19.56; SD=1.83) athletes from a large British university participated in this study. The present study included two data collections over the course of 5 months. Two hundred and fifty-seven athletes took part in the first data collection. An attrition rate of 48% at Time 2 was predominantly due to the absence from practice of the athletes in question on the day of the data collection. Using dummy-coding (stay vs. dropout) to test for possible differences among those athletes who took part in the second data collection (Time 2) and those who did not, they conducted a one-way MANOVA with age, type of sport, the perceived motivational climate, need satisfaction and well-being variables as dependent variables. No significant differences emerged F(11, 237) =1.54, p>0.10. In terms of ethnic background, the sample was primarily white English (97%). On average, the athletes taking part in this study had been participating in their sport for five years or longer (SD =1.41). The participants represented a range of team sports including football (n = 11), rugby (n = 23), netball (n = 20), lacrosse (n= 10), and hockey (n = 64).

Convenient meeting dates and times were then arranged with the coaches. A mufti-section questionnaire was administered by a research assistant either before or after a normal practice in a team clubhouse or a classroom. Two versions of the questionnaire (i.e. each with the measurement instruments ordered differently) were administered at each data collection to control for any potential order effects. At all meetings, instructions on how to fill in the questionnaire were given, emphasising that responses should reflect athletes' own perceptions of the sport experience/environment, that there were no right or wrong answers, and that all responses were anonymous. The terminology was adjusted for each sport (i.e. we used football for football players and hockey for hockey players, etc.). The questionnaire required approximately 20 minutes to complete.

Because they wanted to investigate changes in the study variables, data was collected at two points in time. The first data collection (Time 1) was conducted relatively early (6-8 weeks) in the season. The second data collection (Time 2) was carried put approximately 6-8 weeks before the majority of the teams finished their season. Currently, there exist no formalised guidelines regarding how long it takes for the motivational climate or sense of relatedness to the coach, or other team-mates, to be established. According to some researchers, the perceived motivational climate is likely to be established within 2-6 weeks.

When asked how long they have been playing on their current team at Time 1, 75% of the players indicated that they had done so for 2 years or longer. When asked about how long they have had their current coach, 81% answered that they have had the same current coach for at least 1 year. Overall it seems that most of the players on the team have had some time to establish relationships with each other as well as the coach. Based on the aforementioned information, there is strong reason to believe that the athletes have had enough time to establish relationships with both the coach and fellow team-members, and that the motivational climate had already been established at the time of the first data collection.

Measures

To measure the players' perceptions of the prevailing motivational climate on their respective teams, the Perceived Motivational Climate in Sport Questionnaire-2 was used. The PMCSQ-2 was designed to assess players' perceptions of the degree to which their respective team's motivational climate is characterized in terms of two higher order dimensions which are composites of six underlying characteristics. Task-involving climate items reflect a sense that co-operative learning is encouraged, that each player has an important role on the team, and effort/improvement are emphasized.

Ego-involving items tap the view that mistakes are punished, that recognition by the coach is reserved for the most talented athletes, and that a feeling of intra-team rivalry exists among players on the team. Due to the fact that their predictions stemming from achievement goal frameworks are based on the higher order dimensions of the motivational climate, only the composite higher order scales were analysed in the study. Initial work on the PMCISQ-2 has found the instrument to have adequate internal reliability and factorial validity.

When completing the PMCSQ-2, the participants were asked to think about what the environment is like on their team in general. The stem for each question was: "On this team...'. Responses were indicated on a 5-point Likert scale ranging from strongly disagree (1) to strongly agree (5).

Basic needs

Drawing from research assessing the satisfaction of the need for autonomy in the physical as well as other domains four items were used to tap into the IPLOC aspect of autonomy. Drawing from the same sources, six items were used to assess the choice/ decision-making facets of perceived autonomy. The five-item perceived ability sub-scale of the Intrinsic Motivation Inventory was used to determine the satisfaction of the need for competence. The competence subscale of the IMI has demonstrated acceptable reliability with similar aged participants in previous research involving British athletes.

Satisfaction of the need for relatedness in sport was tapped with the five item Acceptance subscale of the Need for Relatedness Scale. This scale has been found reliable and valid in the context of sport and physical activity. To assess team relatedness, the stem for this scale was "With the other members of my team, I feel...". To tap into perceived relatedness with respect to the coach, the stem was changed to "In terms of my coach specifically, I feel..." The items used to assess perceived relatedness were: supported, understood, listened to, safe, and valued. All responses were indicated on a 7-point Likert scale ranging from strongly disagree (1) to strongly agree (7), except in the case of the relatedness subscale, which was scored on a 5-point scale.

Well-being/ill-being variables

Subjective vitality in sport was measured using the 6-item version of the Subjective Vitality Scale. This instrument taps the degree to which participants feel physically and mentally vigorous and alert while participating in their sport. Responses were indicated on a 7-point Likert scale anchored by not at all true (1) and very true (7). To measure physical symptoms, participants completed the 9-item physical symptom checklist on which they indicated the degree to which they had experienced symptoms such as runny nose,, headaches, stomach-ache/pain, in the past two weeks. Responses were indicated on a 7-point Likert scale anchored by not al all (1) to very much (7). During previous pilot testing of this measure with follow-up interviews, they have found that many participants felt uncomfortable or embarrassed by the question relating to the acne/pimples symptom. Because of this they decided not to assess this symptom. The eight categories were combined into a composite symptom measure.

Alpha coefficients for all scales at both Time 1 and Time 2 ranged from 0.75 to 0.92 and were deemed acceptable on the basis of Nunnally's criterion of 0.70 for the psychological domain.

Results

Means, standard deviations, and alpha coefficients for the study variables are shown in Table 1. On average, participants reported an increase in perceptions of the task-involving climate and a decrease in perceptions of an ego-involving climate from Time 1 to Time 2. They also reported higher levels of need satisfaction, subjective vitality, and reported less physical symptoms across the same time period. Paired sample t-tests showed that all changes were significant ($p < 0.05$) except for assessments of perceptions of an ego-involving climate and coach relatedness. One way MANOVAs were conducted to test for possible type of sport differences (i.e. football vs. hockey). No significant differences emerged. They also examined the effects of gender on all the study variables. No gender differences were found. Therefore, the data were analysed across gender and type of sport.

Pearson product moment correlations at both Time 1 and Time 2 (Table 2) revealed that in line with previous research, the two perceived over-riding dimensions of the motivational climate were significantly and negatively correlated. Perceptions of an ego-involving climate were unrelated to autonomy and conpetence, but significantly negatively related to both them and coach relatedness. A low to moderate correlation emerged between perceptions of an ego-involving climate and reported physical symptoms for Time 2 only. In contrast, perceptions of a sport-environment emphasizing task goals were significantly and positively related to all three basic needs and subjective vitality at Time 1 and Time 2, but were unrelated to reported physical symptoms. The three basic needs were positively low to moderately correlated with each other. They were also significantly positively related to subjective vitality and negatively associated with physical symptoms at both assessment times. The correlations between the two autonomy facets (choice and IPLOC) as well as between the coach and team relatedness ranged between 0.38 and 0.48 indicating that these facets were related and not redundant.

In this study, the researchers used items to assess both the IPLOC and the choice aspects of autonomy. A principal axis factor analyses employing both oblique and varimax rotation were thus conducted on all the .10 items reflecting the two different aspects of the satisfaction of the need for autonomy in sport. As expected, two factors with eigenvalues above 1.00 emerged, collectively accounting for 61°70 (Time 1) and 68°70 (Time 2) of the variance, respectively. Orthogonal and oblique rotation produced very similar solutions and the interfactor correlations of the oblique rotation were all relatively low. As a result, the orthogonal results were maintained. All items loaded appropriately on the two proposed factors with factor loadings ranging from 0.55 to 0.88 at Time 1 and 0.64 to 0.85 at Time 2.

Motivational Climate, Need Satisfaction, and Well-being

A series of hierarchical regression analyses were performed to test the assumption that perceptions of a task-involving and ego-involving coaching emphasis over time would predict changes in the satisfaction of the three psychological needs across the season. The following procedure was used for each of the three basic needs: The corresponding Time 1 score of each need as well as perceptions of the motivational climate (task- and ego-involving) at Time 1 were entered first (step 1); perception's of the motivational climate (task- and ego-involving) at Time 2 were entered second (step 2).

This hierarchical approach to the analysis offers information about how changes in the perceptions of the motivational climate are linked to changes in athletes' reported need satisfaction over the season in that their scores at the beginning of the season were controlled for statistically. That is, the coefficients reported for the second step can be thought of as predicting residual variance in each interest variable, unexplained by the respective variables' initial level.

Results (Table 2) showed that perceptions of an increase in perceptions of a task-involving climate over the season explained significant variance in an increase in the satisfaction for the need for autonomy in terms of the IPLOC (Total $R^2 = 0.40$, $\beta = 0.5\ 3$, $p < 0.001$), and choice (Total $R^2 = 0.45$, $\beta = 0.42$, $p < 0.001$) facets; the need for competence (Total R^2=0.57, (β=0.21, p<0.001), and reported team relatedness (Total $R^2 = 0.43$, $\beta = 0.44$, $p < 0.001$) and coach relatedness (Total $R^2 = 0.41$, $\beta = 0.49$, $p < 0.001$).

In contrast, perceptions of an increase in an ego-involving climate across the season predicted a significant decrease in team relatedness over the course of the season. Next, to test the assumption that changes in need satisfaction predict changes in indices of psychological and physical well/ill-being, subjective vitality and physical symptoms were regressed onto the separate need satisfaction variables (Table 3) using the same method as before. First, the corresponding Time 1 score as well as perceptions of the three needs at Time 1 were entered (step 1); perceptions of the three needs at Time 2 were entered second (step 2).

Results showed that the satisfaction of the IPLOC component of the need for autonomy and coach relatedness across the course of the season were significant predictors of increased feelings of subjective vitality. Changes in the three needs did not emerge as significant predictors for changes in physical symptoms.

Tests of mediation effects

According to SDT, the three psychological needs are assumed to mediate the relationship between social environmental factors (e.g. variations in the motivational climate) and well-being. The procedures suggested by Baron and Kenny were used to test this assumption. Accordingly, a test of mediation should include the three following regression equations: first, regressing the mediator on the independent variable; second regressing the dependent variable on the independent variable; and third, regressing the dependent variable on both the independent variable and on the mediator.

Mediation is established if the following four conditions can be met: (1) the independent variable is related to the mediator variable in the first equation, (2) the independent variable must be shown to affect the dependent variable in the second equation, (3) the mediator has an effect on the dependent variable after the effect of the independent variable is taken into account, and (4) based on a comparison between results obtained under conditions 2 and 3, support for mediation is

Table 1: Descriptive statistics and internal reliability of each measure

	Time 1			Time 2			
	M	*SD,*	*a*	*M*	*SD*	*a*	*p*
Task-involving climate	3.79	0.38	0.81	3.86	0.40	0.84	0.05
Ego-involving climate	2.42	0.47	0.82	2.37	0.54	0.85	0.21
Autonomy (choice)	3.82	1.21	0.87	4.42	1.18	0.91	0.001
Autonomy (IPLOC)	5.18	0.96	0.80	5.40	0.94	0.86	0.05
Perceived competence	5.23	0.77	0.78	5.10	0.91	0.75	0.05
Relatedness team	3.84	0.59	0.86	4.00	0.56	0.87	0.01
Relatedness coach	3.64	0.65	0.88	3.72	0.67	0.92	0.20
Subjective vitality	4.97	1.07	0.89	5.23	0.98	0.92	0.01
Physical symptoms	3.10	1.04	0.79	2.62	1.03	0.80	0.001

provided if the effect of the independent variable on the dependent variable is reduced afters the effect of the mediator on the dependent variable is controlled for.

Table 2: Moderated hierarchical regression analysis for predicting basic needs

Variable	*B*	*SEB*	*β*	*Unique*	R^2
Autonomy (IPLOC)					
Step 1					
IPLOC (T1)	0.26	0.09	0.26	2.93	
Task-involving climate (T1)	0.56	0.23	0.23	2.43	0.15
Step 2					
IPLOC (T1)	0.23	0.08	0.23	3.08	
Task-involving climate (T2)	1.28	0.20	0.54	6.39	0.25
Autonomy (choice)					
Step 1					
Autonomy choice (T1)	0.54	0.08	0.55	6.68	0.30
Step 2					
Autonomy choice (T1)	0.58	0.07	0.59	7.84	
Task-involving climate (T2)	1.21	0.24	0.41	5.02	0.15
Competence					
Step 1					
Competence (T1)	0.60	0.06	0.70	10.88	0.51
Step 2					
IPLOC (T1)	0.61	0.05	0.72	11.71	
Task-involving climate (T2)	0.41	0.14	0.21	2.97	0.05
Relatedness (coach)					
Step 1					
Relatedness (coach) (T1)	0.51	0.10	0.50	5.02	0.22
Step 2					
Relatedness (coach) (T1)	0.46	0.09	0.44	5.14	
Task-involving climate (T2)	0.82	0.14	0.49	5.91	0.21
Relatedness (team)					
Step 1					
Relatedness (team) (T1)	0.41	0.09	4.28	4.67	0.24
Step 2					
Relatedness (team) (T1)	0.36	0.08	0.38	4.76	
Task-involving climate (T2)	0.62	0.11	0.44	5.44	
Ego-involving climate (T2)	-.18	0.08	–.17	–2.11	0.21

Table 3: Moderated hierarchical regression analysis for predicting indices of well/ill-being

Variable	*B*	*SE B*	*β*	*t*	*Unique Rz*
Subjective vitality					
Step 1					
Subjective vitality (T1)	0.40	0.08	0.43	4.76	0.29
Step 2					
Subjective vitality (T1)	0.25	0.07	0.27	3.37	
Autonomy (IPLOC; T2)	0.45	0.10	0.43	4.71	
Relatedness (Coach) (T2)	0.40	0.12	0.28	3.35	0.26
Physical symptoms					
Step 1					
Physical symptoms (T1)	0.55	0.08	0.56	7.30	0.35

Equation 1 Previous results (Table 2) already showed partial support for the first condition of mediation, in that changes in perceptions of the motivational climate (task- and ego-involving features) were significantly related to changes in the satisfaction of the need for autonomy, competence, and relatedness.

Equation 2 Change in subjective vitality and physical symptoms were separately regressed onto changed in perceptions of the motivational climate. Results showed that an increase in perceptions of a task-involving climate was a significant predictor of an increase in subjective vitality during the course of the season.

Equation 3 Subjective vitality and physical symptoms at Time 2 were separately regressed onto the three need satisfaction variables and perceptions of the motivational climate at Time 2, controlling for the corresponding variables at Time 1. Only subjective vitality partially met the demands of the third condition of ı ediation. As can be seen from Table 4, satisfaction of the need for coach relatedness at Time 2 as well as the

IPLOC aspect of the need for autonomy were positive predictors of subjective vitality when controlling for the independent variables (i.e. perceptions of the motivational climate), thus, suggesting partial mediation. Also, the relationship between perceptions of the task-involving climate and the subjective vitality was weaker, although still significant, after taking into account the effect of the mediator (i.e. the three basic needs) into account.

Table 4: Regression analyses testing mediation

Variable	*B*	*SE B*	*β*	*t*	*Unique Rz*
Equation 2: Subjective vitality					
Step 1					
Subjective vitality (T1)	0.41	0.08	0.44	5.23	0.27
Step 2					
Subjective vitality (T1)	0.36	0.07	0.39	5.54	
Task-involving climate (T1)	0.40	0.19	0.57	7.31	0.24
Physical symptoms					
Step 1					
Physical symptoms (T1)	0.57	0.07	0.58	7.72	
Equation 3: Subjective vitality					
Step 1					
Subjective vitality (T1)	0.36	0.08	0.39	4.24	
Autonomy (Choice) (T1)	-0.18	0.08	-0.22	-2.25	
Relatedness (team) (T1)	0.32	0.16	0.19	2.01	0.32
Step 2					
Subjective vitality (T1)	0.24	0.07	0.26	3.22	
Task-involving climate (T2)	0.70	0.25	0.28	2.83	
Autonomy (IPLOC) (T2)	0.33	0.10	0.32	3.35	
Relatedness (coach) (T2)	0.26	0.13	0.18	2.08	0.60

This study set out to investigate whether sport participation might play a role in contributing to .or compromising health and how situational factors can influence the quality of athletes' sport experience and subjective well-being. More specifically, they examined the relationship between changes in facets of the social environment perceived to be engineered by the coach (i.e. the task- and ego-involving features) to changes in need satisfaction and indices of psychological and physical well-well-being among university-team athletes over the course of a competitive season. No previous studies have examined this relationship using a longitudinal design.

Need satisfaction

In line with the hypotheses, the findings showed that an increase in the satisfaction of the needs for autonomy (both in terms of the IPLOC and choice aspects), competence, and relatedness (both team and coach) were all positively predicted by perceptions of the coach's emphasis on task-involving climate structures across the season. By reinforcing effort, personal progress, and the view that everyone has an important role on the team, an over-riding task-involving climate should maximize the opportunities to satisfy all the three needs. In contrast, perceiving the coach to emphasize ego-involving features during the course of the season was a significant negative predictor of team relatedness. Clearly, a team atmosphere which focuses on intra-team rivalry, outdoing others, and recognizing only the most talented players over time would be more likely to reduce feelings of relatedness between members of the same team.

Contrary to the hypothesis, perceptions of an ego-involving motivational climate did not emerge as a negative predictor of the need for autonomy and competence. This finding is, however, in line with the results by Standage et al. who did not find any link between perceptions of an ego-involving climate and the satisfaction of the three basic needs. A possible explanation for these non-significant findings may lie in the theoretical proposition of achievement goal theory suggesting that perceived competence would moderate the relationship of an ego goal emphasis on ensuing achievement-related affect, cognition and behaviour. The findings also make sense from a practical perspective in that even though there may be a strong ego-involving environment operating on a team, it is quite plausible, at least for some players on a team, to have high perceived ability (e.g. if the team is winning). Also, it may be the case that the best players on the team are granted more autonomy (e.g. more involved in decision-making). However, good relationships with, and feeling valued and supported by other team members, does not seem to be compatible with an ego-involving climate.

Need for autonomy

In line with the hypothesis, as well as previous research, the IPLOC aspect of the need for autonomy across the season, emerged as a positive predictor of an increase in subjective vitality from Time 1 to Time 2. This result is aligned with Ryan and Frederick's assumptions that an internal perceived locus of causality may play a particularly important role with regards to feelings of vitality. According to Ryan and Frederick, only those with an internal locus of causality who feel like an `origin' of their behaviour, will experience their energy as `their own, and as emanating from the self and, thus, report higher levels of subjective vitality. These researchers have also proposed that subjective vitality is not directly influenced by physiological factors alone, but by the subjective meaning of these physical factors with regard to the self. For example, an athlete who feels compelled to practice her or his sport may perceive less energy available to her/himself compared to an athlete who feels he or she practices her sport autonomously and wholeheartedly, regardless of observable effort or the objective caloric energy expenditure.

As hypothesised, the IPLOC aspect of autonomy emerged as the strongest (and the only) predictor of psychological well-being. Although perceptions of choice/decision-making were significantly correlated with subjective vitality, it seems that an internal perceived locus of causality is more relevant to feeling energetic and vital. For example, athletes who highly appreciate their coach's expertise and experience can choose to let the coach make the strategic decisions and still feel autonomous in the process.

More research is needed, however, to test whether, the choice/decision-making aspect of autonomy may possibly better predict other indices of psychological well-being such as enjoyment or self-esteem. It is also possible that the choice aspect may perhaps be a stronger predictor of well-being in individual sports. Finally, from a statistical perspective, entering all the three needs simultaneously in the, regression analysis is a rather stringent test given the low to moderate intercorrelations between some of the needs.

In line with the assumptions, perceptions of coach relatedness across the season were also a positive significant predictor of an increase in subjective vitality from Time 1 to Time 2. Team relatedness did not emerge as a significant predictor of any of the well-being variables, despite being significantly correlated with subjective vitality. Again, a reason for this could be shared variance. However, one can argue that coach relatedness does to a large degree express something about the quality of the coach athlete relationship. Several authors such as Jowett and Cockerill; Mageau and Vallerand assert that the quality of this relationship is a central determinant of athletes' satisfaction and well-being.

None of the need satisfaction constructs emerged as significant predictors of physical symptoms. In line with arguments by Sheldon sand Bettencourt, this may suggest that need satisfaction constructs may be more relevant to understanding the presence of positive well-being than for understanding the absence of negative well-being. Stated differently, although one may be made happy by various types of satisfying experiences, it could perhaps be that other difficulties or problems (e.g. rundown with school schedule), that were not measured in this study, may influence one's physical ill-being. In the present study, ill-being was examined with respect to reported physical indicators only. It could be that the consideration of indices of psychological/emotional ill-being may have lead to an observed significant link to need satisfaction. Future research should explore this possibility.

Positive Motivation

Most people have multiple motives rather than single reasons. For example, a tennis player might be attending individual coaching sessions to improve her ranking in order to demonstrate competence, repay the support of her parents and qualify for more prestigious tournaments offering more prize money! Sometimes these multiple motives reinforce each other, but at other times they can cause internal conflicts—as with the young athlete who feels pulled between his athletic career and his academic studies – and then something has to give..

One of the major difficulties for coaches working with groups of athletes with diverse motives and goals is to create a motivational climate that facilitates the development of all these motives—or at least as many as possible. If anyone tells you this is easy, they are lying. As well as being flexible, you will need to have a good grasp of some of the fundamental principles of motivation and knowledge of how to apply them.

Motivation has been defined as 'the direction and intensity of ones efforts'. Direction refers to the decision to commit and to turn up to training on a regular basis. The intensity dimension is about how much people are prepared to give in each training session. In sport, these dimensions are often related, with committed individuals attending training on a regular basis and working hard during their sessions.

Some coaches believe that motivation is a fixed personality trait or characteristic – that you either are or aren't a motivated athlete. In fact, though, motivation is not quite that cut and dried since the motivational climate created by the coach will impact on the motivation of the athletes under his or her guidance.

Reinforcements and punishments can be either positive or negative. However, to avoid confusion, you must think of positive and negative in this case in terms of either adding something or taking something away, not in terms of good or bad.

Whereas classical conditioning works by forming an association between two stimuli (eg a 'clicker' and a treat in dog training), operant conditioning forms an association between a behaviour and a consequence. There are four possible consequences to any behaviour, as follows:

- Something good can start or be presented;
- Something good can end or be taken away;
- Something bad can start or be presented;
- Something bad can end or be taken away.

Anything that increases a behaviour – makes it occur more frequently, makes it stronger or makes it more likely to occur – is termed a reinforcer. Normally a person will perceive 'starting something good' (positive reinforcement) or 'ending something bad' (negative reinforcement) as worth pursuing and will repeat the behaviours that seem to cause these consequences.

Anything that decreases a behaviour – makes it occur less frequently, makes it weaker, or makes it less likely to occur – is termed a punisher. Normally a person will perceive 'ending something good' (negative punishment) or 'starting something bad' (positive punishment) as worth avoiding and will not repeat the behaviours that seem to cause these consequences.

Note that these definitions are based on their actual effect on the behaviour in question – ie they must reduce or strengthen the behaviour to be defined as punishment or reinforcement. Pleasures meant as rewards that do not strengthen a behaviour are indulgences, not reinforcers; would-be punishments that do not weaken a behaviour are classified as abuse.

Sport psychology research evidence overwhelmingly supports the use of a predominantly (80-90%) positive approach, with punishment kept to a minimum. Behavioural modification techniques based on positive reinforcements have been successfully used to increase output during training sessions, improve performance, and reduce errors. It's at this point in lectures that some students tell that they prefer a more authoritarian coach, even one who shouts. That way they know what is expected of them – and that there will be negative consequences if they fail to live up to those expectations.

However, it is important to point out that a positive approach doesn't mean being 'laid-back', having few rules and even fewer expectations of your athletes: far from it. A positive approach is as demanding as a negative one, except that rewards tend to predominate over punishments as the route to better performance.

A predominantly positive approach to coaching will sometimes involve punishment. If, for example, one of your athletes has been late for training a number of times you might need to criticise them in order to ensure better timekeeping in future. Letting someone know you are unhappy is perfectly justified – as long as you limit your criticism to the particular behaviour that has made you unhappy rather than indulging in more general character assassination.

Taking a positive approach to coaching is not about praising athletes continuously, regardless of success or failure, but about giving praise when it is merited. That means recognising and rewarding not just successful overall outcomes – ie winning – but also performance improvements, improved approximations (like a more technically correct forehand in tennis) and effort. One study showed that children who were praised for their efforts following failure were more persistent, enjoyed the task more and performed better than children praised for having high ability.

The scheduling of positive reinforcement is also an important factor. Continuous praise is actually a bad thing – unless you are working with novices–as it devalues the reward, which is seen as too- easily obtained. In this kind of climate, players essentially switch off. You also need to be aware of how your behaviour may be perceived by others. If, for example, you adopt a predominantly positive approach, using positive reinforcements, but for some reason remain fairly quiet during a session, your behaviour may be interpreted as a withdrawal of the normal praise and hence a punishment.

Knowing your Athletes

There are some players for whom a negative approach to coaching might be effective, but you really need to know your athlete before employing such tactics. Creating the most productive motivational climate depends on many interrelated factors, including the characteristics of the group and individuals, their preferred style of coaching, the qualities of the coach (knowledge, expertise etc), situational factors (eg the dangers involved in a given activity) and, of course, the coaching style favoured by the coach.

In experience, the best coaches are flexible and able to adapt to the requirements of different situations. This will nearly always involve criticism or punishment as well as praise, but will rely primarily on a positive approach in order to motivate players to perform at their best.

How to Motivate

Getting your athletes to change an old habit or adopt a new behaviour is often crucial to whether they will achieve their goals or respond correctly to a treatment. Success depends not only on what happens when the athlete is with you but also on what happens when he or she are on their own, looking after themselves.

The following examples should illustrate the point. You coach an athlete who trains very well, achieving all your planned sessions. However, his eating habits are poor and even though you have told him what to eat many times, he doesn't seem to want to change his diet. Or, if you're a therapist, you treat an injured client who needs to do some rehabilitation exercises, such as stretches, at home on his own as well as when he visits you for treatment. Although you've instructed him what to do, he doesn't carry out the exercises regularly to get the benefits required. So what's the solution? Improve your motivational skills.

In 1983, two researchers called Prochaska and DiClementi introduced the Transtheoretical Model of

Behaviour Change (TTM). The TTM very simply describes how people go about changing their health or lifestyle behaviours by defining five 'stages of change'. The TTM suggests that, for people to make positive change, they must go through a process of increasing their readiness to change. In other words, before a new behaviour or action can occur, the individual must have the right attitudes and beliefs to embrace it. Each of the five 'stages of change' depicts a distinct level of attitude and action for behaviour change. For example, the following are the five stages applied to changing eating habits:

– Precontemplation: not changing diet and not intending to start to change.
– Contemplation: not changing diet, but intending to change.
– Preparation: making some changes, but not fully, though intending to change fully.
– Action: achieved all diet changes regularly for less than six months.
– Maintenance: maintained all diet changes for longer than six months.

What the TTM tells us is that the type of strategies needed to get people to change their diets, for example, will depend on their current stage of change. If you give an athlete or client a diet sheet to follow, they will only adopt the new diet if they are at the preparation or action stages. At these stages they would be ready to respond to this 'action-oriented approach'. If, however, the athlete or client is only at the precon-templation or contemplation stages, they will be unlikely to respond to the new diet. So with individuals at these stages of change, the strategy is to motivate and persuade them that changing their diet is important, beneficial and achievable. In short, increasing their readiness to change by taking them on to the preparation stage.

Getting Shot of Pasta and Chips

At these lower stages, the strategies used are not 'action-oriented', such as the diet sheet, but more motivational and attitudinal. To progress from the lower stages, an individual must believe that the new behaviour is important and worthy, and that the 'pros' for adopting it outweigh the 'cons' of changing. This is called 'decision balance' and the strategies used in the lower stages must aim to shift the decision balance in favour of the 'pros'. For instance, the pros for changing diet such as feeling better and losing weight must counter the cons of not being able to eat pizzas and chips every night.

A person must also believe in him/herself to be ready to make a behaviour change. This is known as 'self-efficacy' and is the individual's belief in him/herself to perform a task successfully. Often, individuals at the lower stages have low self-efficacy regarding their behaviour. For instance. they don't feel confident about changing their diets. To progress through the stages, strategies to build self-efficacy must be used to help trigger the change.

Research with the TTM suggests it can be used across a range of health and lifestyle behaviours and that the strategies it supports are effective in helping individuals to make positive changes. For example, Marcus et al found that people in a group became more active when they received motivational materials relevant for their stage of change. Prochaska et al studied why it was than in a worksite weight-loss programme there was an 80 per cent dropout rate. They found that the weight-loss programme had been action-oriented, involving exercise classes and diet plans, and yet most of the participants were still precontemplators and contemplators.

Self-determined Training Programme

The complex and rich phenomenon that affects all of these to some degree is motivation. As you may know, Deci and Ryan in 1985 proposed their Cognitive Evaluation Theory, which posits that intrinsic motivation is maximised when individuals feel competent and self-determining when dealing with their environment. More specifically, intrinsically motivated athletes participate because they find the activity inherently enjoyable, rather than for external rewards, eg, coach recognition, which is called extrinsic motivation.

Goal-setting—SMART

Goal-setting is a simple, yet often-misused motivational technique which can provide some structure for your training and competition programme. Goals give a focus, and the key to effective goal-setting is the S.M.A.R.T principle.

- *First, goals must be Specific.* Research has shown that specific goals work better than general 'do-your-best' goals. For example, if you're a runner, rather than professing a desire to reduce your 5K time, you should state: 'I intend to knock 20 seconds off my 5K time over the next six months'.
- *Your training target ought to be Measurable,* as in the above example. Simply saying that you want to trim your 5K time is insufficient; you need some accurate means of charting your progress. This means that continuous monitoring is needed, but this can become a bore. This can take place once a week or even once a month, but the idea of the day is to reduce your preoccupation with times and

improvement. Certainly, the therapeutic benefits arising from a relaxed (non-timed) workout can help to alleviate stress, reduce symptoms of depression and leave you ready to proceed with an otherwise arduous training schedule.

- *Goals should also be Adjustable.* Goal-setting is a dynamic process. If, for instance, you become injured during a competitive season, you should be able to lower your goals accordingly. On the other hand, you may make such rapid progress that you can raise them. Ultimately this means that they must conform to the first two criteria: being specific and measurable.
- *Goals must be Realistic.* It's all very well saying 'I want to break Daniel Komen's 5K record,' but unless you're his (as yet, undiscovered) identical twin, then that doesn't seem a realistic goal. This is an extreme example, but you also must recognise that your room for improvement shrinks as you get near your full potential, the well-known Law of Diminishing Returns. Conversely, goals should be difficult enough so that you're not struck down by acute boredom because you've achieved them too easily.
- Finally, your training targets ought to be Time-based. If you don't give yourself a specific time frame in which the goal must be achieved, then the urgency for attainment is reduced. The previous example of trimming the 5K time by 20 seconds within six months satisfies this criterion. Try to resist the temptation to move these time constraints back to accommodate life events, such as minor injuries; the result is that the value of the time limit is negated. It is important to identify when this happens, and to set about designing new objectives with new time parameters. This way your goal-setting plan won't lose its effectiveness.

Make no mistake about it, goal-setting is a skill that needs to be mastered just like any other. But by using the following model, you can make the process a little less taxing.

Intrinsic Motivation

Motivational studies have long focused on factors that initiate, influence, and modify behaviour. Early theories dealt essentially with the deterministic aspects of those factors; focusing on instinctual drives, physiological drives, or environmental influences. Although these theories had (and still have) considerable value, their apparent view of people as passive beings that are pushed and pulled around by their physiology or environment has given rise to concern and criticism.

A major development of White's monograph is represented by the addition of a formal statement of cognitive evaluation theory. Cognitive evaluation theory states that intrinsic motivation is driven by an innate need for competence and self-determination in dealing with one's surroundings. The intrinsic rewards for the behaviours motivated by this need are satisfying feelings of competence and autonomy, positive emotions such as enjoyment and excitement, and possibly the sensation of flow (complete absorption in the activity). These feelings, in turn, serve to maintain or increase a person's intrinsic motivation for the particular behaviour.

In a nutshell (according to the theory), an individual's desire to pursue a particular activity depends upon whether his or her feelings of competence, autonomy, and positive affect persist over time. Conversely, if an individual begins to perceive him or herself as incompetent at the activity and/or under external control to do it, then his or her intrinsic motivation is undermined. The outcome is then either a state of extrinsic motivation (the activity might continue dependent on the continuance of external rewards and/or coercion), or a state of amotivation (further activity unlikely because the perceptions of incompetence lead to a sense of futility).

A wealth of studies in general psychology have supported the validity of cognitive evaluation theory. Many studies have clearly shown that when individuals receive information that undermines their sense of competence and/or perception of self-determined choice, their intrinsic motivation declines.

Intrinsic Motivation and Physical Activities

Common sense alone tells us that participation in many sports and physical activities can lead to feelings of autonomy and competence and may produce joy, excitement, thrills, and other satisfying emotions. In that respect it is easy to see that physical activities may be inherently intrinsically motivating. On the other hand, some people say that they would not participate unless there was a material payoff, or unless they were coerced. Others declare that attempting physical challenges leaves them feeling incompetent and humiliated, anxious or pressured. Thus, if we wish to help people reap the benefits of participation and avoid the motivational pitfalls, it is necessary to understand the processes that may lead to specific perceptual outcomes.

Persistence at exercise is related to the motivational constructs described above and has research support. For example, young athletes cite "fun" as a primary reason for participating in sports. Further examination has shown that this feeling of fun depends on experiencing the intrinsic satisfactions of skill improvement, personal accomplishment, and excitement-rather than being a result of extrinsic factors such as winning, getting rewards, or pleasing others. Similar findings have also been related by Gould in a review of the reasons why children drop out of sports, and by Brustad from a study of affective outcomes of competitive youth sport. However, as researchers know well, circumstantial support for the use of a theory of motivation to a particular area (in this case physical activity) is not enough to make a case for its value.

The theory should also hold up under experimental testing. In particular, manipulations of people's perceptions of competence and control should produce changes in their intrinsic motivation. Unfortunately, there is not the volume of evidence in the physical activity setting as there is in general and educational psychology, but several studies do show support for the hypotheses predicted by intrinsic motivation theory.

For example, Orlick and Mosher hypothesised that an extrinsic reward (a trophy) for performance on a stabilometer (balance board) would be perceived by children as controlling-and thus their intrinsic motivation for what is generally an interesting and challenging physical task would be undermined. The hypothesis was supported: When given a free-choice period, the children whose earlier participation was for a trophy showed a decrease in the time they spent voluntarily playing on the stabilometer compared to the children who had no expectation of a reward.

In another study of performance at a stabilometer task, Rudisill hypothesised that training children to understand that their performance improvement was personally controllable (i.e., dependent on practice and effort) would improve their subsequent performance-and would also lead them to persist longer at mastery attempts-even in the face of perceived failure. Again, the results of the experimental manipulation supported the hypothesis that perceptions of personal control enhance intrinsic motivation.

Taking research outside the laboratory, Thompson and Wankel manipulated the perception of exercise choice of adult women who had recently enrolled in a health club. After an initial meeting to discuss activity preferences, the women were randomly allocated to either a perceived choice or a perceived no-choice condition. The initial activity preferences were actually used as the basis for all of the women's programmes. However, the women in the no-choice group were led to believe that they had been assigned a standard programme determined by the instructor. Six weeks later the attendance of the women in the perceived choice group was higher, and they also expressed a greater intention to continue exercising at the health club.

Experimental manipulations designed to affect perceptions of competence at physical activities have also been shown to change intrinsic motivation in line with the predictions of the theory. As before, some studies have employed a stabilometer. For example, Weinberg and Jackson gave subjects bogus success or failure feedback for their balancing ability by telling them that they had either exceeded the 82nd percentile ("...very good..."), or they had fallen below the 18th percentile ("...not very good...").

In line with intrinsic motivation theory, success feedba ck enhanced interest and enjoyment, and reduced boredom with the task-and failure feedback had the opposite effect. Using a similar type of protocol and a stabilometer task, Vallerand and Reid manipulated feedback by making verbal comments to subjects suggesting that they were doing either well or poorly. Like Weinberg and Jackson the results showed that success feedback led to enhanced intrinsic motivation while lack of success feedback reduced it.

Additionally, a more in-depth analysis of the results allowed the experimenters to show that it was not the effect of the feedback per se, but rather it was the effect of feedback on the subjects' perceptions of competence that moderated changes in intrinsic motivation. In other words, this study showed that it was not the feedback itself so much as the meaning of the feedback to the subjects that produced the motivational outcome. Wishing to see if similar results would be obtained from ma ipulations of feedback in a youth physical fitness testing situation,

Whitehead and Corbin set up an experiment in a junior high school using a shuttle run-type fitness test (the Illinois Agility Run). Bogus high or low percentile feedback was given to randomly determined groups, and the results replicated the Vallerand and Reid findings. Again, apparently high percentile scores raised intrinsic motivation and low percentile scores lowered it-and as before, the motivational outcomes were mediated by the subjects' perceptions of competence at the task rather than directly changed by the feedback itself.

Application of Theory

The following recommendations represent an attempt to translate logically the theoretical exposition into guidelines for promoting motivation in practical situations. Note that although these guidelines are presented as a series of Dos and Don'ts, they are not meant to be coercing or controlling.

Competitively Coningent Rewards and Intrinsic Motivation: Can Losers Remain Motivated

Competitively Coningent Rewards and Intrinsic Motivation: Can Losers Remain Motivated, is a research study of Maarten Vansteenkiste (University of Leuven, Tiensstraat,

Belgium) and Edward L. Deci (University of Rochester, New York). The study explored the effect on intrinsic motivation and ego-involved persistence of winning versus losing a competitively contingent reward and, for losers, additional effects of receiving either positive performance-contingent rewards.

In some competitive situations, people's goal is simply to win either because winning is enjoyable and exciting for them or, alternatively, because it helps them bolster their fragile egos. In other competitive situations, people's goal may include not only winning but also obtaining additional outcomes such as symbolic or monetary rewards that have been made contingent upon winning. It is common, for example, to see professional athletes compete in tournaments where the purse runs into tens of thousands of dollars, and the real plum for winning may be product endorsements that yield many times the value of the purse. Remarkably, financial inducements have even made their way into amateur athletics.

Some parents offer financial incentives to their children for winning at sports or other competitive activities, and the use of incentives for amateurs has, to some extent, become institutionalised. Many college athletes receive large scholarships based only on their athletic accomplishments and potentials, and further, for example, in some amateur Belgian soccer leagues, players as young as 16-17 years of age can earn monetary rewards equivalent to about $100 when their team wins a game. Financial incentives are not the only source of pressure on individuals to win competitions. Parents of even very young athletes may become highly ego involved in the outcome of their children's little league or high-school games, pressuring the children to try harder and, perhaps, to win at whatever cost. As well, fans and televisions audiences can add to the stress that some college athletes feel to win big games. It seems that, for some people, playing well is not enough.

Given the importance in modem culture of competition and rewards made contingent upon winning a competition, studies have begun to examine the effects of these factors on people's intrinsic motivation for the activity at which they compete. The following gives an overview of the types of research that have been done.

When people compete against each other, either individually or as teams, doing the same activity at the same time with each side trying to win, it is referred to as direct competition. The current study involved direct competition and previous competition studies that are herein reviewed were also of that type. In experiments of direct competition, the three most basic between-group comparisons that can be made are

1) winners can be compared to losers;
2) either winners or losers can be compared to participants in a control group where participants did the same activity alone, without competing and without any performance feedback (i.e., a no-competition/no-feedback control group); and
3) either winners or losers can be compared to participants in a control group where participants worked in the presence of another person (typically an experimental accomplice) who did the same activity with participants being told simply to do their best, with no mention of trying to win (i.e., a no-competition/implicit-feedback control group). In this third case, the control-group participants get feedback in the sense that they see (or are told) which participant did the activity more quickly (or, in some other way, did it better). Using the former type of control group allows investigators to determine the combined effects of the competition

and the competitive outcome (e.g., competing and winning), whereas the latter type of control group allows investigators to determine the effects of the competition independent of the competitive outcome.

Studies of competition can be further complicated by the addition of rewards. For example, as is frequently done in the real world, participants can be told that the winner of a competition will receive a reward. Such rewards are referred to as competitively contingent rewards, and in real situations with competitively contingent rewards some people are winners and some are losers. Thus, with competitively contingent rewards, the participants (a) compete, (b) have a competitive outcome-that is, they either win or lose the competition, and (c) either receive or do not receive the desired reward.

Competitively contingent rewards differ from performance-contingent rewards, which is another relevant reward contingency, in the following way. Performance-contingent rewards are given to people for doing well at a task. This contingency is frequently instantiated by telling participants that they will get a reward if they perform well according to some normative standard-for example, if they perform better than 80% of the other participants who have done the task. Thus, whereas competitively contingent rewards are given for beating an opponent in a direct competition, performance-contingent rewards are given for doing better than an implicit or explicit normative standard.

Both a competitively contingent reward condition and a performance-contingent reward condition can be compared to either (a) controls group that do not get feedback comparable to that which is implicit in winning (or losing) a competitively contingent reward or in receiving (or not receiving) a performance-contingent reward; or (b) control groups that do get either expected or unexpected feedback that is comparable to the feedback that reward-group participants received implicitly.

An additional complexity of the competition and reward studies is that the interpersonal context within which people compete or get rewards can either be relatively pressuring and controlling or relatively nonpressuring and informational. That is, the individuals administering the competition or rewards can pressure people either to win or to do well enough to get a reward, or the individuals can be relatively nonpressuring, giving people the opportunity to choose f r themselves how hard to try to win or to earn a reward.

Finally, studies of intrinsic motivation have employed two different measures of intrinsic motivation as a dependent variable. Some have used the so-called free-choice measure in which, following the experimental period, participants are left alone in the experimental room with the freedom to either do more of the target activity or to do alternative activities, including j st day dreaming. The amount of time they spend with the ctivity is generally considered a measure of their int insic motivation. The second assessment approach uses selfreports. Because intrinsic motivation for a target activity is assumed to be based in the interest people have for that activity, people's reports of how interesting and enjoyable they find the activity, is also used as a measure of their intrinsic motivation.

There have been a number of studies relating competition (either with or without rewards) to intrinsic motivation, and four findings have emerged that are directly relevant to the formulation of the current study.

First, a study by Deci, Betley, Kahle, Abrams, and Porac found that when two individuals worked in the presence of each other on the same puzzle solving activity, those participants who had been told to try to beat their opponent at solving the puzzles displayed less subsequent intrinsic motivation for the puzzle solving activity than did those who had simply been told to do their best and solve the puzzles as quickly as they could, with no mention being made of winning or doing better than the other person.

Importantly, in that study, participants in the competitive group won the competition and participants in the comparison group got the same implicit positive feedback because they could see that they had solved the puzzles faster than the other participant, who was an experimental accomplice. As such, the comparison group was a no-competition/positive-feedback control group, so the conclusion was that winning a direct, face-to-face competition decreased intrinsic motivation relative to doing the same task in the presence of the other and receiving implicit positive feedback about one's performance. In short, when working in the presence of another and receiving positive performance information were held constant, competition undermined intrinsic motivation, suggesting that competition itself, independent of the competitive outcome, is controlling.

There is some recent evidence that personality factors such as level of achievement motivation may, to some extent, moderate the detrimental effect on intrinsic motivation of direct competition. However, the detrimental main effects has been replicated by various researchers and the moderation effect has been found only with self-reports of enjoyment. Thus, it does appear that there is a detrimental main effect for competition when the information implicit in the competitive outcome is held constant.

The second relevant finding was that the interpersonal climate within which a competition occurred moderated the competition's effects on intrinsic motivation. Specifically, when participants won a competition within a controlling, pressuring interpersonal context, their intrinsic motivation was undermined relative to that of participants who won the competition in a context that did not pressure them to beat the opponent. Thus, a pressuring interpersonal context has a negative main effect on intrinsic motivation when competition and the competitive outcome are held constant.

Further, the Reeve and Deci study introduced a no-competition/no-feedback control group where participants worked alone rather than in the presence of another. Results showed that winning a competition in a context that was not pressuring enhanced intrinsic motivation relative to a non-competition/no feedback control group, whereas winning the competition in a pressuring context resulted in the same level of intrinsic motivation as being in the no-competition/no-feedback control group.

When the Reeve and Deci study is considered together with the Deci et al. study, the findings indicate that winning a competition tends to undermine intrinsic motivation relative to a no-competition/positive-feedback control group where the presence of another and the positive information implicit in winning a competition are held constant. Further, competing in a pressuring interpersonal context can make the experience even more controlling. However, winning a competition does not undermine intrinsic motivation relative to not competing and not receiving any positive feedback; in fact, winning a competition can lead to more intrinsic motivation than this no-competition/no feedback control condition if the competition occurs in a nonpressuring context. In short, then, competition itself tends to undermine intrinsic motivation; positive competence feedback contained in winning or doing well tends to enhance intrinsic motivation; and the interpersonal context can influence which effect is more dominant.

The third relevant finding is that participants who lost a competition had less subsequent intrinsic motivation than those who won. In other words, when competition itself was held constant across conditions, the competitive outcome (i.e., the information contained in winning vs. losing) significantly affected intrinsic motivation. Further, compared to a no-competition/no-feedback control group, those who lost a competition in a nonpressuring setting showed diminished intrinsic motivation whereas those who won the competition in a nonpressuring setting showed enhanced intrinsic motivation. Thus, positive competence feedback inherent in winning tends to enhance intrinsic motivation whereas negative competence feedback inherent in losing tends to diminish it relative to a no-competition/no feedback control condition.

The fourth relevant finding was that, when participants within a group setting competed against the other members of the group to win a tangible monetary reward, the average intrinsic motivation of all participants was less than that of the control group members who did not compete for a reward. In other words, when the winners and losers were considered together, these competitively-contingent rewards undermined intrinsic motivation (relative to a no-competition/no-feedback/no-reward control group). The effect size on intrinsic motivation was very large. However, because the data were collapsed across winners and losers, it is unclear whether the effects of competing for a reward had the same effect for winners as for losers. In other words, it has not been determined whether the negative effect on intrinsic motivation of a competitively contingent reward condition applies to both winners and losers.

Intrinsic Motivation and Ego Involvement

When people are intrinsically motivated for an activity, they do it volitionally and they willingly persist at the activity when no external contingencies are present, experiencing interest and enjoyment while doing so. People can, however, also be motivated by other internal processes that lead them to persist at an activity even in the absence of external contingencies. One such process is ego involvement. When people's egos-that is, their feelings of worth-are contingent on some outcome such as doing well at a task, they may be very motivated to engage that task, with a sense of resolve and determination, feeling pressure and tension about having to do well. Ryan, Koestner, and Deci found that when people became ego involved and then failed to do well at the ego-involving activity, they tended to be persistent and insistent with respect to the activity-that is, they had a high level of ego-involved motivation.

Accordingly, Reeve and Deci found that losers of a competition, although their intrinsic motivation for the task was significantly undermined, did have a high level of ego-involved motivation for the task. Apparently, the competition had gotten them ego involved in the task, and losing made them determined to get better at the task in order to prove their worth. In the current study, participants who lost the competitively contingent rewards would show an enhanced level of ego-involved motivation for the activity, needing to do better at in order to feel better about themselves.

Losers' Intrinsic Motivation

In the present study, researchers also examined possible ways of counteracting what they expected would be strongly negative effects on intrinsic motivation of losing the competitively contingent reward. They began by nothing that, with competitively contingent rewards, losers get the negative performance feedback implicit in losing and they also fail to get the desired rewards. Thus, they considered two possible approaches to counteracting the negative effects of losing the competitively contingent reward: (1) providing positive feedback on the quality of performance, and (2) providing a performance-contingent reward to make up for the competitively contingent reward they failed to win. Consider these in turn.

Positive Feedback for Losers

Positive performance feedback has generally been found to enhance intrinsic motivation. Further, the initial study of the effects of competition on intrinsic motivation indicated that when people received implicit positive feedback, namely seeing that they solved puzzles faster than another participant, they were significantly more intrinsically motivated than people who won a competition. Together these findings suggest that positive performance feedback can be a powerfully positive motivator.

Researchers hypothesised that, if losers of a competitively contingent reward received positive competence feedback about their actual performance at the activity, they would be significantly more intrinsically motivated than comparable losers who did not receive the positive feedback. In other words, the positive feedback should help to counteract the negative feedback implicit in losing a competitively contingent reward. In the present experiment, one of the groups of participants who were told they could win a competitively contingent reward but in fact lost it were also told at the beginning of the experiment that if they solved three out of the four puzzles, they would be doing very well because they would have performed better than 70% of previous participants. These participants, all of whom did in fact solve at least three puzzles, thus got positive feedback about their performance, and they expected them to show significantly higher intrinsic motivation than those who lost the competitively contingent reward but got no positive performance feedback.

Monetary Rewards for Losers

As noted, losing a competitively contingent reward means not only that participants get implicit negative feedback but also that they fail to attain their goal of receiving the reward. As such, it is possible that, even though they lose the competitively contingent reward, receiving a reward for doing well (i.e., a performance-contingent reward) that is comparable in magnitude to the reward they losing the counteract the negative effect of losing the competitively contingent reward.

Tangible rewards, collapsed across type of contingency, have been found meta-analytically to undermine both behavioural and self-report measures of intrinsic motivation. However, the meta-analysis showed that performance-contingent rewards undermined the behavioural measure of intrinsic motivation, but not self-reports of enjoyment. Researchers interpretation of this seemingly disparate result is based in the idea that people enjoy receiving a performance contingent reward because it represents competence affirmation. Specifically, although tangible performance-contingent rewards tend to-be experienced as controlling and thus to decrease self-initiation of the activity, the message of competence conveyed by the performance-contingent rewards promotes enjoyment.

A performance-contingent reward should be nearly as effective as positive feedback in terms of promoting enjoyment because in both conditions people will feel more competent. However, if people are controlled by a performance-contingent reward, they should not self-initiate the activity in the absence of an operative reward contingency, because research has shown that perceived competence does not enhance intrinsically motivated behaviour if people do not feel autonomous. Accordingly, they hypothesised that performance-contingent rewards given to the losers of a competitively contingent reward would lead to less intrinsic motivation behaviourally assessed than would positive feedback given to losers of the competitively contingent reward, but that the levels of enjoyment for the two groups would not differ.

Recently, although the evidence for this is relatively scant, Harackiewicz and Sansone argued that a condition in, which participants get performance contingent rewards for matching evaluative norms should yield higher levels of intrinsic motivation than a condition in which people are told their performance will be evaluated and are then given positive feedback for matching evaluative norms. In the current study, losers in the positive-feedback condition and the performance-contingent rewards conditions were given evaluative norms before they began the puzzle solving. Thus, counter to the predictions that performance contingent rewards would undermine free-choice behaviour but that the two groups would not differ on enjoyment, if Harackiewicz and Sansone were correct, then the performance-contingent rewards condition should have a higher level of both free-choice behaviour and self-reported enjoyment than would the positive feedback condition.

Measuring Intrinsic Motivation and Ego-Involved Persistence

Past experiments have used two different measures of intrinsic motivation. The behavioural measure assesses behaviour during a so-called free-choice period subsequent to the performance period, and the self-report measure assesses participants' reports of interest/ enjoyment for the activity, which is also done following the performance period. Consider the behavioural measure because it relates not only to intrinsic motivation but also to ego involvement that can be easily stimulated in competitive situations.

The free-choice behavioural measure involved leaving participants alone with the target activity and interesting alternative activities for a period of time when the participants assumed that no one would know what they were doing and they would not be asked to work more with the target activity. If participants spent time with the target activity, they were assumed to be intrinsically motivated. The number of seconds spent with the target activity was the measure of intrinsic motivation.

This free-choice behavioural measure has been widely used, and it worked extremely well to assess intrinsic motivation following an experimental manipulation in which an external contingency was presented and subsequently removed. However, it ran into problems when research began to investigate the effects of ego involvement on intrinsic motivation. Specifically, when the experimenter did a manipulation that resulted in people's egos or feelings of self-worth becoming contingent on their performance at an activity, there was no easy way for the experimenter to remove the contingency. In other words, whereas an experimenter can make clear before the free-choice period begins that a tangible-reward contingency is no longer operative, there is no comparable way to terminate an ego-involvement contingency because it is within the person's psyche. Thus, following an experimental period in which people became ego involved in their performance on a task, they may continue to work on the activity during a free choice period in order to buttress a threatened sense of worth. Thus, the free choice period behaviour could reflect either intrinsic motivation or ego-involved persistence.

Two approaches have been used for dealing with this problem. First, Ryan et al. suggested that if free-choice behaviour is really intrinsically motivated, the person should be experiencing interest/enjoyment while doing it; in other words, the free-choice behaviour and self-reports of interest should be positively correlated. On the other hand, if the free-choice behaviour is ego involved, free-choice behaviour and self-reported interest should not be correlated. Ryan et al. further suggested that when ego-involved people do badly at a task, they will be driven to persist during the free-choice period in order to regain a sense of self-worth, whereas if they do well, they will not need to persist because their good performance will have confirmed their worth.

The researchers did an experiment in which, in some conditions, any free-choice behaviour was expected to be intrinsically motivated and in others free-choice behaviour was expected to be ego-involved persistence. Results indicated that in the conditions where intrinsic motivation was expected, free-choice behaviour was significantly positively correlated with expressed interest; whereas, in the conditions where ego-involved persistence was expected, free-choice behaviour was not correlated with expressed interest. As such, Ryan et al. were able to separate the two types of free-choice behaviour. However, the disadvantage to this approach is that the free-choice period behaviour was defined as either intrinsic motivation or ego-involved persistence at the level of the experimental condition rather than within individuals.

The second approach to distinguishing intrinsic motivation from ego-involved persistence during a free-choice period was suggested by Reeve and Deci. They partitioned the free-choice measure into two categories: (a) working with new puzzle configurations, and (b) working with the previously encountered configurations. The reasoning was that, if people are intrinsically motivated for an activity, they would seek novelty and challenge because of interest, so working with new puzzles was considered an indicator of intrinsically motivated persistence. In contrast, if participant are working to regain their feelings of worth-for example, after having failed, while ego involved-they would return to the puzzles on which they had done poorly in order to try to feel better about themselves. Thus, working with old (previously-encountered) puzzles was considered an indicator of ego-involved persistence.

As already mentioned, competition tends to promote ego involvement, and failing at a task in which one is ego involved can promote ego-involved persistence. It was thus necessary to have measures of both intrinsic motivation and ego-involved persistence in the current study.

Method

A total of 25 male and 55 female University of Rochester undergraduates volunteered for the experiment and received extra course credit for doing so. Most of the participants were Caucasian in the age range of 18-23 years old.

The experimental task was a spatial-relations puzzle called Happy Cubes. Past studies with college students working on the Happy Cubes puzzle indicate that participants find it to be a highly interesting activity and persist at it during the free-choice period. Participants were provided with drawings of three-dimensional configurations that they were to reproduce with the mechanical puzzle.

Procedure

Participants arrived at a waiting area where they were welcomed by an experimenter and taken to the experimental room. The experimenter then went to an adjoining room from where he observed participants through a one-way mirror and communicated with them over an intercom. The experimenter explained that the purpose of the study was to examine motivation for working oh a spatial-relations puzzle task. Participants were randomly placed in one of the five experimental conditions. Those in the four competitive conditions were told that their same-sex opponent had already arrived and was settled in the adjoining room.

The experimenter used a sex-appropriate name to refer to that "other participant." In reality, there was no person in the next room, but the purpose of this pretext was to help create a competitive atmosphere. On the table in all five conditions were (a) the Happy Cubes puzzle, (b) two drawings of three-dimensional configurations that the participants would attempt to duplicate with the puzzle during a practice period, and (c) a selection of popular magazines that served as an alternative activity during a later free-choice period. The experimenter explained that there would be a series of six puzzles to solve. The first two of which were there on the table and would be the practice puzzles. The other four would be used subsequently as the actual performance puzzles.

Before starting the practice puzzles, participants received experimental instructions appropriate to their experimental condition. In the no-competition/ nofeedback/no-reward control group (Condition 1) the experimenter simply asked the participants to work on the puzzles, "doing your individual best." In each of the four competitively contingent reward conditions, the experimenter told participants the following: "The purpose of this competition is to try to outperform the other person by solving your puzzles faster than he or she." Thus, participants were led to believe that they would to be competing against the same-sex participant who had been said to be in the adjacent room. "To win the game you will need to solve the puzzles more quickly than your opponent. You will have four puzzles to solve and you will have four minutes to solve each puzzle.

It does not matter whether you figure out how the puzzle works, the important thing is to win the competition. So, focus your attention on being the winner." In all four competitively contingent reward conditions (Conditions 2-5), participants were told that "you can make $3 by winning the competitive game; in other words, you will get $3 if you solve more of the puzzles more quickly than your opponent." People in Conditions 4 and 5 were given the following additional instructions: "if you manage to 'solve three out of the four puzzles correctly, regardless of whether you are slower or faster than your opponent, you will have done better than 70% of the participants in their previous studies. So, the purpose of this competition is twofold: first, to try to beat the other person by solving your puzzles faster than he (or she) does, and second, to try to surpass the 70th percentile performance standard by correctly solving at least three of the four puzzles within the allotted time."

People in Condition 5 were then given an additional instruction, namely that "if you meet the 70th percentile performance standard by correctly solving at least three out of the four puzzles, you will receive a $3 reward. So, there are two ways to earn a reward of $3; one way is through beating the other person and the other is by performing well, namely by solving three out of four puzzles correctly. If you solve three puzzles and win the game you will earn $6." The researchers was to find four puzzles that would be as challenging as possible but would allow all participants to solve at least three of the four.

The amount of money given for the performance contingent reward was $3 just as the amount given for the competitively contingent reward was $3. This was done so the losers of the competitively contingent reward in Condition 5 would receive the same amount of money from the performance-contingent reward that the winners of the competitively contingent reward received in Condition 2, and also so the losers in Condition 5 would lose the same amount as the losers in Conditions 3 and 4 who ended up without any monetary reward. The losers in Condition 5 would have imagined that the winners had made three dollars more than they themselves received (because they would have believed that the winner would get $3 for winning and $3 for solving at least three puzzles). Similarly, the losers in Conditions 3 and 4 would have imagined that the winners had made $3 more than they did from winning the competition (these participants would not have known anything about a performance-contingent reward). As such, for each comparison, the amount of money believed to have been won and/or lost was controlled across relevant comparisons.

Before starting the performance puzzles and after receiving the instructions, participants in all conditions were given two practice puzzles. After the first, participants in the four competitively contingent reward conditons (Conditions 2-5) were informed that their opponent had failed to solve the puzzle in the allotted time, so the participant would have won on that puzzle. After the second practice puzzle, participants were told that their opponent had solved the second puzzle faster than they did. Puzzles had been preselected so that the participants would not be able to solve the second practice puzzle within the allotted time, but could solve the first practice puzzle. This matching of practice outcomes in the competition conditions was intended to convey the impression that the two people were roughly of equal ability and was also intended to create the perception of a challenging game. After the two practice trials the, experimenter told participants the practice period was over.

The experimenter then entered the room to remove the practice configurations and leave six more configurations. Four of these configurations were for the performance phase of the experiment and were put on one end of the table. The other two were placed on the other end of the table so participants could work on new puzzles during the subsequent free-choice period. The period of working on the performance puzzles then began. In each of the competitively contingent reward conditions, the experimenter provided comparison feedback after each trial by telling the participants over the intercom which of them (i.e., the participant or the "confederate" opponent) had won on that puzzle. The feedback that was provided had been predetermined according to condition.

The win versus lose outcome was manipulated by the experimenter as follows. The score of the competitive set of four performance puzzles was always 3-1. Participants in the win condition (Conditions 2) were told

Table 5.

	No-competition, no-feedback, control group (Condition 1)	Winning c-c reward (Condition 2)	Losing c-c reward (Condition 3)	Losing c-c reward, receiving positive feedback (Condition 4)	Losing c-c reward, receiving p-c reward (Condition 5)
Intrinsic motivation as the dependent variable Losing c-c reward relative to winning c-c reward	0	1	–1	0	0
Losing c-c reward relative to no-competition, no-feedback,	1	0	–1	0	0
no-reward control group	0	0	1	-1	0
Losing c-c reward with positive feedback relative to just losing c-c reward	0	0	0	-1	-1
Losing c-c reward, but getting p-c reward relative to losing c-c reward, but getting positive feedback	0	0	0	1	-1
Ego-involved persistence as the dependent variable					
Losing c-c reward versus winning c-c no-feedback, no-reward control group	3	3	-2	-2	-2

they won the first, third, and fourth trial and the opponent had won the second trial. Participants in the lose conditions (Conditions 3-5) were told they lost the first, third, and fourth trial, but they had won the second trial. This way, the score after two trials was equal (1-1) in all competitively contingent reward conditions to further the feelings of competition and challenge. If participants won a puzzle, they had to wait an additional minute or so, in order to give the impression that their opponent was still working on the puzzle.

After the four performance puzzles were completed, participants in all competitive conditions were given the results of the competition, and those in Conditions 4 and 5 got additional feedback. Specifically, participants in Condition 2 were informed that they had won the competition and would receive their $3 for winning at the end of the experiment. Participants in Conditions 3, 4, and 5 were informed that they had lost the competition and would not receive the competitively contingent reward. In Conditions 4 and 5, participants were told that, "although you lost the competition, you still managed to solve at least three out of the four puzzles correctly. I can tell you that you did very well because you reached the performance standard of doing better than 70% of the participants in previous experiments." For participants in Condition 5, the experimenter also said, "So, at the end of the experiment you will receive the $3 reward I promised you." Because the four performance puzzles had been pretested all participants were able to solve at least three of the puzzles within the allotted time, so all competitive losers in Condition 4 received the positive feedback and all competitive losers in Condition S receive the performance-contingent reward.

Table 6: Correlations Among All Variables

	1	2	3	4	5
1. Perceived competence	–				
2. Enjoyment	.56	–			
3. Time spent on new puzzles	.17	.23	–		
4. Time spent on old puzzles	–.03	.05	–.18	–	
5. Total time spent on puzzles	.15	.25	.$8	.32	–

After the four performance trials, the experimenter entered the experimental room and told participants that the puzzle-solving phase of the experiment was over and that he needed to go to another room to get a final questionnaire for them. Because the appropriate questionnaire was to be prepared by the computer based on their performance, it would take him just a few minutes to get the two correct questionnaires and drop off the one for the opponent. The participants were left alone for a 6 mn free-choice period, during which they could do whatever they wanted to do in the experimental room until the experimenter returned.

During this period an observer recorded the amount of time the participants spent on the new and the old puzzle configurations. The observers had been trained to be able to look through the one-way window and identify whether particular puzzles were the performance-period puzzles (i.e., old puzzles) or the free-choice-period puzzles (i.e., new puzzles). After the free-choice period, the experimenter re-entered the room, administered the postexperimental questionnaire, debriefed the participants, and gage the reward to those who had been told they would receive it.

Results

Researchers examining the effectiveness of the two

approaches to differentiating intrinsic motivation from ego-involved persistence, namely, the within-person and the within-group approaches. They used as a criterion that free-choice behaviour theorised to reflect intrinsic motivation would be correlated with enjoyment whereas free-choice behaviour theorised to reflect ego-involved persistence would not. First, they considered the within-person approach by correlating selfreports of enjoyment with the two types of free-choice behaviour-working with new puzzles versus working with previously-encountered puzzles. As in Reeve and Deci, a significant positive correlation was found between working on new puzzles and enjoyment, $r(78) = .23$, $p < .05$, but working on old puzzles was not correlated with enjoyment, $r(78) = .05$, $p < .64$, thus suggesting that time spent working on new puzzles is a good index of intrinsic motivation (Table 2).

Second, they examined the group-level approach by correlating total free-time behaviour (the sum of the time spent working on new puzzles and old puzzles) with self-reported enjoyment in Conditions 1 and 2 versus Conditions 3-5 to examine whether total free-choice behaviour would tend to be more reflective of intrinsic motivation in the former two conditions and of ego-involved persistence in the latter three. Ryan et al. argued that ego-involving conditions (e.g., competition) where people get negative feedback are the most likely to lead to ego-involved persistence during the free-choice period.

Accordingly, in conditions where there was implicit negative feedback from losing the competition (Conditions 3-5), total free-choice behaviour and enjoyment were not correlated, $r(46) = .16$, $p < .40$, whereas, in conditions with no competition or no implicit negative feedback (Conditions 1 and 2), the magnitude of correlation between total free-choice behaviour and enjoyment was more than twice as large and nearly significant, $r(30) = .34$, $p < .06$. This is the first study in which the within-person and the group-level approaches were both considered, and these preliminary results suggest that both approaches are reasonable ways to distinguish the two types of persistence.

Table 7: Correlations Among All Variables

	1	2	3	4	5
1. Perceived competence	–				
2. Enjoyment	.56	–			
3. Time spent on new puzzles	.17	.23	–		
4. Time spent on old puzzles	-.03	.05	–.18	–	
5. Total time spent on puzzles	.15	.25	.88	.32	–

In the next preliminary analysis, they examined perceived competence as a manipulation check using protected t tests. Competitors in Condition 2 who won the reward felt more competent than losers in Condition 3 who got no feedback and no reward, $t(75) = 4.09$, $p < .001$. Losers in Condition 4 who received positive performance feedback felt significantly more competent than loser in Condition 3 who received neither feedback nor rewards, $t(75) = -2.95$, $p < .01$. Finally, losers in Condition's who got performance-contingent rewards did not differ in their level of perceived competence from losers in Condition 4 who got positive performance feedback, $t(75) = -0.32$, $p < .75$. As such, the manipulations did work in that losing diminished feelings of competence whereas positive feedback and performance-contingent rewards enhanced feelings of competence.

Primary analyses

A MANOVA was conducted across the five conditions with all five behavioural and self-report variables included. The overall F-value for the Pillai's procedure was significant, $F(16, 300) = 2.49$, $p < .001$. Subsequently a one-way ANOVA was performed for each of the variables, and then the hypothesised contrasts were tested. The cell-means appear in Table 3.

The five experimental conditions differed significantly on the intrinsic motivation behavioural measure of working on new puzzles, $F(4, 75) = 4.48$, $p < .01$, and on perceived competence, $F(4, 75) = 4.89$, $p < .001$. The conditions were marginally different on self-reported enjoyment, $F(4, 7{,}5) = 2.01$, $p < .10$, on ego-involved persistence (i.e., playing with old puzzles), $F(4, 75) = 2.37$, $p < .06$, and on total free-choice behaviour (i.e., the sum of working on old and new puzzles), $F(4, 75) = 2.02$, $p < .10$.

2

Sports Psychology

Sport psychologists work with sports participants across a range of both team and individual sports and from amateur to elite levels of competition. The aim is predominately to help athletes prepare psychologically for competition and to deal with the psychological demands of both competition and training. Examples of the work they carry out include counselling referees to deal with the stressful and demanding aspects of their role, advising coaches on how to build cohesion within their squad of athletes and helping athletes to deal with the psychological and emotional consequences of sustaining an injury. An exercise psychologist is primarily concerned with the application of psychology to increase exercise participation and motivational levels in the general public.

Examples of the work they do include optimising the benefits that can be derived from exercise participation and helping individual clients with the implementation of goal-setting strategies. Sport and exercise psychologists work in a wide range of sport and exercise settings and with a diverse range of clients. Most sport psychologists combine consultancy work with teaching and research or psychological consultancy in other areas such as the clinical and occupational domains. Some sport psychologists do hold full-time positions with professional sports teams or national governing bodies and opportunities to work as a full-time sport psychologist are constantly increasing in number.

A similar scenario exists for exercise psychologists, with most practitioners combining consultancy with teaching and research careers. The work of exercise psychologists might involve GP exercise referral and setting up and evaluating exercise programmes in employment, prison and psychiatric contexts.

The work of a sport or exercise psychologist is centred on people and can be extremely varied. Although consultancy work may be office-based it is equally likely that consultants will work in field settings such as team premises, competition venues, clinical rehabilitation and recreational exercise settings.

Development and Initial Validation of The Basic Psychological Needs in Exercise Scale

This section discuss, a research study of Symeon P. Vlachopoulos and Sotiria Michailidou. It deals with the development process and initial validation of the Basic Psychological Needs in Exercise Scale (BPNES). This study included the following scale construction steps:

a) the item development and the examination of the content validity of the scale;
b) the item selection for inclusion into the final version of the scale;
c) the examination of the factor structure, internal consistency, generalisability validity, and discriminant validity;
d) the examination of the predictive validity of the scale and the degree to which the BPNES item scores are susceptible to socially desirable responding;

e) the extent to which the psychometric properties of the scale in the calibration sample would be replicable in a validation sample; and

f) the test-retest reliability of the instrument's scores over a 4-week period.

The hypotheses forwarded were that (a) the selected items would confirm the hypothesised three-factor structure; (b) the instrument subscales would emerge internally consistent; (c) the factor structure of the scale would be invariant across the calibration and the validation samples including specifically the factor loadings, factor variances, factor covariances, and item uniquenesses; (d) the instrument's factors would emerge as related but distinct constructs; (e) the subscales' mean scores would be predictive of key exercise-related motivational outcomes and would be related in theoretically expected ways with such outcomes; (f) the items and subscale mean scores would not attract socially desirable responses; and (g) the need subscale mean scores would remain relatively stable over a 4-week time period.

As far as the relationships with the motivational outcomes were concerned, all of the outcomes were hypothesised to be more strongly correlated with autonomy and competence rather than relatedness whereas the external locus of control would be unrelated to all of the need variables because it does not reflect any degree of responsibility on the part of the participants for regulating their exercise behavior. Finally, enjoyment and interest would be more strongly correlated with both autonomy and competence compared to the remaining outcomes.

Methods and Participants

Both samples comprised Greek-speaking exercise

participants, men and women, ages 18 to 64 years who voluntarily participated in organised exercise programs in private fitness centers. Participants were paying to use the fitness centers. This population was targeted because approximately 50% of such participants are at risk of dropping out of organised exercise programs within 6 months from program initiation.

Item selection and initial validity examination of the items tools place in the calibration sample (CS) whereas a validation sample (VS) was used to examine the extent to which the psychometric properties would be replicated in a separate sample representing the same population. Data from the VS were collected 5 months after data had been collected from the CS. Individuals were not randomly assigned to the samples. The samples were different in terms of individuals who comprised the samples, fitness centers used, and the time period in which data collection took place.

There were 508 Greek-speaking exercise participants attending structured exercise programs in five large private fitness centers in Thessaloniki, a city in the northern part of Greece. The gender breakdown was 254 men and 254 women. All participants had attended at least six exercise sessions by the time they provided their responses. The participants' age ranged from 18 to 55 years (M = 30.06 years, SD = 8.13 years). Their exercise experience ranged from a few months to 38 years (M= 8.18 years, SD = 7.30 years). The weekly frequency of their exercise participation ranged from one to seven times per week (M= 3.82, SD = 1.16). Their average exercise class duration was approximately 1½ hr (M= 84.55 min, SD = 29.69 min). For activity type, 102 participants (20.1 %) reported that they were mainly involved in group-type activities such as aerobics, body pump, tae-bo, and cycling, whereas 313 participants (61.6%) were mainly involved in conventional weight-training activities such as free style weight lifting. Finally, 93 participants (18.3%) reported exercise activity involving a combination of the aforementioned activities.

Validation sample

There were 504 participants attending structured exercise programs in five large private fitness centers, different from the centers used for the CS, in Thessaloniki, Greece. There were 246 men (48.8%) and 258 women (51.2%). All of the participants had attended at least six exercise sessions by the time they provided their responses. Participants' age ranged from 18 to 65 years (M= 28.92 years, SD = 8.45 years). The participants' exercise experience ranged from a few months to 45 years (M = 6.88 years, SD = 6.91 years). The weekly frequency of exercise attendance ranged from one to seven times (M = 3.74, SD = 1.07) and the average exercise class duration ranged from 40 to 240 min (M = 85.08, SD = 30.08). For activities, 109 participants (21.6%) reported that they were mainly involved in group-type activities such as aerobics, body pump, tae-bo, and cycling, whereas 280 participants (55.6%) were mainly involved in conventional weight-training activities such as free style weight lifting. Finally, 108 participants (21.4%) reported exercise activity involving a combination of the aforementioned activities.

Retest sample

The retest sample comprised 75 exercise participants. Data were collected from one of the fitness centers used for the VS data collection. There were 46 men (61.3%) and 29 women (38.7%). The participants' age ranged from 18 to 55 years (M = 28.43, SD = 8.36). The participants' exercise experience ranged from a few months to 45 years (M = 8.64, SD = 8.66), and their weekly attendance in the fitness center ranged from one to six times (M= 4.02, SD = 1.03). The duration of their exercise classes ranged from

45 to 190 min (M= 93.46, SD = 33.77). For activities, 10 participants (13.3%) reported to be involved in group-type activities, 44 (58.7%) in conventional weight-training activities, whereas 21 individuals (28%) reported to be involved in a combination of the aforementioned activities.

Seven external variables were assessed. The variables of concentration, attitude, and internal-external locus of control were considered to be cognitive variables. Exercise enjoyment was considered to be an affective variable. Intention for exercise involvement and frequency of participation were considered to be behavioural variables.

Concentration. To assess the participants' concentration levels, four items were used from the Concentration subscale of the Trait Flow Scale. Construct validity evidence has been reported for the TFS through correlations with theoretically related variables. Item wording was modified to become appropriate for use in exercise by substituting the term sport with the term exercise.

Intrinsic Motivation Inventory. To determine the degree to which participants enjoyed their exercise classes, the Enjoyment-Intrinsic Interest subscale was employed from the Intrinsic Motivation Inventory that has been adapted and used successfully with a Hellenic population in school-based physical education classes. Goudas et al. provided evidence for the structural validity of the IMI in a Hellenic sample. Scale items were modified for use in exercise. The respondents indicated the extent of their agreement with the subscales' items on a 5-point Likert-type scale ranging from 1 (do not agree at all) to 5 (very strongly agree). Sample items included the following: "In general, I find my involvement in exercise very interesting," and "In general, I have a lot of fun when I exercise." The alpha value was .78 for the CS and .83 for the VS.

Attitude. Attitude toward exercise participation was assessed by the following question: "I think that participating in exercise five times per week is ... ." In line with recommendations by Ajzen and Fishbein, participants responded to four bipolar adjectives on a 7-point semantic differential scale. The adjectives used were "harmful-beneficial," "pleasant-unpleasant," "boring-interesting," and "important-unimportant." The frequency of exercise participation included in these items falls within the guidelines forwarded by the American College of Sports Medicine for physiological and psychological changes to occur and be maintained through regular exercise participation. Adequate reliability evidence for these items has been provided in a Greek exercise context by Theodorakis. The alpha value for both the CS and the VS was .80.

Intention. To assess strength of intention for continued exercise involvement, three items were used: "I intend/I will try/I am determined to continue participating in this exercise program five times per week for the remainder of this year." In line with Ajzen and Fishbein, participants responded on a semantic differential scale ranging from 1 (extremely unlikely) to 7 (extremely likely). Satisfactory reliability has been demonstrated for the' intention items in a Greek exercise context. Once more the frequency of exercise participation included in the intention items was based on ACSM guidelines for the appropriate frequency of exercise behavior that should be undertaken for healthy adults to obtain and maintain a number of physiological and psychological benefits. The alpha values for both samples were .95.

Athletic Behavior Locus of Control Scale. To assess the degree to which the participants felt they had control over sustaining their exercise involvement, their internal-external locus of control levels were assessed. To this end, the Athletic Behavior Locus of Control Scale was employed. This scale has been modified for a Greek population based on the Exercise Locus of Control Scale. The subscales used in this study were the "Internal Locus of Control" subscale and the "External Locus of Control-Instructor" subscale. Participants indicated their agreement with six "internal locus" and three "external locus" items responding on a 5-point answer scale ranging from 1 (strongly disagree) to 5 (strongly agree). Items adopted the following stem: "Sustaining my involvement in exercise five times per week for the remainder of this year in the present fitness center depends . .. ." Sample items for the "internal locus" subscale were as follows: "totally on me," "on my own actions," and "on my patience." For the "external locus" subscale, sample items were "totally on the fitness instructor" and "totally on the fitness instructor's exercise program." The alpha values for the internal locus of control were .94 for the CS and .91 for the VS. For external locus of control the alpha values were .87 and .88, respectively, for each one of the samples.

Frequency of exercise participation. The weekly frequency of exercise participation served as a behavioral indicator of the participants' persistence in exercise. Weekly frequency was estimated over the last 2 months from the time of the initiation of data collection.

Social Desirability Scale. To assess the extent to which the scale's items may be susceptible to social desirability, Reynolds's Social Desirability Scale was administered with the aforementioned scales. This is a 13-item shortened version of Crowne and Marlowe's Social Desirability Scale that originally comprised 33 items. The items describe culturally approved behaviors that have a low incidence of occurrence. Reynolds provided satisfactory evidence of factorial validity, reliability, and concurrent validity of the scale.

Procedures

Due to a lack of a comprehensive list of the Greek exercising population, nonprobability sampling procedures were used with convenience sampling. Participants were included in each sample to achieve a ratio of participants to parameters to be estimated in the three-factor CFA model greater than 15 to 1. The same procedures were followed during data collection for both samples. Initially, the fitness center managers were informed about the purpose of the study and permission for approaching the participants was secured. The participants were systematically intercepted by research assistants (every second person) around reception areas during various times of day (morning, afternoons, and evenings). Data were collected during both weekdays and weekends. Before administration of the questionnaires, the participants signed an informed consent form for participation in the study while they were informed that no harm or danger of any kind was involved and that their participation would be anonymous. The questionnaires were completed before initiation of the exercise class. Questionnaire completion took approximately 12 min.

Data Analyses

To select the final BPNES items, the model generating approach was employed through CFA procedures using the EQS software. The first phase of the analyses involved estimating three "one-factor" CFA models, one for each BPNES factor. The aim was to identify those items that strongly defined their intended factor and drop those items that were weakly associated with the factor. The second phase involved the estimation of "two-factor"

CFA models with correlated factors representing all the possible pairs of the BPNES factors. The purpose was to identify those items whose presence in the models maximised the overall goodness-of-fit indexes, and drop the remaining items. The items to be dropped were identified by inspection of the goodness-of-fit indexes and the largest standardised residuals provided by EQS. The third phase of the analyses involved the estimation of one "three-factor" CFA model including the final 12 items to be included in the scale.

In line with Hoyle and Panter, the fit indexes used for model assessment were the chi-square statistic (χ^2), the Comparative Fit Index (CFI), and the Non-Normed Fit Index (NNFI). CFI values range between 0 and 1 and are unaffected by sample size. NNFI and CFI values greater than .90 indicate a good fit of the model to the data, whereas values greater than .95 indicate an excellent fit. In addition, the Standardised Root Mean Residual (SRMR), the Root Mean Squared Error of Approximation (RMSEA), and the 90% RMSEA confidence interval (CI) were examined. Values close to .08 for the SRMR and .06 for the RMSEA are indicative of an adequate model fit. The 90% RMSEA CI was examined to assess the stability of the RMSEA across samples. Also, the Akaike's Information Criterion (AIC) was used for comparing competing CFA models because it takes into account both the goodness of fit of the model and the number of parameters that have to be estimated to achieve that degree of fit in a balanced way.

The results section includes three major sections entitled confirmatory factor analysis, predictive validity, and test-retest reliability. The first section includes subsections on descriptive statistics, discriminant validity, and factorial invariance.

Confirmatory Factor Analysis

Statistical description of BPNES items. The univariate skewness values of the BPAS items ranged from -1.02 to -.34 for the CS and from -.78 to -.11 for the VS. The univariate kurtosis values ranged from -.41 to 1.09 for the CS and from -.31 to .75 for the VS. The Mardia's coefficient of multivariate kurtosis was 83.97 for the CS and 47.16 for the VS indicating multivariate normality in both samples. For this CFA model, multivariate normality was indicated by Mardia's values lower than 168 based on the formula p (p+2) where p equals the number of observed variables. The results of the final three-factor CFA model showed an adequate fit of the model to the data for both the CS (χ^2 =166.43, $p < .001$, df =51, NNFI = .96, CFI = .96, SRMR = .04, RMSEA = .06, 90% CI = .05-.07) and the VS (χ^2 = 122.28, $p < .001$, df = 51, NNFI = .97, CFI = .97, SRMR = .03, RMSEA = .05, 90% CI = .04-.06).

In the CS, the factor loadings ranged from .59 to .91. The latent factor correlations were .79 (Autonomy-Competence), .50 (Autonomy-Relatedness), and .41 (Competence-Relatedness). In the VS, the factor, loadings ranged from .60 to .89. The correlations between the need latent factors were .76 (Autonomy-Competence), .48 (Autonomy-Relatedness), and .55 (Competence-Relatedness).

Discriminant validity. To examine the empirical separability of the BPNES factors, a series of CFA models that involved all the possible combinations of the BPNES factors were compared to the three-factor model. Overall, the results showed that the three-factor model was significantly better compared to the other models in both samples indicating that the three factors were empirically separable.

BPNES factorial invariance. To assess the generalisability validity of the scale's scores, the instrument's factorial invariance was examined across the CS and the VS. According to Marsh, the invariance of all factor loadings is the minimal condition for factorial invariance. Byme argued for the usefulness of "partial invariance" of factor loadings that is a less demanding test. According to Bentler, the invariance of measurement errors is the least important hypothesis to test. In line with Marsh, a totally noninvariant multisample model (Model 1) was computed first to serve as a baseline model on which the following models would be compared. In Model 2, factor loadings were constrained to be equal whereas further equality constraints were added to the factor covariances in Model 3. In Model 4, the factor variances were also constrained to be equal whereas in Model 5, equality constraints were added on item uniquenesses.

The goodness-of-fit indexes and results of the chi-square difference tests are presented in Table 4. All the multisample models were in general supported by the data. The Lagrange Multiplier test showed that out of the 12 items, the factor loadings of the third Autonomy and the fourth Competence items emerged as noninvariant, whereas the covariance between the Competence and Relatedness factors was also noninvariant across samples. All factor variances were invariant whereas three item uniquenesses were found to be noninvariant. The chi-square difference tests showed that the more constrained models were significantly worse in terms of fit compared to the less constrained models, except for the difference between Models 3 and 4; however, despite the significance of the model differences, the magnitude of the fit indexes showed that even when all parameters were constrained, the model still had an excellent fit to the data. Overall, for the CS, BPNES item mean scores ranged from 3.75 to 4.03 for Autonomy, from 3.53 to 4.00 for Competence, and from 3.49 to 3.84 for Relatedness.

The Cronbach's alpha values were .84 for Autonomy, .81 for Competence, and .92 for Relatedness. Factor loadings ranged from .60 to .86 for Autonomy, from .59 to .78 for Competence, and from. 80 to .91 for Relatedness. Item correlations with the Social Desirability Scale ranged from .00 to .18, whereas the correlation with the mean Autonomy score was. 13, with the mean Competence score it was .14, and with the mean Relatedness score it was. 17. All the correlation values were significant ($p < .05$, $N= 508$) except for the first Competence item. The values obtained from the VS on the aforementioned statistical indexes were very close to those reported for the CS.

Test-Retest Reliability

To assess the test-retest reliability of the BPNES subscale scores, 75 exercise participants of the VS were re-assessed over a 4-week period. Similar intervals have been used in examining the temporal stability of scores from domain-specific scales assessing variables in the SDT framework in exercise and sport. To examine the stability of the scales, the intraclass correlation coefficient was used. ICC values between .70 and .80 indicate acceptable levels of. For Autonomy, the mean score changed from 3.94 (SD = 0.66) to 3.97 (SD = 0.67) with in ICC value of .97. For Competence, the mean changed from 3.80 (SD = 0.57) to 3.81 (SD = 0.59) with an ICC value of .97. For Relatedness, the mean changed from 3.70 (SD = 0.73) to 3.74 (SD = 0.75) with an ICC value of.97. The results revealed high levels of test-retest reliability for all three BPNES subscales.

The development and initial validation of the BPNES, a domain-specific self-report instrument designed to assess perceptions of the extent to which the innate psychological needs for Autonomy, Competence, and Relatedness are satisfied in exercise, have been reported here. The results of this study largely supported a number of psychometric qualities of the scale including its factorial composition, internal consistency, test-retest reliability over a 4-week period, the reproducibility of the factor structure across two separate samples representing the same population, discriminant validity, predictive validity with respect to a number of motivational outcomes, and low` correlations between the need scores and social desirability scores.

BPNES Factor Composition and Reliability

The results of the CFA supported the three-factor structure of the BPNES. The results revealed that the 12 BPNES items had an acceptable factor structure with strong factor loadings to define their respective factors. Factor correlations were of a moderate size except for the correlation between Autonomy and Competence that was quite strong; however, despite the sizeable correlation between these factors, comparisons of competing CFA models in the context of discriminant validity analyses demonstrated that they represented correlated but distinct constructs.

In the context of discriminant validity analyses, the model in which the Autonomy and Competence items were specified to load onto the same factor resulted into acceptable goodness-of-fit indexes, yet much worse than the fit indexes of the three-factor model. Accepting the two-factor model as correctly specified would imply that the combined Autonomy-Competence factor would be employed for predicting various motivational outcomes; however, the predictive validity results revealed that it was only enjoyment/interest that was independently predicted by both Autonomy and Competence scores whereas all the remaining outcomes except the external locus of control were predicted significantly and considerably only by the Competence factor. These findings in conjunction with the considerably better fit indexes of the three-factor model led us to accept the initially hypothesised three-factor model as the best representation of the latent structure of the BPNES responses.

The extent to which the factor structure that emerged from the CS would be replicable in the VS was examined through tests of factorial invariance. Despite that the factor structure was confirmed in both the CS and the VS independently through CFA, the tests of factorial invariance demonstrated the equivalence of all the factor loadings across the samples except for the third Autonomy and the fourth Competence items; however, in both samples, these particular factor loadings were greater than .750. These results supported the robustness of the BPNES factor composition. In line with calls for assessment of scale dimensionality in populations different from the one on which the scale was developed, the BPNES factor structure should be examined in other exercising populations such as older individuals, and contexts such as community fitness centers and rehabilitation clinics where developing a better understanding of exercise adherence is an important research goal. Evidence of factorial invariance across populations would further enhance the generalisability validity of the scale.

With respect to the sizeable correlation between the Autonomy and Competence factors that reflected 62% common variance in the CS and 57% common variance in the VS, researchers should be aware of the potential problem that this high correlation may cause in predictive analyses. That is, the great overlap between the constructs may mask important relationships with other variables due to collinearity effects. Hence, researchers should attempt to determine the unique relationships between these need constructs and the criterion variables.

The results of this study supported the adequate internal consistency of the BPNES subscales indicating a tight item structure within subscales. Furthermore, the results of the test-retest reliability analyses demonstrated a high level of stability of the subscale mean scores over a 4-week period, indicating that the participants' scores on the instrument are relatively stable over time. These findings are consistent with the assessment of the need constructs at the contextual level; however, because changes in the perceptions of need satisfaction at the context level may require interventions that may last longer than 4 weeks, the stability of the scale scores needs to be examined over longer time intervals in future studies.

Construct Validity of the BPNES

The predictive validity of the BPNES was supported through the examination of the relationships between the need constructs and the motivational outcomes of concentration during exercise, enjoyment/interest, attitude toward exercise, intention for continued exercise involvement, internal and external loci of control, and weekly frequency of exercise participation. The latent variable structural equation modelling analyses supported the predictive validity of the BPNES subscales by confirming the hypotheses.

With respect to the relative contribution of Autonomy and Competence in the prediction of the ;motivational outcomes, the results demonstrated that it was the need for Competence that appeared considerably stronger compared to Autonomy in predicting all of the motivational outcomes except enjoyment/interest and external locus of control. Enjoyment/interest was predicted by both needs whereas external locus of control was not predicted by any of them. That is, except these two outcomes, the need for Competence appeared as the stronger and only significant predictor of concentration, attitude, intention, internal locus of control, and frequency of exercise participation. These findings speak to the importance of the need for Competence in predicting factors that may be responsible for the maintenance of exercise behavior in a context where the physical and athletic element dominates. That is, perceptions of progress with respect to the end result and feelings of effectance with respect to the activity are central to the maximisation of motivational outcomes that may be responsible for the maintenance of exercise behavior.

As far as the contribution of Autonomy is concerned, . was only enjoyment/interest that was predicted by this subscale. According to Deci, intrinsically motivated behaviors are based on people's needs to feel competent and self-determined. Because interest is the prototype of intrinsically motivated behavior, the fact that only enjoyment/interest was predicted by scores of the Autonomy subscale supported the predictive validity of the Autonomy subscale scores. Finally, the fact that neither of the subscale scores predicted external locus of control confirmed theoretical expectations with respect to the relationship between the constructs.

As far as the magnitude of the contribution of the need for Relatedness in the prediction of the outcomes is concerned, the results demonstrated that Relatedness did not contribute to the prediction of any of the outcomes. These findings are consistent with Deci and Ryan's position; they argued for the possibility that the need for Relatedness in some occasions may be less central for intrinsically motivated behavior than Autonomy and Competence, and especially in situations in which people engage in isolation. That is, Relatedness may not be necessary as a proximal factor in maintaining intrinsic motivation. Such a phenomenon may be frequently observed in the exercise domain where many individuals exercise in isolation.

The predictive validity of the BPNES was also supported by the considerable amounts of variance explained in most of the outcome variables such as concentration, enjoyment/interest, attitude, intention, and frequency of exercise behavior but not internal and external locus of control (less than 10% variance explained). At last, the robustness of the predictive validity findings was supported by the large extent of invariance of the structural path coefficients across the CS and the VS. In sum, strong evidence has emerged for the predictive validity of the BPNES scores. Given that the specific names given to scales are based on a priori expectations rather than empirical evidence, future research studies should be designed to aid in clarifying the specific meanings of scores from the three BPNES factors as well as to examine the predictive validity of the instrument with a wider range of behavioral motivational outcomes relevant to exercise involvement such as levels of exercise adherence or dropout in various populations and contexts.

Given the possibility that the BPNES items might be susceptible to the social desirability response bias, the results revealed that they were largely unaffected by this type of bias. According to Paulhus, the Crowne-Marlowe Social Desirability Scale that was presently used assesses the impression management aspect of social desirability; hence, the BPNES scores have been shown to be largely unaffected from this particular response bias.

In general, the psychometric properties of the BPNES have received initial support. Because the BPNES is a new instrument, more research should be conducted to further examine the construct validity of the scale. Furthermore, and in line with the HMIEM, future research attempts may focus on examining social-psychological factors that may enhance or impede the satisfaction of the three innate psychological needs in exercise. Understanding the impact of such factors on the extent to which these needs are satisfied will promote knowledge concerning practical ways to achieve exercise participants' innate need support. Fulfillment of these needs may, in turn, enhance exercise participants' intrinsic motivation and self-determined forms of extrinsic motivation. These, in turn, may result in a number of positive motivational consequences such as long-term exercise involvement.

3
Emotional Control

Emotions can be defined as brief positive or negative feelings occurring in response to meaningful or important situations, which can influence mood states. Basic emotions such as fear, anger, joy and surprise are commonly experienced in sport, although complex mixes of emotions are often evident. Positive emotions can help sustain motivation and enable us to approach events with enthusiasm and energy. Negative emotions, by contrast, are linked to avoidance behaviours and withdrawal. Emotions in the sporting arena can be triggered by many things personal to an individual, including memories, conversations with other people, seeing the competition venue, weighing up the opposition etc.

Researchers have studied emotions in order to determine why they occur and what impact they have on behaviour. At first it was thought that emotions were simply the result of physiological changes, since physiological symptoms, such as increased heart rate, were commonly observed in such reactions. To test this theory, scientists injected volunteers with the so-called 'stress' hormone epinephrine (adrenaline) to see if emotions could be generated in the laboratory.

A small minority of participants reported feeling genuine emotions (usually sadness) while most reported physiological changes (to be expected after administration of adrenaline) and 'as if' emotions—feelings closely associated with being happy, sad or angry, but not the 'real thing'. Subsequent research demonstrated that emotions could be induced by directing participants' thoughts to emotional triggers, such as deceased relatives (sadness) or past achievements (pride). In summary, research in these areas has shown that both physiological arousal and the cognitive interpretation of that arousal are important in determining the emotional response.

During the lead-up to an important competition, the body starts to prepare for the demands to come by releasing hormones such as epinephrine into the bloodstream, setting in motion the physiological changes associated with increased arousal (sometimes referred to as the 'fight or flight' response). In addition, changes occur in the attentional system, as athletes become more focussed and alert, with increasingly active minds. This overall increase in arousal can be your best friend or your worst enemy: and the key to achieving an appropriate mind-set is to analyse the changes in a rational manner and channel your emotions in a positive direction.

This positive interpretation of the arousal response usually leads to more positive emotions and optimistic outlooks. Conversely, some athletes interpret physiological changes like an increased heart rate as anxiety, worry and apprehension, with a negative impact on emotions that is not conducive to good performance. The most important thing to remember is that your interpretation of physiological changes directs your emotional response. However, the relationship between thoughts and emotions works in both directions: although emotions are the result of cognitive interpretations, they can also impact on your thoughts, giving rise to a vicious circle of negative thoughts and emotions.

The good news for athletes who experience unhelpful emotions before competition is that you can gain more control by altering your focus of attention. The next time you feel these unwanted changes occurring try going through the following psychological routine:

- Tell yourself 'this is my body preparing me to perform well', and repeat the affirmation as necessary;
- Try to recall an image of yourself either winning or performing well, and connect this with the feelings you experienced at the time.

You will need to practise this routine on a regular basis in order to establish it as a habitual response that will help you feel more composed and energised before competitions. If negative images jump into your mind during this time, try to visualise the most successful athlete in your sport and the way he or she runs competes, enjoys performing—in short every positive thing about them; Then visualise yourself with similar positive attributes. Even experienced athletes get nervous and irritable before competing, and a little tension (as long as it is controlled) is often necessary to inspire maximal performance.

The techniques outlined above will not remove all the tension, but they should help you to channel your emotions more positively, which is what top athletes have to learn to do. The difference between winners and losers often boils down to coping skills, in that some athletes have learned to cope with competitive situations better than others. It is important to challenge the belief of some athletes that emotions and mood states are simply reactions to external events; in fact, the athlete has considerable capacity for control in this area.

A recent study by Stevens and Lane identified a number of strategies employed by athletes to regulate their moods. Although unique strategies were employed for specific mood dimensions, results indicated that 'changing location' and 'listening to music' were among the most commonly used strategies. Various research studies have demonstrated the ability of music to impact on emotions and mood by either calming or stimulating the individual as required—although careful consideration is needed in the selection of appropriate music. Listening to music or engaging in a mentally active process, such as a crossword, can help to stop the mind wandering in the hours leading up to competition, although immediately beforehand athletes need to be completely focused on the task in hand.

Such a coping response puts the athlete in control by creating a familiar psychological comfort zone regardless of whatever is going on in the external environment. One of the biggest triggers for anxiety is uncertainty, which is, of course, inherent in all sporting events. The key principle for the athlete is to control the things you can control but not to waste energy on things you can't control. Many top athletes have found, to their cost, that giving attention to how opponents might perform or how technically good others were in the warm-up has a negative impact on their focus. The one thing you can control is your own preparation, so that should have your full focus. By developing consistent routines and ways of coping with distractions, uncertainty can be reduced and you are less likely to be negatively affected by external factors. Because athletes have varying requirements, it is impossible to standardise the pre-competition preparation. However, you may wish to adopt some of the ideas below in creating your own pre-performance strategy to achieve the desired emotional state. These ideas are all designed to be put into practice in the hour before competition, although the principles can be adapted for other times.

The warm-up period can be an important psychological aid as well as preparing the body for the rigors of competition and helping to prevent injury. By developing a relatively stable warm-up routine, including mobility work, stretching and increasing deep muscle temperature, uncertainty can be reduced and the athlete's attention directed to appropriate cues, such as quality technique and body awareness. The development of routines in sport has consistently been shown to be important in directing attentional focus to important cues, so aiding performance.

Although during last summer's major athletic events it was impossible to observe what was going on inside the minds of the sprinters, you could clearly observe the regularity of the warm-up routines and the intense concentration written on athletes' faces prior to taking their marks. These routines are not haphazard, but have been systematically designed to promote optimal functioning in the final few minutes before performance.

Golfers have routines that allow them to prepare in the same way for each shot, as do some rugby place kickers, and tennis players before serving. The key to any routine is that it provides the athlete with control and directs attention to the important cues. Coaches and athletes should work together in deciding the key attentional cues and the sequence in which these should occur. Such routines are the opposite of superstitious rituals that take control away from the performer, as with superstitions outcome is essentially believed to be controlled by sources other than the self.

Mental Preparation

The mental aspects prior to performance should involve focussing on what you are going to do during the event. This can include specific strategies, and the establishment of optimal attentional focus. Some athletes will like to use imagery to recall positive past experiences and generate a sense of confidence. Imagery is a very flexible method to employ prior to competition but it needs to be used correctly for maximum effect. Imagery is not just a form of visualisation, but moreover an all sensory experience that should involve the kinaesthetic sense, emotions and auditory experiences to increase the impact.

Many people use imagery to simply see themselves winning but it can be employed to imagine good technique, coping with difficult situations, recreating emotional feelings and rehearsing the up-coming event in the mind. Imagery is a powerful technique since the brain interprets the imagined scenarios very literally, so directly enhancing such psychological variables as confidence. Always keep imagery sessions short (no more than a few minutes) and simple just before competition. Tailoring the imagery to the desired outcome is essential, so if you want to improve your mood, imagine a realistic scenario that makes you feel good. For more advice on incorporating imagery into your preparation, you may like to read a very practical book entitled *In Pursuit of Excellence*.

Mental preparation can include the repeated use of positive self-statements (affirmations) such as 'I have trained hard, and am in great shape'. These affirmations act by occupying our attention in such a way as to change our belief system over time, so that we begin to attend to feelings or happenings than are consistent with these new beliefs. In the example given above, we begin to focus on events that reinforce our belief that we are in great shape, such as a fast training run. In this way negative perceptions can be tuned-out.

Psychologist Jeff Simons has described one of the best ways to organise the last 20-30 seconds before competition in what has become known as the quick set routine. This three-phase routine is designed to provide a quick focus that can be used just before competition or as a means of refocusing quickly following a distraction. It is minimal in content, which appeals to many athletes, and involves a physical, emotional and focus cue.

However meticulous your planning, things often occur at the competition site that are out of your control. Such events have the potential to impact on your emotional state, distract you from your goals and push you out of your optimal state of preparedness. However, it is important to remember that things only become distractions if you let them. They do not have to negatively influence your mood if you can learn to let them go and refocus. Such distractions can by provided by your opponents. It is increasingly common for opponents to use psych-out strategies or mind games to try and break your concentration and consistency.

If you feel yourself attending to them, it is important to become aware that you have lost your optimal focus and need to refocus quickly. First, 'let go' of the distraction and put it out of your mind; say to yourself 'let it go', shake down your body, and refocus on your breathing. Some people might prefer to use their quick set routine to refocus in such circumstances. Remember that some opponents are actively seeking to unsettle you, and that by reacting to their comments or behaviours you are falling into their trap and allowing them the psychological edge.

By engaging in this psychological duel you run the risk of disrupting your emotional state, becoming over-aroused and suffering a catastrophic decline in performance that is difficult to recover from quickly. Reacting emotionally often means that you discard your carefully laid plans and operate a strategy of reprisal. Self-control is best regained by not reacting to provocation. This, in turn, can make your opponent worried or angry as it demonstrates that his or her attempts to undermine you have failed. Attempts to engage in such antics can, in any case, be a sign that your opponent is worried about you.

A classic example of how emotions can affect sport performers came in a famous boxing match between Sugar Ray Leonard and Roberto Duran. Leonard was considered the better boxer who was expected to outclass Duran with slick movements and long-range punching. However, before the fight Duran insulted Leonard in front of his family and this, to the dismay of Leonard's Trainer Angelo Dundee, sent Leonard into a rage, which completely altered the course of subsequent events. Instead of fighting to the pre-planned strategy devised with his trainer, Leonard let his emotions take over and decided he was going to 'beat-up' his opponent. Duran's actions amounted to a psychological masterstroke as Leonard ditched his boxing skills and opted for a brawl. It was exactly what Duran had hoped for, and he won a points decision.

There are many other potential distractions for the athlete, including the actions of friends or family, coaches or team mates, the environmental conditions, memories, delays and irrelevant thoughts. All of these can detract from your preparations, so be ready to clear your mind and refocus as necessary. Additionally/alternatively, remove yourself physically from the source of these distractions if possible. Learning any physical skill takes time, effort and practice.

Psychological skills are no different in this respect, so don't expect miraculous overnight changes in your performance. If you are a serious athlete, it is best to work with your coach to devise routines and mental plans. Once you are happy with these, they can be introduced first to practice situations and later to competition. Give yourself a few weeks to use these new techniques before re-evaluating them and adding or deleting parts as necessary. It is unlikely that the initial plans or routines will be perfect, so do not be afraid to develop them. It is also sensible to add distractions to your training sessions in order to simulate more realistic conditions.

This can include attempting to refocus while people are trying to distract you. You might even practice your refocusing skills using imagery, by envisaging potential distracting scenarios in your mind. Only when you are comfortable with your strategies should you start to use them in competitions. Remember to give it time, as improvements take time to show through.

Emotions are an essential part of sport and competition, but if you don't gain control of them before competing they might control you and hinder your performance. While it is true that some people are more emotionally sensitive than others, taking mental charge by implementing psychological plans and routines can help all athletes to a more optimal state of readiness for performance.

Thought Suppression

Pay attention now: don't think about the referee and his biased decisions. Are you succeeding in not thinking about him? If you have ever tried to suppress disruptive or irritating thoughts, you will know that it is easier said than done—and recent research suggests we might actually achieve the opposite, just as trying hard to go to sleep may actually serve to keep us awake.

A team of researchers from the University of Western Australia have examined the dubious benefits of thought suppression in a sporting context in two studies using videotaped clips of Australian Rules Football. In the first study, involving 102 under-graduates, participants watched a video with short sequences focusing on players, coaches and umpires, and were then asked to complete a brief questionnaire to assess their awareness of target images. Before this task, they were divided into three groups, as follows:

- General—asked simply to view the video and answer a questionnaire describing what they had seen;
- Suppression of intention to harm—additionally asked not to pay attention to players attempting to harm others;
- Suppression of umpires—asked not to pay attention to umpires.

The researchers also manipulated 'cognitive load' (played distracting background noises to simulate increased stress levels) to test the theory that stressful conditions would aggravate the difficulties of thought suppression. As predicted, analysis of the results revealed that subjects asked to suppress their attention to umpires actually paid more attention to them than those whose thoughts were allowed to roam freely. However, this effect was not apparent in the group asked to suppress awareness of intention to harm, and was not aggravated by distracting external stimuli.

The researchers offer two possible explanations for this discrepancy: first, there were significantly fewer 'intention to harm' images than those featuring umpires; secondly, intention to harm may have been too subjective a focus to be interpreted meaningfully by the students. The research was later extended using a further 64 students, who viewed the same footage but were assigned to one of just two conditions:

- Suppression of umpires, as in the first study, and
- Suppression of umpires plus cue word (a word to aid refocusing of attention to task-relevant cues, such as the ball).

The results of this study showed that under conditions of high cognitive load (with distracting background noise—considered similar to that of stressful conditions) the additional use of a task-relevant cue word was significantly more effective in suppressing unwanted focus than suppression alone (36% v 65%). A suggested explanation for these findings is that when thought suppression is attempted without a new focus, the unwanted thought is likely to return quite quickly. The key to effective thought-suppression thus seems to be replacing the undesired thought with a preferred option.

From a practical viewpoint, this research demonstrates that thought-suppressing techniques have to be carefully applied. Simply instructing someone not to attend to a distracting stimulus may be ineffective or, even worse, damaging to performance. To gain maximum benefit from the process, the Australian researchers argue that it is essential—especially in conditions of high stress—to follow any attempts to clear the mind and stop unwanted thoughts with an effort to refocus on a task-relevant cue.

Pressure Training Sessions

Coping under pressure is the hallmark of success in any sport. As often as not, the best performers are those who keep the skill elements of their game or event together under the most severe physical and psychological duress. Such ability is not simply a result of natural talent, although genetic endowment is a requisite for elite-level performance in modem-day sport. Well-structured training programmes and sessions draw the best from an athlete, conditioning him or her to perform at the highest level when it matters on competition day.

Normal training sessions may work on biochemical adaptations within the body to enhance various fitness attributes. They require some sort of biochemical overload to the body systems to trigger adaptations, given sufficient recovery in between. Technique work, when fresh, will enhance skill learning and improve the ability to perform the particular skill in the correct manner when required. This is fine for the improvement of skill in the training environment, but sometimes added stimulus is required to make the situation more specific to actual competition. Such training can come in the form of pressure

There are few sports where the element of skill does not come unto play for optimal performance. Even a basic sport like running can reveal poor technique under conditions of fatigue. Picture, for example, Coe at his best, gracefully kicking away from the opposition. His form would be perfect, leaving a trail of athletes spread along the home straight, with tight upper bodies and shoulders near their earlobes as they struggled to maintain form.

Technique drills for running should normally be done when the body is fresh. The same is true for virtually any quality or skill-based session. However, every so often it is appropriate to perform somc high-intensity skill work under conditions of fatigue. This enables practice of the skill when it becomes uncomfortable and ragged, thus mimicking the demands of actual competition.

Speed endurance work, such as high-intensity effort off a short recovery, is one possible means of achieving this. Another is to perform the skilled sprint work after a standard training session, like intervals or even a steady run. It must be stressed that normally such skill work is done when fresh; it is only for a pressure session that the element of fatigue is established first.

Hurdlers use another method of practising their skill when fatigued. Naturally, they have to concentrate on running form as well, but their event requires the successful negotiation of barriers. Turnabouts are a method of practising the skill of hurdling under pressure. These are performed indoors or out, as necessary. Quite simply, hurdles are placed in pairs next to each other, with one facing one way and the other in the opposite direction. A series of these pairs can be laid over a stretch of 20-60 metres, as appropriate.

The athlete then runs in one direction clearing the hurdles facing the correct way, and when he reaches the end simply turns about face to take the other hurdles, which are now facing the right way for the return journey. The whole point about turnabouts is that the skill is practised under fatigue, so a series of repetitions are used with a very short recovery. This means that the session is a fine form of physical conditioning in its own right as well as being extremely specific to the demands of the event.

Performers of racket sports can use pressure sessions to great effect. A series of different strokes from different positions can be used, before changing quickly to a different drill. In between these, physical work such as shuttles on the court or circuit-training exercises can be included. Jumping exercises are particularly good, as they promote the explosive leg strength required in a match and are sufficient to induce the fatigue required. Other exercises for the back and abdominals are also good as these muscles of posture are often neglected in general conditioning programmes.

Overtraining and Depression

Overtraining syndrome is a very common pitfall for athletes and sports people, affecting more than 60% of distance runners during their athletic careers, more than half of professional soccer players during a five-month competitive season and 33% of basketball players participating in a six-week training camp, according to published research. Yet there is no agreed definition, no objective diagnostic test for the condition, while the underlying mechanism remains unknown. And despite elaborate annual periodisation programmes designed to prevent OTS, even the most experienced coaches admit that they cannot predict which team members will experience performance decrements—the only universal sign of the syndrome. However, in a comprehensive review of this mystifying syndrome—known variously as staleness, chronic fatigue, overstrain and burnout—a pair of US sports scientists point the way to a greater understanding of the syndrome and even towards a cure.

The critical OTS diagnostic factor is a chronic decrease in performance, not simply the existence of [signs and symptoms]...complete recovery from OTS requires from several weeks to several months'. Up to 90 signs and symptoms of OTS have been identified, of which the most common are:

- Decreased physical performance.
- General fatigue, malaise and loss of vigour.
- Insomnia.
- Change in appetite.
- Irritability, restlessness, excitability, anxiety.
- Loss of body weight.
- Loss of motivation.
- Lack of mental concentration.
- Feelings of depression.

All except the first of these are also recognised signs and symptoms of major depression.

Thought Control

When it comes to doing your best, it's the thoughts that count. When it comes to running—or any other endurance sport—your mind can be your biggest asset or your worst enemy. Enjoying your training and achieving your best performances is not simply down to physical conditioning: your mental states and, particularly, the thoughts that run through your mind can affect the way you feel during exercise. It is normal for athletes to plan their race strategy in minute detail, but how many systematically plan what they are going to think about during training or competition?

In fact the nature and quality of your thoughts can make the difference between winning or losing, enjoying or hating your training, and may impact on your decision to stay with an exercise programme. Much of this scientific evidence comes from studies of marathon runners. Neuroscientists have shown that we have thousands of thoughts running through our minds each and every day. Athletes spend a large percentage of their time thinking sport-related thoughts, but most of these are unplanned and random. The first step towards becoming more organised and purposeful in your thinking is to become more aware of them. So when you next go for a training run, cycle or swim, try to become more aware of what you are thinking about.

Depression, Training and Overtraining

Overtraining syndrome is a very common pitfall for athletes and sports people. Laurence Armstrong and Jaci VanHeest outlined OTS and clinical depression share remarkably similar signs and symptoms, brain structures, neurotransmitters, endocrine pathways and immune responses. This suggests that the two syndromes have similar causes and raised the possibility that medications prescribed for depression—i.e. antidepressants—may also be effective in the treatment of OTS. OTS is defined in the review as a set of persistent physical and psychological symptoms that occur subsequent to prolonged application of heavy training loads. The critical OTS diagnostic factor is a chronic decrease in performance, not simply the existence of [signs and symptoms]... complete recovery from OTS requires from several weeks to several months.

Part of this disappointment stems from the athletes realisation that they are not living up to pre-established aspirations or goals, despite having invested much in their training programme. Frustration then leads to increased practice time each day and increased training intensity, which results in less regeneration, increased fatigue and worsening of performance. This progressive cycle of decline also results in deterioration of an athlete's mental well-being. Depression then may manifest itself as altered mood states, sleep disturbances and a loss of zeal for training and competition.

Exercise-related Behaviours

Physically active lifestyle plays a great role in maximising and maintaining both physical and mental health. Specifically, participation in physical activity programs has been linked to improved health status for many different physiological and psychological conditions, including cardiovascular disease, hypertension, diabetes, obesity, osteoporosis, depression, and anxiety.

As children grow and develop it is important for them to increase their level of self-determination. For young children, it is appropriate for parents, caregivers, teachers, and professionals to make decisions and direct children to leisure opportunities. Parents make decisions for their children based on what they have deemed appropriate for their child and within the capabilities they believe the child possesses. The role of parents and teachers is to assist children with exploration of multiple leisure options, gauging interests, and creating opportunities to learn skills and behaviors in the activities preferred by the child.

However, as the child gets older, he or she needs to more actively be involved in leisure decision-making. If not, then the child will continue to be dependent upon others to make decisions for them and to direct them to activities and experiences that may have more appeal to the decision makers than to the child. The process of making decisions independently is referred to as self-determination. Simply put, self-determination is one's ability to act as the primary decision maker in his or her life and make choices free from external influences or inference. An adolescent may not be developmentally ready to make appropriate decisions about all aspects of his or her life. However, by having the opportunity to make decisions or choices about participating in various leisure experiences, your child is able to develop valuable skills.

One aspect of self-determination that is very important to understand is the concept of intrinsic motivation. Intrinsic motivation is an internal or personal desire to do something, for example, a person plays soccer on a daily basis, simply because he loves the game. Self-determination is said to both direct and be directed by intrinsic motivation. If a person is intrinsically motivated to do an activity they will continue doing a particular activity for longer periods of time because they enjoy it, and additionally, learn, adapt and develop skills that contribute to overall well-being.

It is important that youth have the ability to make decisions and act on their own choices as they mature. Meaningful leisure experiences come when an individual is free to participate in an activity that he or she choose because it is something interests him or her. Therefore, being self-determined gives an individual the skills and confidence to speak up for him or her self, letting others know what he or she thinks and desires.

4

Sports Education

Physical education (PE), also called physical training (PT) or gym, though each with a slightly different connotation, is a course in the curriculum which utilises learning in the cognitive, affective and psychomotor domains in a play or movement exploration setting. The term physical education is most commonly used in this way; however, this denotes rather that "they have participated in the subject area, not studied it." The primary aims of physical education vary historically, based on the needs of the time and place. Often, many different types of physical education occur simultaneously, some intentionally and others not.

Most modern, Western, school systems claim their intent is to equip students with the knowledge, skills, capacities, and values along with the enthusiasm to maintain a healthy lifestyle into adulthood. Some schools also require physical education as a way to promote weight loss in students. Activities included in the program are designed to promote physical fitness, to develop motor skills, to instill knowledge and understanding of rules, concepts, and strategies, and to teach students to work as part of a team, or as individuals, in a wide variety of competitive activities.

Physical Activity

The rate of participation in physical activity by American adolscents has decreased dramatically over the last decade.

In the United States, the physical education curriculum is designed to allow students to experience at least a minimum exposure to the following categories of activities: aquatics, conditioning activities, gymnastics, individual/dual sports, team sports, rhythms, and dance. Students are encouraged to continue to explore those activities in which they have a primary interest by effectively managing their community resources. In these areas, a planned sequence of learning experiences is designed to support a progression of student development.

In all states in the United States, physical education is offered to students from grades K to 12. However, Illinois is the only state that requires physical education in all schools (even private schools) for all grade levels. Mandatory physical education is up to each individual State and school district. Most states do require physical education 6th-9th grade and offer "elective" physical education classes 10th-12th grades. Many school districts, especially those with limited budgets, cut back or eliminate on physical education from the curriculum.

In Canada, physical education is required up to grade, although some provinces are considering extending this to grade 12. In the United States, individual states determine the requirement for physical education in their schools; requirements in middle schools and high schools vary widely from state to state.

In France, physical education is required from age 6 to age 16 (mandatory schooling period). It is actually taught by specialised state teachers to all secondary school students, mostly in coeducational classes: 4 hours/ week at age 11, 3 hours/week from age 12 to 15 and 2 hours/week from age 16 to 18.

In the United Kingdom, sports like netball, cricket and rugby are also played. In Romania and Moldova, oina (which is similar to baseball), rugby, basketball and soccer are popular sports played in PE classes.

In New Zealand and Australia, softball, cricket, Australian rules football and sometimes rugby are played. In Japan, physical education is more like what are known as health classes in the United States, although some Japanese high schools, especially in Hokkaido, have the more common version.

In Sweden, sports like floorball and brännboll are played, along with internationally known sports such as soccer, basketball and volleyball.

In Spain, sports like soccer, basketball, handball and volleyball are played from primary education to bachillerato.

Clothing

The majority of schools require pupils to changes into a different set trainers or barefoot. A common uniform consists of a white t-shirt and shorts in the school colour, but this is not a universal rule. For safety, some schools require boys to wear an athletic supporter as part of the physical education uniform.

Occasionally, certain activities will require a special uniform. For example, some schools require swimming as part of the physical education curriculum. In this case, students typically have to wear a bathing suit in either the school colour or black with a swimming cap of the same colour. Also, in games with two or more teams, students usually have to wear coloured jerseys or capelike garments over the usual uniform as a way of identifying team members.

There is some disagreement about required PE classes, especially in the upper grades and at the college level. Physical Education is promoted as a way to teach students about teamwork and sports, but also is a means to develop and maintain physical fitness. The latter goal requires regular activity. PE grading scales should be based on more than just athletic ability so that students who do not excel in sports have an opportunity to receive respectable grades, as these grades may be included in their GPA (which colleges look at when considering students for admission).

Many schools are implementing grading systems in that if a student is absent, excused or unexcused, points are deducted from their grade. Many parents and students find this policy unacceptable, as a person who is legitimately sick can get a lower grade just for being out of school a few days. While this applies to all classes, it is especially bad in PE classes because it is nearly impossible to make up work in these classes.

Another reason some people look down upon required PE classes is that bullying takes place in them. As long as students are playing the game, teachers are rarely concerned with what the students say or do to each other. This often gives bullies an opportunity to harass other students without being caught. Also, PE classes put emphasis on athletic ability, which gives bullies something to harass them about. The same rings true when teachers bully students.

Another criticism of PE classes, especially in the high school level, is the emphasis on body image and weight loss. Students often already have negative thoughts about how they look, and PE classes can encourage this, sometimes to the point that it cause eating disorders in some students. In some school PE classes, students are weighed on a regular basis, and their weight is recorded. In these cases, even if weight loss is not the school's primary concern, it can add to the worries of students who may be insecure about their weight.

Quality Physical Education

Physical activity is critical to the development and maintenance of good health. The goal of physical education is to develop physically educated individuals who have the knowledge, skills, and confidence to enjoy a lifetime of healthful physical activity.

Meaningful Content

The national content standards clearly identify what students should know and be able to do as a result of a quality physical education program. The most current research and theory about physical education.

- *Standard 1*: Demonstrates competency in motor skills and movement patterns needed to perform a variety of physical activities.
- *Standard 2*: Demonstrates understanding of movement concepts, principles, strategies, and tactics as they apply to the learning and performance of physical activities.
- *Standard 3*: Participates regularly in physical activity.
- *Standard 4*: Achieves and maintains a health-enhancing level of physical fitness.
- *Standard 5*: Exhibits responsible personal and social behaviour that respects self and others in physical activity settings.
- *Standard 6*: Values physical activity for health, enjoyment, challenge, self-expression, and/or social interaction.

Physical Education in K to 7

The new physical education programme emphasises active living through participation in a balanced variety of movement experiences. Physical education is a requirement for all Kindergarten to Grade 10 students, and schools are expected to allocate 10% of instructional time to the subject. However, facilities, equipment, and time allocation vary widely. Therefore, the suggested instructional and assessment strategies in this Integrated Resource Package must be moulded to meet the needs and circumstances of particular school and community programmes.

Quality Physical Education Programme

Quality physical education programmes are structured so that the duration, intensity, and frequency of activities motivate students and meet their individual needs. When appropriate, students participate in the selection of activities from all movement categories. All students are given equal opportunity to participate in a balanced physical education programme. It is intended that a quality physical education programme will:

- foster the development of positive attitudes,
- foster active participation,
- require problem-solving skills,
- recognise the difference in students' interests, potential, and cultures,
- develop personal and career-planning skills.

Organisation of the Curriculum

The physical education curriculum is arranged under three curriculum organisers:

- Active Living.

- Movement.
- Personal and Social Responsibility.

These organisers form the curriculum framework. Under each organiser, learning outcomes reflect the knowledge, skills, and attitudes that students are expected to demonstrate at each grade level.

Planning for physical education requires a progression from a long-term overview to short-term units and the development of individual lesson plans. Teachers can do this by first selecting a main concept, skill, or theme. Once they have identified the focus, they may select prescribed learning outcomes. They can design a series of lessons that reflects the sequential nature of skill development and meets a number of prescribed learning outcomes. When selecting appropriate activities for students, teachers should consider their own expertise, available resources, and facilities within the school and community. It is recommended that no less than 15% of instructional time be spent in any one movement category. This minimum-time percentage provides flexibility for teachers to allocate additional time in areas that best meet the needs of their students.

Learning Environment

It is essential that teachers address the following questions prior to, during, and after an activity has taken place:

- Is the activity suitable to the student's physical age, and mental and physical condition?
- Has the instruction been sequenced progressively to ensure safety?
- Have students been given specific instruction about how to use and handle the equipment appropriately?

- Is the equipment in good repair, and has it been suitably arranged?
- Are the students being properly supervised?
- Are the facilities in good repair?

Teachers should ensure that the following safety practices are implemented. This is not an all-inclusive list but a guide to help teachers establish a safe learning environment in physical education classes.

The body image components of the physical education curriculum address issues and concerns that may be a source of sensitivity for some students and their parents, such as self-image, body image, eating difficulties, and eating disorders. Concerns may arise about a student having an eating disorder, or a student may disclose this information directly. Eating disorders are a serious medical concern. The following are some suggested guidelines for dealing with such sensitive issues:

- Obtain the support of the school administration before beginning instruction on any potentially sensitive issues.
- Inform an administrator or counsellor when a concern arises. Warning signals may include some or all of the following: excessive perfectionism, compulsive exercising, depression, very low or high body weight, or avoidance of wearing standard gym attire.
- Be aware of provincial and district policy and legislation on disclosure related to child abuse and eating disorders or suicide.
- Do not promise that information disclosed will be kept in confidence.
- Obtain appropriate inservice training before beginning instruction in these sensitive areas.

Participation in physical education is important for all students. Some students with special needs may require programme modification to facilitate their participation. When students with special needs are expected to achieve the learning outcomes, with or without adaptations, teachers should follow regular grading practices and reporting procedures. When students are not expected to achieve the learning outcomes because of special needs, teachers should make programme modifications. Reports should be in the form of structured written comments rather than letter grades.

Gender Issues in Physical Education

Research indicates that upon reaching secondary level, girls' participation and interest in physical education decreases significantly. Most young women do not select optional physical education in grades 11 and 12 and may develop a lifelong distaste for physical activity. A decline in interest has been particularly evident in physical education programmes that emphasise highly structured and competitive sports. However, the research shows that young women tend to be more involved in physical education programmes that provide a balance of co-operative, competitive activities from all movement categories.

Assessment is the systematic process of gathering information about students' learning in order to describe what they know, are able to do, and are working toward. From the evidence and information collected in assessments, teachers describe each student's learning and performance. They use this information to provide students with ongoing feedback, plan further instructional and learning activities, set subsequent learning goals, and determine areas requiring diagnostic teaching and intervention. Teachers determine the purpose, aspects, or attributes of learning on which to focus the assessment. They also decide when to collect the evidence and the assessment methods, tools, or techniques most appropriate to use. Assessment focusses on the critical or significant aspects of the learning students will be asked to demonstrate. Students benefit when they clearly understand the learning goals and learning expectations. Since the emphasis in physical education is on activity, teachers should use a variety of strategies to assess the ongoing development of skills in the various movement categories.

Physical Education in High Schools

The study investigated the attitude toward physical education of 1107 high school students from four countries, Czech Republic, Austria, England, and the United States. Survey data were gathered and measured using the Adams Scale survey instrument. While the data revealed individual differences, the overall sample indicated a decidedly positive attitude toward physical education. Students from the Czech Republic had significantly higher attitude scores than both U.S. and English respondents ($p < .001$), and males showed a more favorable attitude toward physical education than females ($p < .001$). Several notable differences were also found when the combined effect of gender and country of origin was measured.

The harmful consequences of the sedentary lifestyle adopted by a rapidly increasing segment of our population are apparent to even the casual observer. As Thompson made patently clear:

– Humans are designed and constructed for one thing—movement. Yet our society does everything it can to prevent movement. Our children have access to every "labor-saving" device that exists. They are not being saved at all, however, but rather being exposed to potential overweight, illness, and physiological deterioration.

In 1987, Siedentop cautioned that high school physical education was an endangered species; a subject matter that might gradually become extinct in secondary curricula. He argued that an increasing lack of expectations for significant outcomes in high school physical education and, even more alarming, concern that students have stopped caring about physical education would bring about its demise. Physical educators have a duty to alter the expectations of high school students, but the best curricula and most heroic expectations will be ineffective if negative attitudes toward the course lead students to ignore its value. Attitude, then, is the agent that can change perceptions and the catalyst that can make physical education a positive educational experience. Although some of the researchers questioned the correlation between attitudes and actual behavior most researchers suggested that attitude and the individual's underlying belief system are considered the best indicators of the decisions people will make throughout their lives.

According to Nunnally, "attitude" refers to a state of mind or feelings about particular social or physical objects such as significant people, social institutions, or physical activity. Identifying attitude as an important variable in the role and perceived importance of physical education dates to Alden's research into the attitudes of female university students and various aspects of their physical experiences. Later research efforts in the 1950's and 1960's determined that students generally had positive attitudes toward physical education.

More recently, Greenockle, Lee, and Lomax identified student attitudes at the middle school level as being strongly influenced by their peers and less positive than those of past students. Eighth grade students (13-14 years of age) were seen to be at the crucial incipient stage of dissatisfaction with physical education programs. The researchers catalogued a variety of negative student comments evidencing this growing dissatisfaction such as the "discomforts of exercise," "lack of choice of sports," the inconvenience of clothing changes, "getting sweaty," "messing up make-up," and getting "messed-up hair."

Other research efforts suggest that as middle-school students matriculate to high school, these attitudes tend to become more negative and participation in physical activity declines. For example, Tannehill and Zakrajsek investigated middle school and high school students' attitudes toward physical education and found that while students imply that physical education was important to their overall education, they participated in competitive sports less frequently in high school than in middle school.

Other researchers have explored the relationship between attitude toward physical education and participation in physical activity as well. Macintosh and Albinson compared the attitudes of two groups of eighth grade students (N=670); those opting out of secondary school physical education and those electing to take it. Students who chose not to take part in physical education reported less positive attitudes toward physical activity and physical education and were less pleased with the aspects of the program than students electing to participate.

The relationship between attitude toward physical education and fitness level was also investigated by Abu-Saley. He surveyed male college students from two Saudi Arabian universities and found a positive correlation between attitude and scores on the Health-Related Physical Test. Papaioannou obtained similar results from his study. He used the Learning and Performance Orientations in Physical Education Classes Questionnaire to explore the relationship between attitude toward physical activity and learning outcomes. He found that learning corresponded directly with positive attitude toward the lesson and the level of motivation for students of both sexes. This finding led Papaioannou to conclude that student interest in the lesson and the overall usefulness of the activity can be directly related to his or her attitude.

Existing research supports the notion of a strong correlation between increasingly negative attitudes toward physical education and the decline in physical activity and fitness levels that occurs as young people progress through the early stages of maturation. The deleterious long-term consequences may already be evident in the dramatic increase in obesity and other related health issues that have recently come to light. Adolescence is the time when personal limits are explored and lifetime attitudes and habits shaped. If positive attitudes toward physical education and physical activity are not promoted in the formative school years, they may never be adopted.

While existing research has established the link between attitude and the relative role of physical education, efforts to explore a wider range of attitudinal issues are absent from the literature. Studies exploring cross-cultural attitudes and relationships between gender, country of residence, and socio-economic status and physical education are non-existent. This study addresses most of that shortcoming. It investigates the important question of whether there are cross-cultural or gender differences in attitude toward physical education. The findings provide useful information for educators interesting in improving or reforming physical education programs or those involved with policy formulation.

Feminine Values in Sport and Physical Education

Women's sport has made great progress in recent decades. We observe, for example, that women are increasingly being admitted to types of sports that have traditionally been perceived as masculine sports. Thus the argument that sports and physical activity in general have been considered a male domain and that the participation of women in sports as "... a woman in man's territory" might seem to be rather outdated today. However, a closer look at sport and physical activities reveals several gender differences regarding participation, physical self-concept, and values.

Across many countries in the Western world (e.g., Norway, Spain, Germany, Great Britain, USA, France) several studies have suggested that girls and women are less likely to participate in physical activities and sport than boys and men are. In cases where there are as many girls and boys participating in sport, boys seem to exercise more often than girls. This does not necessarily mean that girls are less likely to do regularly physical activity in their leisure time. Many girls, for example, take dance lessons, or do cheerleading, yoga, or aerobics. However, many of these activities are not affiliated members of a sport federation; thus these girls are neither considered by sport organizations nor by researchers as active in sport.

Although, on a general basis, the gender gap in sport participation seems to be decreasing, there is evidence that boys and girls still seem to participate in different sport activities. Despite cultural differences, more boys than girls participate in sports such as boxing, ice hockey, martial arts, bandy, and football, whereas more girls participate in sports such as ballet, dance, horse riding, figure skating, and aerobics. These sports may, based on their characteristics, be defined as masculine and feminine, respectively.

Certain characteristics and activities in the sport domain have traditionally been assigned to boys and others to girls; in essence some sports have been defined as either having masculine or feminine characteristics and activities. We regard these distinctions between masculine and feminine characteristics and activities in sport to be social-constructions based upon how people think boys and girls differ, and not upon how they actually differ. More specifically, these gender differences are the result of generally held images or stereotypes of boys and girls.

Sports regarded as masculine often consist of one or more of the following characteristics: danger, risk, violence, speed, strength, endurance, challenge, and team spirit. In addition courage and aggression are traits associated exclusively with masculine sport. Examples of sports traditionally classified as "typically masculine" are: bandy, baseball, bobsled, boxing, martial arts, football, handball, soccer, ice hockey, motor sport, rugby, weight lifting, and wrestling.

Feminine sports, on the other hand, are found to score high on aesthetic features such as gracefulness, and sports such as aerobics, dance, figure skating, gymnastics, tennis, riding, and synchronized swimming are regarded as feminine sports. In addition, ballet, which is an art form, is also considered a femininc activity. Being graceful, non-aggressive, and conforming to the stereotyped expectations of femininity, such as beauty, seem to be traits that have survived over the years and are still closely tied to women's sport. The component of beauty as an element of the sport seems to be an important aspect of the perceived femininity of a sport. This is probably because it is an important aspect in the general concept of femininity.

The female body continues to be identified as an object; girls and women are also socialized to use their bodies to please others and to compare their appearance to that of the dominant feminine ideal. Sports that seek to provide beauty and visual pleasure are thereby not only acceptable for girls but well in line with stereotyped expectations of femininity.

Metheny was one of the first scholars to identify gender stereotypes in sport. In her classic analysis of sporting activities she also emphasized that the aesthetic qualities often recognized in women's sport are frequently individual activities in contrast to direct competition and team sports. Although Metheny offered her analysis almost 40 years ago, gender stereotypes have remained strong. For example, Kane and Snyder24 years later confirmed the gender stereotyping in sports suggested by Metheny.

Many studies have demonstrated that girls score lower than their male counterparts on physical self-concept. Klomsten et al. demonstrated in a recent study that not only did girls score lower on general physical self-concept than boys did, they also scored significantly lower than boys on 8 of 9 sub-domains of physical self-concept: appearance, body fat, sports competence, physical activity, endurance, strength, coordination, and health. No gender difference was found on the flexibility dimension.

Research from sport science has shown that boys believe that doing well in sports is much more important than do girls, and both boys and girls think that it is more important for boys than for girls to have abilities in sports. The features of these studies, however, have been general in nature. For example Eccles and Harold asked adolescents "how important is it to you to be good at sports?" It might be fruitful to look at feminine and masculine values in sport more specifically.

From previous research we know that sport is thought to be a male domain, but we also know that the number of girls participating in sport has been increasing. It might well be that boys and girls rate various values within sport differently; for example it could be reasonable to believe that strength and visible muscles are more important to boys, whereas girls are more concerned about being slender and thin.

Some research has shown gender differences in general sport values that favor boys (i.e., boys' value being good in sport as more important than girls). Few researchers, however, have investigated gender differences in sport values more specifically, for example masculine and feminine sport values. Thus, the first aim of the present study was to examine boys' and girls' perceptions of feminine and masculine characteristics within sport and physical education.

Data were collected from 357 secondary school students, 190 girls (Mean age = 14.34; SD = .71) and 167 boys (Mean age = 14.50; SD = .74). The participants were students in eight to tenth grade in four different public schools in Trondheim, Norway. All of the students participated in the organized physical education (PE) during school time, and 277 (130 = 77.8% of boys; 147 = 77.4% of girls) of the students participated some sort of organized sport in their leisure time. Boys and girls participated in different kinds of sports and also in a variety of combinations of sports. Some sports were more common among boys (i.e., soccer, ice-hockey, boxing, martial arts), whereas other sports were more common among girls (i.e., dance, handball, gymnastics, horse riding, and aerobics).

Students from four secondary schools participated in the study. After the schools granted permission to perform the study, information letters were sent to parents by way of the class teachers. The letters briefly explained the purpose of the study. Only those students who agreed to participate in the study completed questionnaires. The questionnaires were filled out during class hours, and information about the study and questionnaire was read aloud before we handed out the questionnaires. Participants were informed that they were to answer the questionnaires anonymously, and they were assured that their answers would be kept confidential.

Students were informed that the questionnaire was not a test, that there were no right and wrong answers, and that they could stop participation in the study at any time. They were asked not to talk with anyone during the questionnaire session, except to ask for help from the researcher if something in the questionnaire was unclear. Because of differences in reading and writing skills, participants were allowed to complete the questionnaire at their own pace, and usually they finished within 35-40 min.

Preliminary psychometric support

Based on responses of 357 students the questionnaire demonstrated a good internal consistency (coefficient alpha) on all dimensions except for the femininity dimension. The internal consistency coefficients for the 10 factors were: Appearance good looking face = 91; Appearance good looking body = .86; Endurance = .88; Flexibility = .71; Sports competence = .79; Appearance strength = .89; Appearance slender = .86; Strength = .86; Femininity = .60; and Masculinity = 74. A confirmatory factor analysis (CFA) was conducted to test the factor structure in the questionnaire using LISREL, version 8.54. Following the recommendations of Hu and Bentler, several fit indices were used to test the factor structure: the chi-square ([chi square]) statistic, degrees of freedom (df), Root Mean Square of Error Approximation (RMSEA), the Tucker-Lewis index (TLI), and the relative noncentrality index (RNI). For RMSEAs, values less than .05 and .08 were taken to reflect a close fit and a reasonable fit, respectively. The TLI and RNI vary along a 0-1 continuum in which values greater than .90 and .95 are typically taken to reflect acceptable and excellent fits to the data. The results showed a reasonable fit, with RMSEA = 0.071, df = 360, [chi square] = 1126.05, TLI = 0.95, and RFI = 0.96. The TLI and RFI indexes further support our assumption that the data fitted the model.

The first aim in the present study was to examine how the adolescent boys and girls valued the importance of the following characteristics: Appearance good looking face; Appearance good looking body; Appearance strength; Appearance slender; Strength; Endurance; Sports competence; Flexibility; Masculinity; Femininity. All variables were found to be approximately normally distributed and within [+ or -]1 in both kurtosis and skewness. Gender differences were evident in 8 of the 10 characteristics. Boys had significantly higher means than girls did in Appearance strength, Sports competence, Endurance, Strength, and Masculinity, whereas means for girls were significantly higher than those of boys in Appearance good looking face, Appearance slender, and Femininity.

The boys and girls did not only differ in how they valued feminine and masculine characteristics, but also in their involvement in sport activities. More boys than girls participated in masculine sports such as soccer, ice hockey, boxing, martial arts, and motor cross, whereas girls to a greater extent participated in feminine sports such as dance, gymnastics, horse riding, figure skating and aerobics. The classification of different sports as masculine, feminine or neutral was based upon previous research.

One way to categorize sports as masculine, feminine, or neutral is by traits or characteristics, as suggested by previous researchers, but another method is to classify sport based upon the number of male and female participants. The national participation numbers from a number of sports in Norway clearly differentiate between sports that are dominated by men and women respectively. Men dominate in most sports. More men than women play soccer, ice hockey, tennis, basketball, and golf. Men are also involved in boxing, motor cross, martial arts, skiing, skating, athletics, bike riding, and archery to a greater extent than women are. Women, alternatively, dominate in handball, dance, gymnastics, horse riding, and swimming. Participation numbers in the present study supported the same pattern, even though there were few participants in some of those sports.

To categorize sport as masculine, feminine, or neutral, a ratio was calculated for the gendered sport variable (i.e., masculine, feminine, and neutral sport variable), in both the national sample as well as in the present study sample. The ratio for each sport was calculated by the use of the following formula: male participants/(male participants + female participants). Using soccer as an example, the ratio was computed as follows 265.538/(265.538 + 85.680) = 0.76. The ratio varied along a 0-1 continuum in which lower values (0.0 - <0.4) indicate feminine sports, a value of 0.5 indicates neutral sports, and higher values (>0.6-1.0) indicate masculine sports.

Categorizing sports based upon participation numbers from Norway, both national and in the current sample, suggested that most sports focused upon in the present study were masculine. Quite a few sports were feminine, and few were categorized as neutral sports. According to Eccles and her colleagues, activity choice is linked to the importance or the value individuals attach to the available options. If this theory can be used to explain whether activity choice is linked to the importance of feminine and masculine values, then differences in the adolescents' perceptions of masculine and feminine values should lead individuals to participate in feminine, masculine, and neutral sport activities at different rates. The results revealed that the majority of boys (80.8%) were involved in masculine activities, and quite a few (17.7%) participated in neutral activities, whereas a very small percentage (1.5%) reported that their main sport was feminine. Most girls (60.5%), on the other hand, reported that their main sport was feminine, 11.6% participated in sports that were categorized as neutral, and quite a few (27.9%) were involved in masculine activities.

However, a real test of the Eccles et al. model requires a demonstration of the role these perceived values play in shaping the gender differences in participation in gendered sport. Discriminant function analysis and path analysis are two techniques that can be used to demonstrate such an effect. A multiple discriminant function analysis was performed using 10 variables as predictors for membership in three groups. Predictor variables included perceived importance of Appearance good looking face, Appearance good looking body, Appearance slender, Appearance strength, Endurance, Strength, Sports Competence, Flexibility, Femininity, and Masculinity. Membership in the three groups was based on participation in feminine, masculine, or neutral sports. There were 277 cases in the analyses.

Stepwise analyses was then used to ensure that only those variables that contributed substantially to discrimination entered the analysis. The analysis shows that 4 of 10 feminine/masculine characteristics were able to discriminate significantly among the three sporting groups. Two discriminant functions were calculated, with a combined [chi square](8) = 94.15, Eigenvalue = .37, Canonical correlation = .52, df = 3, $p < .0001$. After removal of the first function, there was still an association between groups and predictors, [chi square](3) = 8.26, Eigenvalue = .03, Canonical correlation = .17, df = 8, $p = .04$. Even though function 2 is significant at .05 level, this function is regarded as weak, because of a low [chi square], very low Eigenvalue, and low canonical correlation.

The two discriminant functions accounted for 92.3% and 7.7% respectively, of the between-group variability. The group centroids indicate that the first discriminant function maximally separated the masculine sport group (.53) from the feminine sport group (-.81), whereas the neutral sport group (-.09) showed a score close to zero. For this function a higher score is indicative of a lower value on Appearance slender, and a lower value on flexibility, accompanied by a higher value on Appearance strength, and a high value on Masculinity. The second function mainly discriminated between the masculine sport group (-.09) and the feminine sport group (-.06), on the one hand, and the neutral sport group (.42), on the other hand. For the second function a higher score was indicative of a lower score on Flexibility, accompanied by higher scores on Appearance slender, Appearance strength, and Masculinity.

The standardized canonical discriminant function coefficients suggest that Appearance strength (.63), Masculinity (.43), Appearance slender (-.45), and Flexibility (-.23) were the most important predictors in function 1, whereas Appearance slender (.80), Flexibility (-.20), Appearance strength (.31), and Masculinity (.31) were the most important predictors in function 2. The classification procedure revealed that 65.3% of the original grouped cases were correctly classified. The relations between gendered sport and four latent variables were then examined by the means of path analysis using Lisrel.

In addition to the quantitative scales, the open-ended questions revealed adolescents' thoughts about an ideal male body and an ideal female body, as well as about gender appropriate sports. Students could include as many characteristics about an ideal male body and an ideal female body, as they liked. Also, they could include as many gender appropriate sports as they liked. Characteristics are categorized with the most frequent feature mentioned first. An ideal male body is described by adjectives such as fit and strong, with well-defined muscles, especially on the shoulders, upper arms, chest and belly ("six-pack"). Among girls, 66% (n = 126) included one or more of these adjectives in their description of an ideal male body, compared to 49% (n = 81) of the boys.

The majority of boys and girls emphasized that an ideal female body was associated with the characteristics thin, slender but fit, nice "boobs," "tight butt," sexy, and pretty face. Whereas 67% (n = 127) of the girls included one or more of these characteristics in their description of an ideal female body, 79% (n = 132) of the boys shared their point of view. Participants had certain opinions of what would be appropriate sports for girls and boys, respectively. More girls (98%, n = 186) than boys (45%, n = 75) reported that some sports (e.g., dance, ballet, aerobic, gymnastics, and handball) are more appropriate to girls than to boys. The reasons for this were that the girls ... "are graceful," ... "are flexible," ... "have good rhythm," and they are ... "caring." Many students reported that there were typically boys' sports as well (e.g., soccer, boxing, ice hockey, motor cross, football, and rugby). The reasons were that boys are ... "tough," ... "big and strong," ... "boys like to fight," ... "boys have muscles," ... "one could get injured," and ... "it is nothing for weak females actually." More girls (55%, n = 105) had this point of view than did boys (45%, n = 76).

Exercise physiologists help people achieve better health and control of their bodies through physical activity. They combine two areas of expertise: exercise and the science of the human body. They often work in schools, hospitals, or rehabilitation centers. They use a variety of tests to understand a person's body composition and stress level. "It's our job to take everything into consideration," such as diseases, physical limitations, or weight issues, explains Michael Lapolla, an exercise physiologist at the Wellness Center of Saratoga, in New York. "We look at the big picture and develop a long-term exercise and wellness plan—one that somebody will stick to, not one that will provide a quick fix for weight loss."

LaFountain has many roles as an exercise physiologist. He's the youth bureau director of Oneida County, N.Y., where he runs one of the state's largest summer recreation programs for kids. He writes a fitness column for his local newspaper and is the wellness director of the Utica City School District. Kids' health is LaFountain's primary area of interest—and worry.

"I'm most concerned with those 80 percent of kids who don't exercise enough," says LaFountain. "Physically gifted students almost always will succeed in PE classes, sports, and recreational activities. Those who are less gifted are the ones left behind to become the health risks of tomorrow." LaFountain develops appealing fitness programs for kids in schools and in the community, such as school-based wellness centers as an alternative to traditional team sport-based physical education programs.

Fitness trainers teach people how to exercise properly for good health. Individual fitness training was a natural career choice for Tiffany Crate, a personal trainer in Chicago. "I was never a team sports person. I was a dancer, gymnast, weight lifter, skater, and runner," Crate says. "In junior high school, I vowed that I would create my own job doing what I love: being physically active, creative, and inspiring to others."

As a college freshman, Crate became certified to teach group fitness classes, and she taught aerobics while earning her bachelor's and master's degrees in exercise physiology, from the University or of Illinois at Chicago. Today, Crate says, "I provide lots of ways to get people ... fit and healthy."

In a typical training session, Crate and a client plan a fitness goal. Crate then recommends a series of exercises, coaches the client on good form, and educates him or her on the muscle groups that are getting a workout. Her clients use activity monitors to track their heart rate and calories burned. Crate says, "Certain people are very motivated by the objective, immediate feedback of the monitors." Once a client masters a workout, Crate helps the client set new, more challenging goals.

"Some people like working on cars or machines. I feel that the body is the perfect machine," says Brian Beane, who works in New York as an athletic trainer at the Regional Therapy Center of Saratoga. Athletic trainers work with athletes to prevent and rehabilitate sports-related injuries. They may be employed by schools, professional teams, fitness centers, or clinics. For example, they might show a basketball team how to use lateral drills to strengthen the muscles the players need to move around the court. "One of our main goals is to condition the athletes, whether it's to better their performance or to decrease the risk of injury," Beane explains. "It's not enough that we tape up an ankle. We want to strengthen that ankle."

You may have already seen an athletic trainer at work. If someone gets hurt during a sporting event, the athletic trainer is the first one to run onto the field or the court. The trainer examines the injury and sometimes provides emergency first aid. "The athletic trainer isn't going to have a 9 to 5 day," notes Beane. "We can get up at 5:30 and go to basketball practice in the morning and work until midnight, when a baseball game is ending."

Physical therapists are experts in the skeletal-muscular system. They help people with injuries or disabilities to relieve pain and build strength and mobility. When someone is sent to a physical therapist by his or her doctor, the therapist first tests the patient's mobility, balance, posture, strength, and muscle function. Then the therapist creates a treatment plan and works with the patient to most effectively carry out that plan, which may include a number of flexibility and strength exercises.

5

Sports Health

Comprehensive health education and physical education are best delivered within the context of a coordinated programme that includes all eight elements, linked by a common network and philosophy. Schools with coordinated and comprehensive programmes in place are considered *health-promoting* environments. Coordinated school health programmes include:

- Policies and procedures that support and reinforce classroom instruction. Health messages are clear and consistent.
- Access to health services and referrals to community healthcare providers. Classroom instructors, school nurses, parents, and community healthcare providers work as a team to support student health.
- In-school support and referral for those needing counseling services. Classroom instructors and school counsellors work in concert with social workers and mental health specialists to provide immediate care in time of crisis and to facilitate long-term care for those who need it.
- A safe school environment. School staff work to provide a clean, safe, drug-free and weaponfree environment.

- Nutritious and appealing food choices. The food services staff provides meals that reflect the tenets of sound nutrition yet are appealing to young people.
- School staff that promote and support wellness. School staff members are supported in their own efforts to achieve health and well-being.
- Parental and community support. Schools involve parents and community members in health promotion efforts and policy making.

Coordinated school health programmes are an integral part of school reform efforts. These programmes reflect a collaborative school community seeking to enhance the health and well-being of its members. Instructional programmes grounded in a health-promoting environment tend to be more successful, more consistent, and more effective. The comprehensive curriculum includes a variety of topics such as personal health, family health, community health, consumer health, environmental health, sexuality education, mental and emotional health, injury prevention and safety, nutrition, prevention and control of disease, and substance use and abuse.

Instructional programme delivery varies at the elementary and secondary levels. Many factors contribute to this variation. At the secondary level, programmes tend to be implemented by departmentalised content specialists. At the elementary level, the comprehensive health and physical education programme may be implemented by the classroom teacher, with the assistance of a content specialist. Additionally, school facilities may impact the delivery of instruction.

Most high schools have dedicated gymnasiums with separate food service facilities. Many elementary schools provide physical education instruction in an "all-purpose" room that serves as the hub for lunch, school assemblies, and special exhibits such as science fairs. This practice may limit the number of hours per day the facility can be used for physical education instruction. Teachers in rural or suburban schools may be able to compensate by taking students outside for structured activities. Their counterparts in urban areas may not have access to safe playgrounds, open play areas, and athletic fields.

Physical Education in the Elementary Level

The classroom teacher can integrate instruction in all content areas. It provides for flexible scheduling and enables the teacher to relate content to actual classroom activity (e.g., address conflict management when fights occur, reinforce hand washing).

Once again, this approach supports interdisciplinary instruction and links instruction to classroom life. It allows the physical education specialist to focus on specialised movement and fitness content and skills.

The certified school nurse has a strong background in health content and can be most helpful to the classroom teacher. The school nurse is able to connect classroom behaviour and health room behaviour and adjust instruction accordingly. Additionally, the school nurse is more comfortable addressing sensitive issues.

This approach uses professionally prepared staff to deliver health and physical education instruction. Instruction can be delivered in an integrated manner, using a wellness approach. The school nurse can use his/her expertise in healthcare to bridge the gap between knowledge and application. The physical educator can focus on developmentally appropriate practices in movement and fitness.

Disadvantages

The classroom teacher has minimal preparation in health

and physical education. This lack of professional preparation translates into less emphasis on content and skills, especially in areas considered sensitive or controversial. The teacher is more likely to concentrate on what "gets tested" rather than on important concepts and skills. Due to a lack of knowledge and skills in physical education, the classroom teacher may focus on games and unstructured play instead of developmentally appropriate movement and fitness activities. In addition, classroom teachers may not be familiar with the safe use of equipment used in physical education activities.

The classroom teacher and the physical education specialist must collaborate to support related instruction. This may be difficult to accomplish if the specialist teaches at several schools. Unless the classroom teacher is committed to health instruction, the subject may not be taught in sufficient depth to meet the Standards.

The school nurse's schedule may preclude regular instruction or may interrupt instruction if emergencies arise. Because of the classroom teacher's discomfort or lack of professional preparation, the school nurse may be assigned to deliver instruction in family life education. This creates a fragmented approach to instruction rather than an integrated one. This approach requires both parties to jointly plan instruction; this may be difficult if the school nurse serves more than one school.

The school nurse may be required to "travel"-that is, move from classroom to classroom with no home base. This limits the use of some materials and classroom strategies. The school nurse, the physical educator, and the classroom teacher need to schedule planning meetings to discuss issues and concerns that require reinforcement by the classroom teacher. This may be difficult to accomplish due to scheduling and school building assignments. When the school nurse teaches, emergencies may interrupt instruction. For such instances, contingency plans must be developed to provide classroom coverage and instruction.

Physical Education in the Secondary Level

As movement and fitness instruction becomes more complex, the physical educator can address safety and management issues and focus on more difficult content and skills. The school nurse can use his/her background to address the myriad of sensitive and complex issues presented by adolescents. This team approach can provide students with instruction that is accurate, wellnessfocused and sensitive to their developing needs.

The science teacher has a strong background in the life sciences. The family and consumer science teacher has strong preparation in nutrition, family health issues, and parenting. The social studies teacher has a strong background in sociological and psychological principles that impact relationships. This approach provides for a natural integration of related areas and increases interdisciplinary opportunities. The physical educator focuses on developmental movement and fitness applications and can work with the other instructors to reinforce movement theory.

This approach enables the teacher to coordinate instruction during the entire school year. If facilities allow, the programme can be structured to provide content and skill instruction on separate days.

The extended class period allows the teacher to implement a conceptual physical education programme, one that emphasises the skills and concepts to become an intelligent consumer of physical activity. This approach links health and physical education and allows more time for discussion, project work, technological approaches, and critique.

Disadvantages

Instruction may be fragmented; a team approach is needed to avoid this pitfall. The physical educator and school nurse may not be supervised by the same administrator, making collaboration more difficult. The school nurse may have additional responsibilities at this level (e.g., core team) that preclude a regular instructional commitment. Additionally, secondary school physical education teachers often focus on interscholastic athletics rather than classroom instruction.

The science teacher may focus on life science approaches to the exclusion of skill-based instruction (e.g., refusal skills, negotiation skills). All teachers have a responsibility to teach critical inquiry and problem solving; however, subject area teachers are less likely to teach these strategies from a health perspective. It is important that these skills be taught within a situational context so students can readily apply them when needed. Collaboration with the physical educator may be difficult.

This approach may provide only one-half year of physical activity. Students tend to lose skills over time. If the content is organised as separate courses, it may be difficult to facilitate the mastery of important interpersonal skills (e.g., refusal skills) that need constant practice and reinforcement. In some schools, more time is devoted to games and sports in physical education than to important health and fitness concepts.

Students participate in physical activity for only one-half year. This approach may have a minimal impact on fitness and skill development. Because the course is limited to one-half year, it does not allow the teacher to address relevant health issues that arise during the school year.

Interdisciplinary Instruction

Interdisciplinary instruction occurring within the context of health education and physical education means that the central theme and content of instruction is determined by the content specialist (e.g., the physical education teacher or health educator). Various aspects of that content are taught within the context of other subject areas. The health and physical education content specialist(s) retains accountability to ensure that all students receive adequate preparation to meet the *Standards*. Collaboration is the key to this kind of instructional programme.

For the most part, the professional literature considers health education and physical education as separate entities. This distinction is clearly evident at the national level, where two separate standards documents were developed and sponsored by different professional organisations.

Physical education programmes are one means to reduce the incidence of life-threatening disease-an educational response to a public health challenge. Supervised physical activity, such as that occurring in school physical education programmes, provides students with opportunities to explore and refine a wide range of life-enhancing physical activities that can become part of the student's daily routine.

The *Standards* support the notion that physical education is an academic core subject. With this belief comes accountability. The *Standards* clearly establish levels of achievement and affirm that mere participation in physical activity is not the same as education. We must embrace a new philosophy of physical education, one that emphasises the principles of movement, fitness, and wellness and empowers students to incorporate physical activity into the fabric of their daily lives. Recent research by Dale, Corbin and Cuddihy demonstrates that *conceptual physical education,* a programme that combines a cognitive, theory-based approach with a sport-based approach, enhances participation in physical activity.

Curriculum Development Framework

In order to best utilise the comprehensive health education and physical education standards in curriculum development, teachers and curriculum developers need to understand the language of standards-based instructional programmes. Here are a few key terms used in this framework. The comprehensive health education and physical education standards and cumulative progress indicators follow.

- A core curriculum content standard (or simply *content standard*) describes what students should know and be able to do in a particular discipline. Standards outline the broad concepts and skills deemed an essential part of every student's instructional programme.
- A cumulative progress indicator also describes what a student should know and be able to do but in a more specific manner. It illustrates the standard, focusing on specific knowledge and skills necessary at certain benchmark grades. Students at each benchmark level are expected to master all the cumulative progress in their cluster and continue to maintain that mastery as they move through the more advanced clusters. Each *standard* has numerous cumulative progress indictors
- A framework is a compendium of sample learning strategies, background information, and resources to assist school district staff in the development of an instructional programme that will enable all students to meet the *standards.* Activities in the framework are

samples; that is, they reflect the creative energy and best practices of teachers from across the State but do not comprise a required curriculum. The framework illuminates the comprehensive health education and physical education standards and cumulative progress indicators, giving teachers a better picture of content and expectations.

Physical Education Standards and Cumulative Progress Indicators

Health-literate and physically educated students seek to improve personal, family, and public health. Using health promotion and disease prevention principles, nutritional concepts, and injury prevention strategies, students modify personal behaviours based on risk factors and adopt health practices to reduce or eliminate preventable health problems. Health-literate and physically educated students recognise the importance of prevention, early detection, and treatment in enhancing personal wellness.

By the end of Grade 4, students:

- Describe a healthy child and identify factors that contribute to good health.
- Describe the basic structure and function of human body systems.
- Identify and demonstrate responsible health behaviours for children.
- Explain how childhood injuries and illnesses can be prevented and treated.
- Describe potentially dangerous or threatening situations related to childhood activities, develop personal protection strategies, and cite resources for help.
- Identify common health products and foods found in the home and correctly interpret labels, information, directions, and warnings.

Building upon knowledge and skills gained in the preceding grades, by the end of Grade 8, students:

– Describe a healthy adolescent, discuss injuries and illnesses common to this age group, and identify ways to prevent, reduce, or eliminate these health problems.
– Explain how health is influenced by the interactions of body systems and nutritional intake.
– Analyse how family, peers, culture, media, technology, and the environment affect wellness.
– Identify and demonstrate health practices that support and enhance personal and family physical and mental health.
– Analyse a health profile to determine strengths and potential health risks resulting from risk factors and health-enhancing behaviours.
– Describe situations requiring health services and locate community health care providers comparing their services, benefits, and costs.
– Examine health product and food labels and advertisements comparing accuracy, content, directions, and value.
– Analyse the influence of peers and the media on risk behaviours, injuries, and violent behaviour.

Building upon knowledge and skills gained in the preceding grades, by the end of Grade 12, students:

– Describe a healthy adult, discuss adult physical and mental health problems, and use health assessment data to develop strategies for reducing health problems and related risk factors.
– Analyse the impact of genetic, nutritional, behavioural, cultural, and environmental factors on the functioning of the body systems and use this information to identify responsible health practices.

– Analyse situations that require professional health services, analyse the costs and sources of payment, and discuss how these factors influence the accessibility and delivery of healthcare.

– Discuss and compare the influence of public health policy, government regulations, research, medical advances, and the healthcare industry on current and emerging health problems.

– Describe the principles of injury prevention and risk management, analyse factors that contribute to the incidence of injuries and violence, and develop strategies for prevention.

– Analyse the influence of the media on risk behaviours, disease prevention, and the incidence of injuries and violent behaviour.

Health-literate and physically educated students communicate effectively. These students set health goals, solve health-related problems, and resolve conflicts. They use health-enhancing personal, interpersonal, and life skills to initiate and maintain healthy relationships that contribute to wellness.

School district curriculum committees need to examine the big picture as they review, revise, and create a context for student achievement. When creating this vision, the most important factor is linking the core curriculum content standards to the programme development process. Before any actual writing occurs, curriculum specialists and teachers need to become fully cognisant of the scope of the comprehensive health education and physical education standards and this accompanying framework. Curriculum committees need to update their district goals, soliciting input from school administrators, the board of education, teachers, students, parents, and community members. Creating a vision and pathway for student achievement requires retrospection, data collection, analysis, and an honest examination of the needs of students.

To accomplish this, curriculum developers need to become familiar with various national documents that support and enhance our own state *Standards.* School staff involved in developing curriculum should become familiar with national reviews of health and physical education programmes. Too many times, teachers are given an unreasonable amount of time to adequately prepare for the process of curriculum development. Before one can ever begin to actually write, much research and preparation must take place.

Developing curriculum, or even reviewing and revising an existing programme, necessitates extensive fact-finding, research, and preparation. Collecting the data, however, is only the beginning. To assist districts to use public health data to support coordinated school health programmes, numerous "howto" manuals have been developed.

Most school districts will not need to develop a health and physical education programme from ground zero. The curriculum renewal process offers a streamlined, yet still comprehensive, approach to align the existing programme with the comprehensive health education and physical education standards. The school district committee charged with this task should include a district level administrator, building supervisors/ principals, grade level teachers, and health and physical education content specialists. Parents, community leaders, and representatives from business and industry should be invited to participate in the process. Student input is extremely important and most valuable when debating the "appropriateness" of content and materials. The local board of education has the authority to approve curriculum; the committee acts in an advisory capacity only.

Curriculum should be developed before purchasing materials. Too many times, school districts select a textbook or programme and tailor the curriculum to meet the programme. Curricular goals and instructional objectives, based on the *Standards,* should drive instruction. Even a well-researched commercial programme will not be effective if teachers have limited access to programme materials or if school staff are not properly trained to utilise the materials. All teachers need access to the entire curriculum in order to envision the spiraling content.

Teachers not normally involved in health education and physical education programmes need to become familiar with the curriculum so health and physical education content and skills can be incorporated into daily classroom activities for reinforcement. By the same token, health and physical education teachers need to know other content area requirements and plan activities that match programme goals and objectives.

Articulation between grade levels or between schools (e.g., regional sending districts) may be difficult to accomplish but is necessary so that all students can be prepared to meet the *Standards*. Communication and collaboration are essential for effective curriculum development and implementation. This can be accomplished through regularly scheduled articulation meetings, the establishment of content networks, newsletters, and shared professional development opportunities.

The development of a "new" curriculum aligned with the *Standards* is not enough. School district curriculum committees should develop an action plan for curriculum implementation, staff development, and expanded local assessment of student knowledge and skills. The plan should clearly delineate the roles of teachers, supervisors, and administrators and should be grounded in the extensive data collected by the committee. The action plan lays the groundwork for teacher/student accountability in the implementation and achievement of the *Standards.*

Role of the Content Experts

As members of the school district curriculum committee, teachers of health education and physical education are the content "experts." It is imperative that health education and physical education specialists (including school nurses and family and consumer science teachers) are cognisant of the major changes in the field, the most current and relevant topics, and the teaching strategies found to be most effective. As content experts, health education and physical education teachers are expected to define terms, summarise research, and suggest strategies that support the research base.

For some districts, this may be the first time a health and physical education programme is offered for students in early childhood programmes. Classroom activities may need to be modified for these younger students. As content experts, health educators and physical education teachers may be called upon to actually instruct students in early childhood programmes. In other school districts, content specialists may be called upon to assist or train early childhood teachers to provide such instruction. The specialist may be asked to serve as a content resource, providing the early childhood teacher with articles, information, and supportive materials. It is imperative that health education and physical education content specialists take a lead role in the development of a comprehensive and coordinated programme that articulates across grades, schools, and perhaps even districts.

When developing the comprehensive health and physical education curriculum, schools need to be cognisant of issues and concerns that may impede instruction. The labeling of topics or teaching methods as controversial could deprive students of valuable information and skills and significantly impact their ability to learn. Controversy in health and physical education develops when a cherished belief, economic interest, or basic principle is threatened.

Traditionally, health and physical education has had its ardent supporters as well as its ardent opponents. Curriculum developers and teachers need to recognise that not all students and their families feel the same way about each issue. Ideas about wellness develop over time and are strongly influenced by family upbringing, past experiences, socio-economic status, and culture. An issue may be very sensitive and personal for one student yet have little impact on another.

Educators need to develop a reasonable and consistent plan to deal with sensitive issues. The plan should allow for an open forum and examination of student and parental concerns. The process of curriculum development and materials adoption can promote proactive, positive interaction, actively engaging students and their families in the development of an instructional programme that is relevant and meaningful.

To effectively implement the intent of the statute, school districts need policies that clearly outline the application process, any required meetings with school staff, alternative student assignments, educational assessment, grading, and accountability for both student and teacher. In addition, the student, his/her parents, and the teacher need to discuss the transition into the regular instructional programme once the "objectionable" content is covered. Teachers and administrators need to be familiar with such policies and implement them with consistency.

Generally, a clear, concise, and honest response to a parental concern will clear up any misconceptions. On the other hand, objections are different from questions. Objections are differences of opinion that are highly emotional, rooted in very personal experiences. School districts need to develop a more detailed plan of action to deal with objections. Objections to health and physical education instruction may be handled informally by the classroom teacher or school administrator. These types of objections most often involve policy or process.

If a teacher responds to this type of objection, he/she should inform the building administrator by the end of the school day and should follow-up with a written summary of the objection and response within five days. If the objector is not pleased with the informal response, the building principal should address the concerns. If this does not effectively address the issue, the objector should be advised to submit his/her concerns in writing to the school district administration.

Dealing with controversy in health and physical education is inevitable. The very personal nature of the discipline-discussing death, sexuality, substance use, and even body image-cause some individuals concern. When handling conflict teachers and administrators need to:

- Listen to the whole concern.
- Seek comfort-sit in a relaxing area.
- Personalise the meeting by using the individual's name.
- Speak softly and use "I" messages.
- Ask questions and clarify meaning.
- Never assume anything.

- Pay attention to detail.
- Offer the individual thanks for his/her concerns.
- Involve others in the process, as appropriate (e.g., principal, supervisor).
- Provide alternatives for action.
- Apply the principles of teaching and learning to the discussion. Vary the approaches used to be sure the individual understands the school's position.

Teachers and administrators need to be proactive, developing policies and procedures to address potential concerns. Most of all, school staff should be cooperative and collaborative when reviewing, revising, or developing the health and physical education instructional programme.

Learning and Behaviour

The cognitive sciences have seen a number of developing theories and research studies that use biological processes to explain learning. While these research approaches are easier to control and study, it is difficult to assimilate the information into concrete principles that teachers can implement. Neuroscientists still disagree on some of the inner workings of the brain.

With each new stimulation, experience, and behaviour the brain can rewire itself. A *stimulus* to the brain starts the process. If we are repeating something we have already learned, the neural pathways become more efficient. Research has shown that many areas of the brain are involved in new tasks but less and less of the brain is involved as the task is learned. The brain's neural networks combine to process an object or event; each area is responsible for a particular element of the task (e.g., colour, spatial movement). The daily chemistry of the human brain complicates things even more.

The human brain contains dozens of types of neu-*rotransmitters,* classified both functionally and chemically. Neurotransmitters send either an excitatory or inhibiting message to the receiving neuron, much like an on/off switch. This mechanism enables the brain to focus attention or limit activity. Chemically, these substances include amino acids, such as glutamate; *monoamines,* such as dopamine or serotonin; and peptides, such as endorphins or vasopressin. An in-depth understanding of neurotransmitters is essential for all teachers but particularly necessary for health and physical education teachers.

For example, peptides play an important role in modulating emotional states and consequent behaviours. These substances play an important role in the body's response to stress. In addition, exercise and positive social interactions can elevate endorphin levels and help people feel good about themselves. The implications for teachers of health and physical education should be obvious.

Theory of Multiple Intelligences

In his Theory of Multiple Intelligences, Howard Gardner suggests that intelligencc has more to do with the capacity for solving problems and fashioning products in a contextreal and naturalistic setting. Gardner's theories have been embraced by educators as a way to map the broad array of abilities seen in the classroom.

The theory proposes that all individuals have capacities in all seven areas. Most people are highly developed in some intelligences, modestly developed in others, and relatively underdeveloped in the remaining areas. Most people can develop each intelligence to an adequate level of competency. If given the appropriate encouragement, enrichment, and instruction, most people can develop all seven intelligences to a reasonably high level.

Intelligences usually work together in complex ways. Intelligences are always interacting with each other. In a kickball game, a child must kick the ball, run to the appropriate spot, and keep score, using three kinds of intelligence to participate in the activity. There are many ways to be intelligent within each category. This theory emphasises the many ways individuals show their gifts within their intelligences as well as between the intelligences.

Numerous theories and models have been used in behavioural and social science research to study and promote health-enhancing behaviours. These theories have major implications for classroom instruction and for school and community programmes that support and reinforce classroom instruction. The theories are particularly significant when designing prevention and intervention programmes that are synergistic, coordinated, and complementary.

At one time, it was thought that providing students with facts would result in behaviour change. Through research, it has been determined that lack of knowledge is only one of many factors that influences decision making. Given that experts in both health and education have recognised the variety of factors that influence learning and behaviour, it seems prudent to institute multiple interventions to foster the adoption of health-enhancing behaviours. Students need to be armed with the knowledge and skills to address a myriad of problems, now and in the future. The decisions made now can have a significant impact on one's quality of life in the future.

Student Assessment

The purpose of student assessment is to provide meaningful feedback that reflects the student's individual growth and allows the student and teacher to plan purposeful and appropriate learning experiences. Meaningful assessment focuses on the knowledge, skills, and behaviours evidenced in the curriculum. Various levels of assessment occur-national, state, local, and classroom-each with a distinct opportunity to provide teachers, students, and parents with important information about student progress.

In the near future, comprehensive health education and physical education will become part of the statewide testing programme. Teachers of health and physical education are held to the same high levels of accountability as their math and science counterparts. It is no longer acceptable to simply test students at the end of a unit. Physical education teachers who only measure sport and fitness skills and pay little or no attention to cognitive assessment are denying students important information that can assist them to achieve the *Standards*. Health teachers who only measure content knowledge and never evaluate student progress in skill development are short-changing students. Student assessment is a critical element of instruction, providing the student with important information about his/her progress. This information enables the student and teacher to collaborate on specific instructional goals so that every student can achieve the core curriculum content standards.

Student assessment is a complex, ever-changing issue. New forms of assessment result from educational reform, developments in psychology and neuroscience, and advances in technology. Classroom teachers need to expand their repertoire of assessment tools and ensure that they are inextricably linked to standards-based instruction.

Choosing the appropriate assessment measure requires careful consideration of the instructional content; student learning styles; the teacher's comfort level; and space, facilities, and time. Special attention needs to be paid to the correlation of the measure to the content and skills prescribed in the core curriculum content standards.

A rubric is a fixed scale listing the characteristics of performance for each point on the scale. Rubrics are most often used to rate performance tasks, essays, and portfolios and can be modified to serve as a self-assessment tool for students. In physical education, a task card used by a second-grade student to rate overhand throws is an example of a simple rubric. In health class, students utilise a critical elements card to review and assess a partner's response to a problem-solving scenario. As students and teachers become more comfortable using rubrics, they can be used to address student performance, content knowledge or collaborative qualities.

Professional Development

Professional development is undergoing profound changes to meet these demands. There are 11 major paradigm shifts in staff development designed to focus energies on meaningful and productive professional experiences. Staff development is moving:

- From district-focused to school-focused approaches;
- From individual development to individual development and organisational development;
- From fragmented, piecemeal, one-shot efforts to staff development driven by a clear and coherent plan;
- From a focus on adult needs and satisfaction to a focus on student needs, learning outcomes, and changes in on-the-job behaviours;
- From training conducted off-site as the primary delivery system to multiple forms of job embedded learning;
- From the transmission of knowledge and skills by experts to the study by teachers of teaching and learning;

- From a focus on generic instructional skills to both generic and content specific skills;
- From staff developers who function as trainers to those who provide consultation, planning, and facilitation as well as training;
- From staff development provided by one or two department staff developers to staff development being a critical function and responsibility of all administrators and teacher leaders;
- From activities directed solely at teachers to programmes involving everyone who impacts student performance; and
- From staff development as a frill to staff development as an indispensable process.

This expanded version of staff development requires significant planning on the part of teachers and school administrators. "Learning to practice in significantly different ways can occur neither through theoretical imaginings alone nor through unguided experience alone. Instead, it requires a tight coupling of the two." Research supports the notion that teachers learn in much the same ways as students. Rich professional development is centered on the critical elements of teaching and learning: planning, evaluation, development, investigation, and professional discourse.

Professional development experiences that succeed provide teachers with experiential engagement in concrete tasks involving teaching, assessment, and observation. The activities are connected to and derived from the teachers' work; thus, teachers are involved in questioning, experimenting, and researching. Professional development enhances collaboration and supports systemic school change efforts. Finally, effective staff development opportunities are sustained and intensive, utilising such strategies as modeling, peer coaching and mentoring, observation, and collective problem solving to institutionalise the effects .

Effective Staff Development

Staff development experiences should be varied and intensive and allow time for practice and reflection. Adult learning can take place in many forms and use various processes. Professional development planners need to vary the content and format of these experiences to meet the needs of all school staff. Essential topics for effective staff development experiences are listed below.

Subject matter

It is imperative that health educators and physical education teachers remain keenly aware of frequent changes in content knowledge. Professional development experiences should focus on the following:

- Current information on topics (e.g., new diseases, cures, drugs, data)
- Relationships between content (e.g., multiple risk behaviours)
- Current research in the field
- Connections to everyday life (e.g., decisions about sex, drugs, driving)
- Content as a foundation and how ideas can be linked and assembled (e.g., teaching the relationship between physical activity and mood).
- How to determine existing student knowledge and tailor content accordingly.
- Laws relevant to content.
- Trends in the field (e.g., healthcare, insurance).
- Resources.

- Certification in specific content areas (e.g., water safety).
- Technology as a tool in instructional delivery.
- Skill practice and behaviour change.

Adolescent development

Teachers of health education and physical education deal with a wide range of physical, social, and emotional levels of development. It is imperative that teachers have an understanding of the following concepts:

- Normal growth and development.
- How students think and behave.
- Goals of students.
- Student interests.
- What students know.
- Concepts that may be difficult for some or all of the class to grasp.
- Culture, language, family, and gender issues.
- Prior schooling.
- Knowledge of the community.
- Intelligences demonstrated in the class.
- Preferred approaches to learning.
- How students view the curriculum.
- Motivation and feedback.
- Student self-images.
- What students care about.
- What success means to the students.

Teaching and learning

Professional development opportunities that focus on teaching and learning should include:

- The kinds and purposes of learning.
- The context for learning.
- Strategies to support different kinds of learning, materials, and tasks.
- Specialised instructional tools (e.g., adaptive equipment).
- Modes of cognition.
- Information processing.
- Neuroscience/brain research.
- Communication skills (e.g., language acquisition).
- Motor development.

Assessment

Teachers of health and physical education need time to practice and refine assessment skills. Staff development in this regard should focus on the following:

- Identifying student strengths.
- Testing various intelligences.
- Interdisciplinary measures.
- Reasoning skills.
- Developing rubrics, task cards, and self-assessment measures.
- Developing performance assessments.
- Planning lessons and using assessment.
- Instructionally embedded assessment.
- Special needs adaptations.

Curriculum development

Too often teachers are left to their "own devices" when it comes to developing curriculum. Professional development experiences, designed to prepare teachers for curriculum development, should include information about the following:

- State, national, and local standards.
- Available resources.
- Text and material review and selection process.
- Goals and objectives and how they link with assessment.
- Interdisciplinary opportunities.
- Research based programmes.
- Articulation (e.g., grade levels, school-to-school, district-to-district).
- Curriculum revision process.
- Analysing test results, health data, and student behaviour to refine and improve programme.

Collaboration

An effective comprehensive health and physical education programme requires the players (students, teachers, other school staff, parents) to collaborate to foster student achievement and success. Professional development opportunities should focus on the following:

- Instructional activities that promote student collaboration (e.g., cooperative learning, teams).
- Productive discourse in the classroom.
- Strategies to promote parent involvement.
- Strategies to support school and community wellness.
- Collaboration with community health resources.
- External funding support for programmes and projects.

- Extracurricular links to classroom instruction.
- Peer mentoring, peer mediation, coaching, and cross-age teaching.
- School and community partnerships.
- School staff networks.

Improving Teacher Performance

Effective comprehensive health education and physical education programmes depend on trained teachers. Research indicates that the classroom teacher is the key to student achievement. New and exciting trends in the field, along with emerging health issues and knowledge, necessitate planned professional development experiences that allow teachers to validate existing practices and develop their competence and confidence to implement innovative and effective teaching strategies.

Comprehensive health education and physical education deal with sensitive and sometimes personal issues in both students' and teachers' lives. Effective teacher training builds commitment, understanding, skills, and attitudes that foster instructional practices to support the achievement of the *Standards*. Professional development programmes in health and physical education should be designed to:

- Develop positive attitudes towards and commitment to health and physical education;
- Provide teachers with the structure, content, and philosophy of the district's health and physical education programme;
- Increase the teacher's understanding of learning theories and principles of behaviour change as specifically related to wellness;
- Improve teaching and facilitative skills;

- Prepare teachers to deal with sensitive issues and controversy; and
- Acquaint teachers with school and community health resources that support instruction.

Professional development experiences need to balance health and physical education content and theory with ample opportunities for hands-on experiential learning. Many teachers, accustomed to "read the book and answer the questions" modes of instruction, have a great deal of difficulty adjusting to an interactive classroom and a facilitative role. These same teachers may have difficulty using cooperative grouping, role-play, and case-study approaches. Becoming comfortable with these modes of teaching increases the likelihood that the teacher will at least try to employ the methods in the classroom.

Teachers may benefit most from observing master teachers or working with another teacher who is comfortable in a more facilitative role. As new classroom practices are adopted and implemented, coaching and circles (networking groups) reinforce and enhance skill development. Teachers need to become comfortable with these mechanisms in much the same way as students do.

The effectiveness of any health and physical education professional development experience is greatly enhanced by continued support that deals with new questions and problems as they arise. Students often ask questions that may seem inappropriate or may be difficult to answer. How the teacher deals with such questions may determine his/her credibility for the remainder of the year. Practicing similar situations with other professionals enables teachers to anticipate such situations and handle them more effectively when they do arise. Booster sessions, where health and physical education teachers can discuss problems, issues, and successes, help address gaps in preservice educational experiences and provide on-going opportunities for collegial exchange.

Effective staff development addresses the needs of the participants. No doubt the range of content knowledge, skill performance, and commitment will vary among staff members. To develop effective experiences with benefits for all participants, staff development planners should solicit information using a simple needs assessment and use the information obtained to plan experiences focusing on the needs of the participants in relation to the core curriculum content standards. At the conclusion of the session, participant feedback enables the planners to adjust the content and training as necessary and can be used to support additional training sessions.

Professional development in health and physical education is not limited to attendance at workshops or training sessions. Professionals must remain cognisant of emerging health and social issues that profoundly impact health and physical education instruction. Teachers should attend medical seminars and state, regional, and national conferences. In addition, professional health educators and physical educators can be involved in research; take advanced college work in the field; and apply their knowledge and skills in other venues such as healthcare facilities, camps, and recreational programmes.

Childhood Illnesses and Deaths

The higher rate of mortality in lower income countries is primarily due to the high incidence of acute respiratory infections, malaria, diarrhoeal diseases and injuries due to road traffic and drowning. Injuries are also dominant causes of death in higher income countries along with congenital abnormalities and leukaemia. WHO estimates that between 25% and 33% of the global burden of disease can be attributed to environmental risk factors.

About 40% of the total burden of disease due to environmental risks falls on children under the age of 5. Disease burden can be expressed in *Disability-Adjusted Life Years* (DALY), which combines the burden due to death and disability in a single index. The DALY index allows comparison of the impact of different diseases, and the contribution of environmental and other risk factors to these diseases.

It is important to remember that children are affected disproportionately by environmental exposures as compared to adults. Unfortunately, more specific data on the environmental burden of disease in children or on additional environmental risks are currently not available. WHO and UNICEF are co-leading a Global Initiative on Children's Environmental Health Indicators, launched at the World Summit on Sustainable Development, which intends to provide richer data on children's health and the environment in the near future. Preventing childhood exposure to environmental hazards may prevent injuries, immediate illnesses, such as respiratory infections and diarrhoeal diseases, and diseases with longer latency periods, such as cancer.

Respiratory infections are the most common among all diseases in children, and pneumonia is the primary cause of childhood mortality worldwide. Indoor and outdoor air pollution may be to blame for as much as 60% of the global burden of disease brought about by respiratory infections. The most recent estimates suggest that 36% of acute lower respiratory infections, including pneumonia, are attributable to solid fuel use. More than half of the world's population relies on solid fuels such as dung, wood and coal for cooking and heating needs, leading to very high levels of indoor air pollution.

Exposure to such indoor air pollution has been linked with respiratory infections in children, chronic illness such as bronchitis and, in the case of coal, lung cancer in adults, and may be associated with low birth weight, tuberculosis, cataract, and many other diseases. Indoor air pollution is the fourth most important risk factor in developing countries (behind malnutrition, unsafe sex, and unsafe water and sanitation). Outdoor air pollution remains a serious threat to health in cities throughout the world. In Latin America, for example, air pollution limits are routinely exceeded in many cities including Sao Paulo and Rio de Janeiro, Brazil; Santiago, Chile; and Mexico City, Mexico. Both ambient air quality and a school's indoor air quality affect the respiratory health of school children.

Diarrhoeal Diseases

Diarrhoeal diseases, the second most common global illness affecting young children and a major cause of death in lower income countries, are closely linked with poor sanitation, poor hygiene, and lack of access to safe and sufficient supplies of water and food. Each year, nearly two million children under the age of five die of diarrhoeal diseases caused by unsafe water supplies, sanitation, and hygiene. Interventions such as simple hand washing have been shown to reduce sickness from diarrhoeal diseases by up to 47%, and could save up to one million lives. Although diarrhoeal diseases are most prevalent in the developing world, they are also a significant health threat in developed countries.

Salmonella and Campylobacter jejuni, tiny organisms that spread through eggs, chicken or milk, are two of the most common causes of diarrhoea in the developed world. Outbreaks of food poisoning in the United States of America, Canada, Europe, and Japan have been linked with the parasite Cyclospora and a new form of E. coli bacteria. Contaminated water can also be a cause of diarrhoea in the developed world. The largest outbreak of diarrhoea in the United States affected over 400 000 people when the municipal water supply of Milwaukee, Wisconsin was contaminated with Cryptosporidium, a parasite from farm animal waste. School children everywhere need to have access to safe and sufficient water and sanitation and need to be taught basic hygiene.

Injuries and Poisonings

In high income countries, road traffic injuries are the most common cause of death among children aged 5 to 14, and account for approximately 10% of deaths in this age group. In low and middle income countries they are the fifth leading cause of death in the same age group behind diarrhoeal diseases, lower respiratory infections, measles and drowning. Schools located near busy roads or water bodies have increased risks of these types of injuries. Falls and injuries within the school grounds can occur as a result of poorly maintained schools or poor construction management.

Poisonings in children account for about 2% of all injury deaths in children in developed countries, and about 5% in developing countries. There is potential for children to be poisoned at school by pesticides due to improper storage or improper pesticide applications; lead in paint chips and in water contaminated by metals; and by chemicals in cleaning products. In addition, the effects of long-term exposure on children's health and development, even to low levels of pesticides, are suspected of having lasting effects that could extend over a lifetime.

Cancer

Cancers of all types claimed more than 7 million lives in 2001. This figure is likely to underestimate incidence, since disease surveillance efforts are often inadequate or non-existent. Genetic factors in combination with a wealth of environmental factors, such as exposure to chemical pollutants, and behavioural factors, such as unhealthy lifestyles, are believed to cause the vast majority of cancers. Some environmental causes of childhood cancer such as ionising radiation are well known. Other childhood exposures, such as excessive exposure to sunlight and environmental tobacco smoke, pesticides, solvents, radon (a radioactive gas) and arsenic may contribute to cancers that develop in adulthood.

All children are exposed to ultraviolet radiation from the sun and almost half of the world's children are regularly exposed to environmental tobacco smoke. Some evidence suggests that childhood cancer may be associated with a variety of other products and exposures. Children may be at higher risk of developing cancer due to some exposures, such as radiation and pesticides, than similarly exposed adults. Therefore, it is important to minimise children's exposure to such agents in the school environment.

Developmental Disabilities

Developmental disabilities include a variety of conditions that occur during childhood and cause mental or physical limitations. These disabilities include autism, cerebral palsy, epilepsy, mental retardation, and other neurological impairments. Many researchers believe an epidemic of learning and behavioural disabilities is occurring among children. Developmental disabilities are believed to be a significant and frequently undetected health problem in developing countries. Malnutrition and parasitosis (especially helminth infections) may contribute to these illnesses.

In India, undernourished rural children 10-12 years of age demonstrated a range of learning deficiencies when compared to normally nourished children.

Considering the estimate that a third of the world's children suffered from malnutrition during the 1990s, the potential for widespread learning deficiencies is staggering. Schools could play an important role in ensuring that students have nutritious food to eat several times per day. Schools that offer a lunch programme give children an opportunity for at least one safe and nutritious meal a day. This also serves as a motivation for families to send children to school.

Exposure to toxic substances also places children at risk of developmental disorders, particularly in developing countries where regulations are lax or non-existent. In many developing countries where leaded gasoline is still used, lead presents a threat to more than half of urban children. Populations in at least 100 countries are still exposed to air polluted with lead from gasoline. Also, past use of leaded gasoline in countries that have already phased out leaded gasoline leaves behind a reservoir of lead in the soil which will continue to pose a hazard to human health for years to come.

In the United States, 17% of children younger than 18 years have been diagnosed with one or more developmental disability. It has been estimated that 25% of major developmental deficits may result from a combination of environmental and genetic factors. These estimates are based on known toxic substances. Since little is known about the developmental effects of most chemicals, this percentage could be much higher. Exposure to lead, mercury, organic solvents, substances such as polychlorinated biphenyls (PCBs), and pesticides (particularly organic compounds such as organophosphates) occur worldwide. All of these chemicals are known to affect the nervous system and are particularly harmful to children. Schools need to reduce or eliminate student exposures to these chemicals.

Asthma

Asthma and chronic respiratory illnesses such as bronchitis are growing problems, especially in intensively developed nations. Since the middle of the 20th century, the worldwide prevalence and severity of asthma have increased considerably, especially among children. In Taiwan, the prevalence of childhood asthma has risen to around 10% in contrast to a 1% prevalence rate in the 1970s. Currently, Australia and New Zealand report the highest asthma prevalence rates in the world (>15%), and in the United States, asthma is now the most prevalent chronic disease among children, affecting about 7% of all American children.

Between 1980 and 1995, the asthma prevalence rate for children increased 75% in the United States. Asthma rates are increasing among all ethnic groups, both sexes, all age groups, and in all regions of the United States but asthma prevalence is highest among urban children and is the primary cause for childhood hospitalisation in urban areas.

Experts acknowledge that in conjunction with genetic susceptibility, indoor and outdoor air pollution are an important factor in the increasing incidence and severity of asthma. Exposure to house dust mite allergens and secondhand smoke has been associated with the development of asthma as well as the exacerbation of asthma symptoms. Other indoor asthma triggers include allergens from cockroach, pet dander, and mold. Recently, ozone has been implicated as a factor contributing to asthma among children who exercise in urban settings. By reducing exposure to allergens and irritants, the incidence of asthma attacks can often be reduced. Schools represent an important setting for effective control measures. Wood smoke, environmental tobacco smoke, molds, and many volatile chemicals found in indoor environments can reduce respiratory function in school children. School absenteeism associated with these respiratory diseases can adversely affect both intellectual and emotional development.

Importance of Healthy School Environment

Children under five years of age experience over 40% of all environment-related illness. Children living in poor populations in rural and peri-urban areas in developing countries are particularly affected. These children face health risks from living in an environment that lacks clean air, water, and food, and from hazardous chemicals associated with rapid economic and urban development. Children are more susceptible to the harmful effects of chemical, biological and physical threats in their environment for the following reasons:

- Children are in a dynamic state of growth and their nervous, immune, respiratory, endocrine, reproductive and digestive systems are still developing. Their ability to detoxify and excrete toxins differs from that of adults. Exposure to environmental toxicants during certain stages of development can irreversibly damage the normal development of organs and systems.
- Young children breathe faster, and eat and drink more in proportion to their body weight than adults. They drink 2.5 times more water, eat 3 to 4 times more food, and breathe 2 times more air. Children therefore absorb more toxicants contained in air, water or food, which makes them more vulnerable to acute and chronic effects of environmental hazards.
- Children often have a greater exposure to environmental hazards than adults: they are closer to the ground where many contaminants settle and young children commonly put their hands into their mouths.

– The longer lifespan of a child increases the risk of developing diseases with long latency periods such as cancer.

Water and Sanitation

Around 1.1 billion people (one sixth of the global population) lack access to improved drinking water sources. Even sources of water thought to be safe may be affected by microbiological or chemical contamination. For example, where the water distribution systems in urban areas function intermittently, contaminated water may infiltrate into the pipelines. In Bangladesh as well as many other parts of the world, contamination of groundwater with arsenic is a major public health problem.

The Global Water Supply and Sanitation Assessment reported that 2.4 billion people globally did not have access to any type of improved sanitation facilities in 2000. These facts indicate that billions of people around the world, especially the poor, are at serious risk of contracting diseases such as diarrhoea, intestinal parasitic infections, trachoma, schistosomiasis, and of being exposed to high concentrations of heavy metals or chemicals.

Indoor Air Pollutants

For many children, much of their school day is spent indoors. The air they breathe inside their school may be more polluted than outdoor air. Poor indoor air quality may increase rates of asthma, allergies, and infectious and respiratory diseases, and affect student performance of mental tasks involving. In many rural schools in developing countries, fuels such as dung, wood and coal are used for heating and the preparation of school meals, exposing students to high levels of particles and other toxic pollutants.

Cooking and heating with simple fuels is likely to be the most prominent source of indoor air pollution in developing country schools but additional pollutants may include airborne bacteria and viruses, molds and fungal growths, and particles from building materials. In schools in industrialised countries, indoor air pollution may be the most prevalent of all environmental hazards. Over half of the schools surveyed in the United States reported at least one environmental problem affecting indoor air quality.

Problems include molds and toxic fungi; pesticides; volatile organic chemicals emitted from cleaning products, photocopiers, and classroom furnishings; radon gas and outdoor pollutants entering the school buildings; airborne asbestos from insulation, and lead released from paints and other building materials. Faulty heating, ventilation, and air conditioning systems can exacerbate air quality problems. "Sick building syndrome," manifested by headaches, nervous system effects, and respiratory problems, is routinely reported to American school nurses. The syndrome became prevalent in the 1970s and continues today with the construction of airtight buildings designed to conserve energy.

Outdoor Air Pollutants

In urban settings, children are exposed to outdoor air pollution from industry and traffic exhaust fumes on their way to school, and outdoor air pollutants may enter into the classroom. These health effects are difficult to quantify, but WHO estimates that worldwide about 800 000 annual deaths and 0.8% of all DALYs are caused by outdoor air pollution. Air pollution is a global health threat to children. Nearly 80% of 105 European cities surveyed exceeded WHO air quality standards for at least one pollutant.

In Western Europe, asthma cases have doubled in the last ten years. In the United States, the number of asthmatics has leapt by over 60% since the early 1980's and deaths have doubled to over 5 000 per year. In the Russian Federation, over 200 cities often exceed pollution limits and air pollution has been implicated as a contributing factor to 17% of childhood illnesses. Air pollution in developing world cities is estimated to be responsible for 50 million annual cases of chronic coughing in children younger than 14 years of age. In Beijing, Delhi, Jakarta, and Mexico City, pollution levels sometimes exceed WHO air quality standards by a factor of three or more.

In some of China's major cities, particulate levels are as much as six times the WHO guidelines. Throughout the world, as many as 1.5 billion urban residents breathe air exceeding WHO air quality standards. While all school children incur health risks as a result of exposure to air pollution, children with asthma need to be particularly concerned because they are 40% more likely to have an asthma attack on high outdoor pollution days. Even short-term increases in air pollution levels have been associated with an increase in asthma symptoms in children.

Children may be particularly sensitive to the cancer-causing and other adverse effects of pesticides, and accumulate a large percentage of their lifetime health risk during childhood. Exposure to pesticides at school may result from their application both indoors and outdoors. Children in both developing and industrialised countries may also be exposed to pesticide residues in drinking water, food and objects such as books and toys.

Pesticides are widely misused due to misunderstanding of their toxicity by applicators. Labels rarely provide a complete and accurate summary of pesticide health threats. Pesticides like DDT have been banned or restricted in many countries, but are still widely available in others. In a school in Costa Rica for the children of workers in a banana plantation, health problems were reported to be overwhelmingly respiratory and eye infections. The school was located in the center of the plantation and was regularly sprayed with insecticide from the plantation's aircraft.

Several recent studies in various parts of the United States found that nearly 85% of schools were treated with pesticides, with no notification or vacancy requirement prior to spraying. Some of the pesticides used have the potential to cause short-term or longterm health effects, including vomiting, diarrhoea, convulsions, headaches, skin irritations, liver damage, neurological problems, and behavioural and emotional disturbances. Other pesticides used in schools were labelled with warnings of health effects that may include reproductive system disorders, flu-like symptoms and asthma-like problems. In addition to using pesticides in and around school grounds, many industrialised countries use "pressure treated lumber" that has been impregnated with pesticides to build play sets and picnic tables. In the United States, new regulations on pressure treated lumber will help avoid this problem in the future.

Food

In 2002, UNESCO estimated that nearly 5 500 children die each day from bacteria in food. Unsafe food remains a widespread public health problem in all parts of the world. Surveys in New Zealand, Europe, and North America suggest that each year up to 10% of the population suffer from diseases caused by unsafe food. *E. coli* bacteria are a major cause of diarrhoea and kidney failure that can be fatal in children. The largest ever outbreak occurred in 1996 in Japan, affecting 6 300 school children and 92 staff members and resulting in two deaths.

The probable cause was determined to be fresh radish sprouts. Another large *E. coli* outbreak occurred in Africa: contaminated drinking water and cooked maize infected thousands of people. In developing countries, a polluted environment, lack of a safe water supply and poor sanitation increase the likelihood of food contamination. Worldwide, most outbreaks result from improper food handling such as use of contaminated equipment; contamination by infected persons; use of contaminated raw ingredients; cross-contamination; and addition of toxic chemicals or use of food containing natural toxins.

Hazardous location

Lands near or directly beneath schools in many parts of the world may pose health threats to children. Schools located near transportation corridors, bus depots, industrial sites, abandoned lots, landfills, military bases, utility plants, and construction sites may present health problems to the students and staff occupying the school. New schools are difficult and expensive to site and are often constructed on undesirable lands.

In developed countries, enormous sums of money are spent remediating schools that have been built on hazardous land. Many schools are located adjacent to highways causing students' and staff's exposure to high concentrations of vehicle exhaust, which is known to contain several cancer-causing substances and at least 50 toxic air pollutants.

Application of Changes in the School's Environment

There are potentially many changes that can be implemented to improve a school's physical environment and, ultimately, the health of students and staff. These changes can serve to educate students, teachers, and parents about the relationship between the environment and health. For example, providing shade from a sweltering sun either by planting trees or building shade structures and encouraging the use of clothes, hats and sunglasses can reduce exposure to the damaging effects of ultraviolet radiation.

Minimising the use of pesticides in schools while educating teachers and students about why this is important can lead to a heightened awareness about the hazards of pesticides in the community. Implementing changes in the physical environment to improve indoor air quality with the goal of reducing respiratory illness and asthma will educate students about managing their own environment to improve respiratory health. Students can, in turn, educate their parents about these management techniques. Health education activities brought home from school by children have been found to positively influence parents' self-management of asthma. Schools can implement policies and procedures that can improve the health of students at little or no extra cost.

In the developing world, providing separate sanitation facilities for girls is an important contributing factor in reducing dropout during and before menses. Educated girls marry later in life, have fewer children and are more likely to seek health care for themselves and their children. An increase in the number of girls who stay in school is likely to lead to a reduction in childhood mortality, improved children's health and nutrition, and a deceleration in population growth.

Female education has the greatest return on the dollar of all investments available in the developing world. Eliminating air pollutants that trigger asthma attacks and other respiratory illnesses can help improve attendance in high and low income nations. In the United States, asthma is believed to be the most common reason that students miss school.

Building capacity to protect children's health and educational potential will demand changing knowledge, perspectives, and priorities. It will also require collective decisions to adopt new policies, and make commitments to pursue specific plans for health risk reduction. Procedural steps toward creating a healthy physical environment at schools are:

- *Participation*: Organise broad participation to design and implement plans to create healthy school environments. Participants could include school administrators; managers of facilities, transportation and grounds; parents; students; community leaders; and experts in public health and environmental protection.
- *Threat identification*: Conduct research to identify the magnitude and relative importance of significant threats to health within the school environment. Threats may be associated with the following: water quality, sanitation, air quality, food safety and nutrition, vector-borne diseases, waste management, pesticide use, hazardous chemical management, transportation, adjacent land uses, structural integrity, renovation, purchasing, and grounds management.
- *Goal identification*: Establish clear and measurable goals to reduce significant threats.
- *Design of intervention plans*: Design specific intervention plans to improve healthpromoting practices in the following areas: water quality, sanitation, air quality, food safety and nutrition, waste management, pesticide use, hazardous chemical management, transportation, facility siting,

structural integrity, renovation, purchasing, and grounds management.

– *Implementation of plans and evaluation of progress*: Implement the intervention plans. Define timetables to meet goals, and assign clear responsibility and accountability. Routinely evaluate progress in goal attainment, and the effectiveness of interventions. Adjust policies, intervention plans, and methods of implementation in response to evaluations, changing conditions and availability of resources.

Protecting Environmental Threats

Successful protection of children from environmental threats at school requires careful definition of problems and goals to resolve them. Goals are grouped into two categories: substantive goals and procedural goals.

Substantive goals

– *Hazard reduction:* Reduce exposure to significant physical, biological and chemical threats to children's health within the school environment.

– *Education:* Educate school administrators, teachers, parents, health providers, political leaders and community members about direct and indirect relationships between the school environment and health.

– *Surveillance:* Create an effective system to monitor and record infectious and chronic disease prevalence, and environmental hazards within the school environment.

– *Health service delivery:* Develop capacity to provide fundamental emergency medical care within each school.

Food: Provide safe and nutritious meals for students.

- *Water:* Provide safe water at schools for drinking, cooking and washing.
- *Sanitation:* Provide clean and well maintained sanitary facilities, separate for males and females.
- *Transport:* Provide safe passage between homes and schools.
- *Waste:* Create a secure and effective system for waste collection, storage and removal.
- *Facilities:* Ensure structural integrity of school buildings, use of safe building materials, and health protective renovation procedures.
- *Grounds:* Prevent students from exposure to dangerous conditions on grounds, such as rivers, ravines, flood prone areas, rockslides, or highways. Manage grounds to prevent diseases carried by rodents or insects.
- *Hazardous materials storage:* Ensure that hazardous materials are stored safely and securely, preferably in a structure detached from educational facilities. Hazardous materials include fuels, solvents, some cleaning supplies, paints and wood finishes, pesticides, and vehicle fluids.
- *Pesticides:* Restrict use to situations where pesticides will confer a health protective benefit, such as reducing insects that carry diseases, and then employ only the least toxic alternatives.
- *Tobacco:* Eliminate use of tobacco on school grounds.
- *Green purchasing:* Develop criteria to guide purchasing of products and services that will better protect the environment and children's health. Categories of products for which low risk options should be identified include: food, vehicles, fuels, furnishings, cleaning products, building materials, pesticides, paints and wood finishes.

Procedural Goals

- *Participation:* Create decision-making processes that encourage broad community participation in goal formulation, policy development, intervention design, implementation and evaluation.
- *Transparency in decision-making:* Make decisions and deliberations in open meetings.
- *Freedom of information:* Information and records on hazards in the school environment should be publicly accessible.
- *Protection of privacy:* The privacy of individual medical records should be protected.
- *Fair warning of significant hazards:* If school officials recognise unusually hazardous situations, the community should be promptly warned (e.g. lead water piping, bacterial contamination of food or water, pesticide applications, asbestos in renovation debris).
- *Timely response:* The community should expect a timely response by school officials to credible evidence of health hazards.
- *Equity:* Implement interventions to achieve an equitable reduction in exposure to hazards within school environments.

Planning Process

Effective protection of health and enhancement of education require school and community involvement in the planning of interventions. Two important groups that could be involved in the planning process are a school health team and a community advisory team.

School health team

A school health team may be designated to coordinate

and monitor health-promoting policies and activities. If a school does not have a health team, planning to improve the school's physical environment can provide the opportunity to form one. Valuable members of the school health team could include teachers, administrators, school nurses, students, parents, transport managers, facilities managers and groundskeepers. Specific task forces can be organised to focus on specific health concerns such as health surveillance and evaluation, health service delivery, sanitary facilities, water quality, food preparation and safety, waste management, transport, vector-borne disease management, pesticide use, structural facilities, renovation, purchasing, and grounds.

Planning improvements to the physical environment provides an opportunity to work outside the school with those who have an interest and expertise in the relationship between the environment and health. Potential partners from the community include parents, childcare centers, local government representatives, businesses, residents, non-governmental agencies, health service providers, environmental organisations, and experts in facility design, construction, renovation, grounds management, waste management, transport, and infectious diseases.

Intervention Plans

Schools could develop intervention plans that include:

- *Purpose statement:* A general purpose statement should address the need for hazard reduction, environmental quality, safety assurance, education, surveillance, and health service delivery.
- *Problem identification:* Problems should be identified and ranked in order of relative significance to provide priorities given limited budgets and time.

- *Goals and objectives:* General goals and specific objectives should provide clear and measurable targets for environmental improvements.
- *Procedural policies:* Policies should be adopted to structure participation, transparency in decision-making, access to information, confidentiality and privacy of medical records, warning of significant hazards, timely response to significant threats, and equitable reduction in exposure to hazards within school environments.
- *Specific intervention strategies:* Specific strategies should be designed to protect or improve the following components of the school environment: nutrition and food safety; water quality; air quality; sanitation facilities; transportation; waste; facilities design, construction, renovation and maintenance; grounds; hazardous materials storage; pesticide use; and purchasing.
- *Educational strategy:* Each plan may also include an educational strategy, addressing important problems through curricular and extracurricular efforts.
- *Responsible parties*: Specific individuals should be assigned responsibility to develop and implement components of intervention plans.
- *Financial analysis:* Each plan should include a financial analysis estimating the cost of goal attainment, and potential sources of funding or voluntary service and materials.
- *Evaluation:* Each plan should include criteria for evaluating progress and goal attainment.
- *Community outreach:* Each plan should consider how the expertise, labour and financial resources of community members might be helpful in achieving goals.

Both qualitative and quantitative data are necessary for planning effective environmental health interventions, and to establish a baseline for evaluation. Qualitative data include perceptions, beliefs, and attitudes; quantitative data include numerical information. The following information could help determine local needs and priorities in relation to the school environment:

- Health trends at the national, regional, local and school level, if available.
- Environmental status and trends at the national, regional, local and school level, if available.
- Knowledge, attitudes, beliefs, values, behaviours and conditions related to the environment and health.
- Available resources, both personnel and financial, and commitment to health within the school and community.
- Ongoing initiatives in the community, in other schools, or in the country that may provide support.
- Status of existing school and community programmes that might help to implement improvements to the physical environment.

Commitment and Policies

Making improvements to a school's physical environment will require understanding and commitment from a wide range of individuals and groups, including relevant government departments, health and education authorities, community and business leaders, educators, parents, students, and the community.

Successful reduction of environmental health threats within schools demands political commitment at all levels of government. Political leaders will need to understand the importance of the threat. Experience in some nations suggests that recognition of school environmental health problems results from the educational efforts of community and grass roots organisations. National legal authority, expertise, and financial support may be necessary to implement change, especially within the poorest communities. Political commitment and support may occur in the form of:

- *Support for research*: Research to understand more fully the extent and distribution of environmental health threats faced by children in schools is often necessary. Although hazards may vary from classroom to classroom, national and regional governments and universities can show commitment by providing support and/or expertise to implement needed research. Results of such research can also be publicly acknowledged and disseminated by national authorities.
- *Authority and responsibility*: National authority to set standards for physical school improvements may be necessary to bring about significant change. This authority could require the provision of safe food and water; attainment of sanitary standards; and establishment of pollution limits and building standards.
- *Financial commitment*: Financial support for construction, maintenance, health surveillance, medical services, and environmental hazard assessment and intervention may all be necessary to assure sufficient health protection for children in schools. Training, equipment, and materials may be required to enable schools to develop and implement physical improvements. Many communities lack the financial resources necessary to provide these services, and will need financial commitments from provincial or national levels.

A healthy school environment requires community support. Parents and community members need to participate in the development and evaluation of interventions to improve school health. Commitment and the support of many parties on a variety of levels are necessary to share expertise, facilities, and resources. Community group meetings, parent-teacher conferences, open houses, and formal presentations are all opportunities for involving family and community members early in the development process. Community commitment may be enhanced by:

- Public recognition of the association between health and the environment by community leaders, local government representatives, health and education authorities, and other relevant organisations.
- Establishment of a designated committee for coordinating efforts to improve the physical environment of schools.
- Provision of local resources for interventions to improve the physical environment of schools.
- Coordination of interventions with other programmes in the community (e.g. malaria control, food safety initiatives, asthma education, pesticide awareness, recycling initiatives, implementation of environmental management systems).
- Efforts to attract community and media attention (e.g. though printed material, community forums, school events).

Environmental Health Education within Other Components

A health-promoting school draws on the school's full organisational capacity to improve the health of students, school personnel, families and community members by improving the physical environment of the school and educating the school community about environmental health threats. Physical improvements to schools can serve as an entry point for the development or enhancement of policies, planning groups, and various components that serve as a framework for a health-promoting school.

The effectiveness of interventions integrated into each of these components is influenced by the extent to which they are supported by a variety of people, policies, and trained staff and by the extent to which interventions in each of these components combine with other health promotion efforts to complement and reinforce each other. Most schools will not have the resources to address all the environmental health issues that might be identified at once. Each school must establish its own priorities, in collaboration with all parties concerned, to decide the extent to which identified issues should be addressed.

A health-promoting school should enable students, parents, teachers and community members to work together to make these decisions. Schools should start with small changes that are feasible rather than waiting until resources become available to address all of the issues at once.

Create a Healthy School Environment

All members of the school community need clean air to breathe, clean water to drink, a safe place for recreation, a safe way to travel to school to avoid accidents, and protection from extreme temperatures and ultraviolet radiation. A safe and healthy physical environment requires a good location and safe buildings; protection from excessive noise; natural light; clean indoor air and water; a healthy outdoor environment; and healthy school-related activities including safe management and maintenance practices, use of non-toxic cleaning supplies, careful use of pesticides, vector control, and use of non-toxic art supplies.

School Location

Before a school is constructed, planners and community groups need to consider potential environmental risks in relation to the school's location, e.g. the vicinity of a chemical plant or former waste site, an area prone to flooding, or a busy, noisy road. Options for improving existing schools on poor sites include hazardous waste removal, construction of footpaths or bridges for getting to school, and construction of school barriers to provide a buffer to hazardous areas. Adjustments in behaviour can be made to account for poor environmental conditions such as avoiding recreation activities during periods of the day when air pollution is at a peak or the sun is most intense.

In areas where school children are required to cross busy roads, crossing guards or older children can assist younger children. If children are required to travel to school by bus, these buses should be in good running order and exposure to diesel or gasoline exhaust fumes should be minimised.

The structure of a school building should protect students and staff, but poorly designed school buildings and play areas may present serious health risks instead. School buildings are often larger than traditional domestic or residential buildings. Special construction techniques may be required to ensure safety, particularly in areas prone to natural disasters such as earthquakes and typhoons. In addition to being structurally sound, school buildings and play areas should be constructed without asbestos and with the safest, non-toxic materials available. Schools should be designed to prevent temperature extremes inside classrooms.

Indoor School Environment

Fecal material contaminates drinking water. Children

dipping their unwashed hands into a shared drinking-water supply provide a typical route of contamination. In areas where this occurs, providing schools with a ladle to dip into water sources may be a low-cost solution to cleaner water. A safe water supply is free from bacteria, parasites, and toxic chemicals. Where there is uncertainty about the quality of the drinking water, it should be tested regularly. If the water has not been chlorinated, it is important to disinfect it through chlorination, boiling or any other acceptable method. Safe storage of water at school and at home should also be promoted.

Where helminth infections are a problem, store drinking water for over 24 hours and then decant to help remove helminth eggs that may have fallen to the bottom of the container. Boiling is an effective way to kill worms, eggs, and other germs that may have contaminated the water. A filtration system made from stones and sand or gauze/filters in guinea worm areas can also be used to make water safe from worms.

In the industrialised world, water supplies at school can be contaminated by chemicals present on-site as a result of former land-use practices, adjacent land uses, or plumbing fixtures. Many school water fountains have lead-soldered or lead-lined tanks. Patterns of intermittent water use from these fountains result in water standing in tanks longer than in typical residential situations, increasing the amount of lead that is absorbed into the water from the tanks. Schools need to be aware of these potential risks and have their water tested regularly.

Human excreta are the biggest source of disease-producing organisms including parasites, bacteria, and viruses. Success in eliminating fecal material from the school environment is dependent on: informed and responsible students; supervision of young students; a fence or structure to stop animals from defecating in areas where children play; toilets conveniently located, reliable, clean, odor-free, private, and well-maintained. Separate facilities for girls can reduce dropout rates during or before menses. A variety of latrine systems are used in different parts of the world depending on cultural, environmental, and economic conditions. Education and health officials need to make sure that construction of latrines is technically appropriate and acceptable.

The quality of indoor air is a function of building ventilation, construction materials used, and pollutants released inside the building (such as tobacco smoke, cleaning supplies, pesticides, and art supplies). It is also a function of policy, as in the case of environmental tobacco smoke. WHO strongly recommends that schools and their grounds should be completely tobacco free.

Breathing environmental tobacco smoke (e.g. side-stream and exhaled smoke from cigarettes, cigars and pipes) causes serious health problems. It can aggravate allergies and increase the severity of symptoms in children and adolescents with asthma and heart disease. It is also associated with lung cancer because environmental tobacco smoke contains essentially the same cancer-causing substances and toxic agents that are inhaled by the smoker.

In developing countries, the indoor burning of dung, wood and coal for cooking and heating within schools can cause high levels of fine particles in indoor air that can lead to respiratory illness and trigger asthma attacks. Adequate ventilation should be provided whenever possible and students should be educated about the health effects of poor ventilation, and particles and other combustion by-products in smoke. Schools in the developing world can promote the use of improved stoves, ensure that fuel wood is dry, time cooking activities when students are outside, and ensure that smoke is vented away from places where students may study or play.

A study on the causes of indoor air quality problems in schools throughout the developed worldfound that most problems in school facilities could be avoided by:

- Providing adequate outdoor air ventilation on a continuous basis (15 cubic feet per minute per student).
- Controlling the space relative humidity between 30% and 60%.
- Providing effective filters to remove fine particles from the outdoor air.

Outdoor Environment

The probability that children with asthma will have an attack is estimated to be 40% higher on high outdoor pollution days, and research indicates that children that play active sports are more likely to develop the disease in polluted cities. Many schools should be concerned with outdoor air quality. Equipped with some knowledge about air quality in their area, schools may choose to avoid involving students in intensive outdoor exercise during periods of high air pollution. Ozone levels usually peak between midday and evening. Avoiding outdoor activities during high pollution periods and in areas adjacent to highways or near other sources of air pollution will help to minimise asthma attacks in sensitive children and other short- and long-term health effects associated with exposure to air pollutants.

Play areas should be designed to be more than "play" areas. There is an urgent need for children to be able to take part in regular and appropriate physical activity. Schools offer a unique setting to promote and provide opportunities for physical activity as recreation and sport. Regular and appropriate physical activity is an essential stimulus for children to reach their potential of growth and development. It is necessary for optimal health and functional capacity. It also counteracts disabilities and diseases common to ageing.

Regular physical activity helps children and adolescents develop strong muscles and bones, normal body weight, efficient function of the heart and lungs, and skills of movement. To provide an environment that encourages and enables children to engage in regular and appropriate physical activity, schools should:

- provide play areas that are safe and have facilities for physical activity;
- establish and enforce policies and standards for the use of equipment and grounds to prevent physical activity-related injuries;
- provide time during the day for children to have access to play areas for unstructured physical activity;
- provide access to community recreation areas when insufficient space prevents children from regular physical activity on the schools grounds.

Children need to be protected from injuries that could occur outside the school buildings, and areas where children play or exercise should be free from hazards. Busy roadways, water bodies, waste sites, rockslides, and ravines should be considered threats to children. Play areas should not be located near these areas. When selecting wood for playgrounds or outdoor furniture that children and staff will use, avoid lumber treated with chromated copper arsenic, creosote and pentachlorophenol. Potentially toxic levels of arsenic can leach from the wood to the hands of children and contaminate the soil below where children play. Existing treated play sets can be sealed with polyurethane or painted to reduce exposure to toxic wood preservatives.

School Health Services

School health services help to treat health problems and to prevent, reduce and monitor them. In a health-promoting school, health services work in partnership with and are provided for students, school personnel, families and community members. School health services should be coordinated with members of the school and community to recognise and treat health problems resulting from exposure to environmental threats. These threats vary from community to community.

School nurses can help raise awareness of health problems among students, teachers and staff, and play an important role in referring students to specialists. They are responsible for "de-worming" at regular intervals, managing health outcomes such as an asthma attack or injury, and recognising severe diseases such as malaria, severe diarrhoea and respiratory infections for correct referral. Ideally, they should receive training in environmental health issues prevalent in their community. School nurses should be responsible for tracking illnesses among students to help identify potential environmental health problems within the school.

A health-promoting school should involve students, school staff, families, and community members in efforts to improve health in the school. Children who participate in efforts to create a cleaner and safer environment learn about protecting themselves and their environment, and can acquire the knowledge, attitudes, values and skills needed to adopt healthy lifestyles as adults. Family and community members can serve on the school health team or community advisory committee; participate in activities and services offered through the school such as helping to build a safe play structure for children or helping to clean up school grounds; or provide support and resources by offering financial or technical assistance to improve a school's building structure or ventilation system.

It is important for parents to understand the relationship between their child's health and their environment both at school and at home. A health-promoting school can help to educate parents about potential environmental health threats in the home. This can be accomplished at a school health fair or at a health-related workshop for parents on environmental health threats to children. In addition to learning about maintaining a healthy environment for children to thrive, parents can contribute their services or resources to the school to make improvements in the school's physical environment.

Both the school and the community can benefit from working together to create a safe physical environment at schools. For example, a school can use the services of a local company to improve its ventilation system. Parents may subsequently utilise their services to improve the indoor air quality of their own homes.

Heath promotion and training school staff to understand and recognise the relationship between the environment and health is necessary if staff are to be positive role models for students. Additionally, well-trained school staff will be able to recognise problems in their school environment that may be contributing to poor health in both students and staff.

6

Health Education

There are variations across countries, and disparities between regions, provinces, districts, cities and areas. While there has been a significant decline in tooth decay in some developed countries during the past few decades, a large number of children worldwide are still suffering from the disease, much of which is active and untreated, leading to toothache and restricted activities. Such problems are particularly prevalent among children of deprived communities.

Similar to tooth decay, gum disease affects children in all countries and, in many countries, it is one of the most common diseases. The prevalence of gum disease in children is very high worldwide, with the majority of children being affected. Unintentional injury is one of the leading causes of death in the world, with 1 in 5 deaths among children under the age of 15 years. In some developing countries, unintentional injuries account for 80% of all deaths in children. Sport and playground related injuries, as well as general and road traffic accidents, often affect the head, neck and mouth. These injuries have a significant impact on oral health. Throughout the world, the number of cases of head and face injuries is increasing in both urban and rural areas.

With the increase in road traffic, poor lighting on the road and a lack of legislation regarding road safety, this is particularly significant in some developing countries. The front teeth are most vulnerable. In some countries, over 50% of children have experienced oral trauma, with a quarter of cases being children under the age of 5 years. According to the 1993 UK Child Dental Health Survey, 5% of 12-year-old children (45.7 per 1000) exhibit trauma to their front teeth. The corresponding figure for Syria is 12%. In the US, over 20% of children aged less than 15 years have been admitted to the emergency room sustaining head and face injuries.

While the most commonly sustained damage is fractures to tooth enamel, some injuries can lead to permanent tooth loss. The significance of intentional head and face injuries should not be overlooked. In addition to potential direct damage to the teeth and, possibly, other head and face structures, they may be signs of child abuse, a problem that could scar the child for life. Defects and the colour of tooth enamel affect the appearance of teeth which, in turn, may have a impact on quality of life. The prevalence of enamel undesirable and defects is rising in some countries.

Demarcated opacities (white marks on the teeth) are often found on the upper front teeth, while diffuse opacities or fluorosis (discolouration of the teeth) affect all the teeth generally. Some childhood systemic diseases and malnutrition during tooth formation could lead to hypoplasia (discolouration and structural damage to the teeth). In some countries, about 25-40% of children have opacities (demarcated or diffuse opacities) of the tooth enamel on one or more teeth. In Malaysia, it has been reported that over 75% of 12-year-old children have some form of enamel defects and opacities, regardless of whether the area is fluoridated or not. However, severe enamel defects are not common.

In many countries, a considerable number of children have limited knowledge of the causes and prevention of the most common oral disease. Similarly, mothers' oral health knowledge is generally poor and schoolteachers' oral health knowledge, while better than that of the mothers', remains unsatisfactory. It is evident that cultural beliefs play an important role in the perception of the causes of dental decay and gum disease. Only a small proportion of children, parents and schoolteachers is aware of the harmful effects of hidden sugars and sugary drinks.

Moreover, while many parents recognise the importance of tooth brushing in general, some do not know how to prevent tooth decay and gum disease and the role of fluoride in the prevention of dental decay is poorly understood. In many countries, less than half of mothers have received oral health advice from dentists. While the harmful effect of smoking is generally acknowledged, other forms of tobacco use are not regarded as risk factors for oral cancer. Many children are exposed to smoke because their parents smoke at home. Improving the parents' awareness, attitudes and behaviour toward tobacco is therefore paramount.

As part of oral hygiene routine self-care, children should clean their teeth and gums every day with fluoridated toothpaste. However, in many countries the proportion of children who brush their teeth every day is still unsatisfactory. A small proportion of children does not clean their teeth at all. Some may not have access to a toothbrush. The use of traditional cleaning aids such as 'Miswaki', a traditional chewing stick, is common in some communities. Furthermore, the availability, affordability and quality of fluoride toothpaste remain a major problem in developing countries.

Only a small proportion of children used fluoridated toothpaste. In some countries, toothpastes are considered as cosmetics with high taxation, leading to exorbitant retail prices that are out of reach of most families. The need for promoting affordable fluoride toothpaste is evident. In several countries, many households do not have access to safe water for drinking, let alone for cleaning teeth. Given that schools may be the only place where children can carry out oral hygiene practices, it is therefore vital that sufficient safe water and sanitation facilities are provided in schools.

Healthy dietary behaviours are essential to growth and development and to maintain good oral health. The relationship between diet and oral disease is well established. It is therefore essential to reduce the amount, and more importantly the frequency, of sugary foods, snacks and drinks (including carbonated drinks and fruit juices) in a well-balanced diet with sufficient fresh fruit and vegetables. However, a high proportion of schoolchildren aged 11 to 17 years consume sugary snacks daily, according to a recent international report on health behaviour in schoolchildren.

In many countries, over 50% of 15-year-old children drink at least one can of soft drink everyday. In order to reduce the risk of oral cancer in later life, it is important to start at a very young age to have a balanced and healthy diet, to avoid using tobacco and consuming alcohol, to limit the exposure to the sun and to protect the lips from overexposure. Addressing these risk factors also helps prevent other oral diseases and general health conditions. However, in many countries, children and adolescents are increasingly developing a habit of tobacco use, in the form of cigarette smoking or smokeless tobacco. In Greenland, over 50% of 15-year-old children smoke daily and 3 in 4 smokers in the region of the Americas start smoking during adolescence.

Over 50% of children as young as 8 years old have experienced chewing tobacco in some communities. In some cultures, children chew betel quid that contains tobacco and other carcinogens. The high sugar content in some chewing tobacco is also a cause for concern. Professional care is an important component for attaining and maintaining optimal oral health. However, a significant proportion of children have no access to dental care, particularly among children in developing countries.

A staggering number of children have not visited a dentist before starting school. In some countries, a significant proportion of school children has never visited the dentist. For example, in Tanzania, over 75% of 12-year-old children have never been to the dentist. Consequently, few have preventive oral care.

Most advanced oral diseases are irreversible. For example, once tooth decay in permanent teeth is established, it will last for a lifetime. Even when the decayed teeth have been restored, the fillings remain in the mouth for life and may need to be replaced from time to time. However, it must be emphasised that, with appropriate measures, early onset of gum disease and dental decay is reversible. In contrast, advanced or established lesions progressively become more serious and difficult to treat. Clearly, prevention is better than cure.

Consequences of Oral Disease

The oral health of children is a significant public health issue. Oral disease is one of the most costly diet- and behaviour-related diseases. Childhood oral diseases, if untreated, can lead to irreversible damage, pain, disfigurement, more serious general health problems, lost school time, low self-esteem, poor quality of life and, in the case of noma, death. The delay in treatment not only results in aggravation of disease, but also costs of care are substantially escalated as a consequence. Adverse dental experience during childhood may lead to dental phobia, impacting on attitudes to oral health and self-care as well as dental visiting behaviours for life. These could have further personal and treatment costs.

Oral diseases result in considerable costs. Dental services constitute about 5% to 10% of the total health expenditure in industrial countries each year, costing billions of dollars. This poses a problem to many developing countries. The cost of dental treatment could easily exhaust the country's entire health budget, a budget that is already fully stretched or simply does not exist. The social and educational costs are also significant. For example, over 50 million school hours in learning are lost due to dental problems in the US.

The interference with daily activities, sleeping pattern, quality of life and parents' work output is considerable. Prevention, early diagnosis and timely treatment are therefore crucial in efforts to contain the costs of oral diseases. Children with disabilities are at increased risk of oral diseases, infections, delayed tooth eruption, gum disease and enamel defects. The exposure to special diets, medications and therapies, compounded by difficulty in maintaining effective self-care practices and in accessing professional care, have a serious adverse effect on their oral health.

Costs of neglect are also high, in terms of financial, social and personal impacts. Advanced disease may necessitate more complex, costly and, possibly, more traumatic treatments, such as surgery, root canal therapy, extractions and treatment under general anaesthesia and hospitalisation. Playground related injuries, including injuries to head and face, among children aged 15 years or under cost the US government an estimated 1.2 billion dollars annually. There are also indirect and intangible costs that should not be underestimated.

Poor oral health in childhood often continues into adulthood, impacting on economic productivity and quality of life. It has been reported that investment in oral disease prevention and health promotion decreases costs in health expenditure and is more cost-effective in the long-term.

The experience of pain, endurance of dental abscesses, problems with eating and chewing, embarrassment about the discoloration, damage or shape of teeth can distract children from play and effective learning. Oral health affects general health. If left untreated even for a short period of time, oral diseases can have adverse consequences. Oral infection can kill. It has been considered a risk factor for a number of general health conditions. Systemic spread of germs can cause, or seriously worsen, infections throughout the body, particularly among individuals with suppressed immune systems, heart disease and diabetes.

Studies have suggested that oral diseases (such as dental decay and gum disease) are associated with a variety of problems. For example:

- failure to thrive;
- poor nutrition;
- speech impairments;
- psychological problems;
- cardiovascular disease;
- diabetes;
- cancer.

Furthermore, some common medications and therapies used to treat general health conditions can compromise the health of the mouth and oral functioning. In recent years, much research has demonstrated the impact of oral health on quality of life. A number of oral health related quality of life measures have been developed to assess the functional, psychological, social and economic consequences. In general, poor oral health has a negative impact on quality of life, influencing eating abilities, personal confidence, mental health, social interaction, personal relationships, general health and well being and enjoyment in life.

Low quality of life scores are also related to poor oral health status and reduced access to professional care. Similarly, general health risk factors also affect oral health, such as excessive alcohol intake, smoking, tobacco use and poor dietary practices. The correlation between these lifestyle behaviours and increased risk of tooth decay, gum disease, oral infections, head and face defects, oral cancer and other oral conditions has been evidenced. There is a need to adopt an integrated approach to address these important risk factors for both oral and general health. Promoting oral health provides a valuable opportunity to integrate oral health promotion into general health promotion. Such an approach is likely to be more efficient and effective than those programmes targeting a single disease or condition.

Nutrition and Oral Health

Nutrition plays a critical role in a number of oral diseases including dental decay, gum disease, toothwear and oral cancer. Nutrition and oral health have a particularly intricate relationship. They form a vicious circle; poor oral health disrupts nutritional intake and poor nutrition affects the development of oral tissues including teeth, making them more susceptible to oral disease. Chronic deficiencies of some micronutrients, such as ascorbate, zinc and iron, may also impair the oral defence mechanisms.

Poor oral health is associated with stunted growth and compromised nutrition. Early childhood caries (ECC) could lead to failure to thrive. ECC has been considered an indicator for malnutrition, a condition that affects growth and development of children. Mental development and, subsequently, learning abilities are compromised. In more severe cases, malnutrition can cause death. Nutritional deficiencies could also lead to many general health problems in later life such as cardiovascular diseases and poor pregnancy outcomes. In contrast, good oral health helps promote nutritional intake in children, enhancing their learning potential and school performance and enabling them to lead a more productive life.

Effective oral hygiene practices, good dietary behaviours and appropriate use of fluorides, together with sustainable, effective and accessible professional care, are keys to good oral health. The school provides an excellent setting for delivering oral health services for children. Individuals, families, community, schools, education authorities, healthcare providers and government departments should work collaboratively to reduce risk factors and to promote oral health, incorporating the guiding principles for health promotion:

- develop healthy public policies;
- create supportive environments;
- strengthen community actions,
- develop personal skills to improve knowledge, attitudes and behaviours;
- reorient health services to provide a sustainable, effective and accessible system.

Prevention is a critically important strategy for promoting good oral health among young people. Most risk behaviours and lifestyles stem from school-age years. Equally, good habits that are developed at a young age are more sustainable. Oral hygiene practices can easily be adopted and incorporated into daily routines such as eating and cooking. Hence, daily tooth brushing with fluoridated toothpaste is a habit that should be encouraged to become a norm early in life. Good dietary patterns should also be fostered at a young age, particularly in preventing children from acquiring a 'sweet tooth' that leads to a habit of eating too much sugar.

Early dental visiting experience enables children to develop a good rapport and relationship with the dental team, so that preventive measures can be implemented before oral disease begins. Parents also play an important role in shaping the positive attitudes and influencing good oral health behaviours at home. With regular reinforcement and encouragement at home and in schools, these healthy behaviours are more likely to continue into adulthood, becoming life-long habits.

Oral Health Promotion

Oral health promotion activities can easily be integrated into school curriculum and activities, coordinated and delivered by school teachers or other school personnel. In Thailand, school teachers are responsible for oral health education, supervising tooth brushing drills after lunch and oral health screening and surveillance. Many of these activities are also incorporated into general health promotion. For example, oral hygiene forms part of the personal hygiene and grooming programmes such as hair and hand washing.

Dental trauma prevention is included in injury prevention. Oral health surveillance is an integral part of growth and nutrition surveillance that takes place twice a year. Some schools also include oral health in family planning and sex education. Oral health can also be featured in various grade levels throughout the school curriculum, with community projects and home-based activities that involve other members of the family. Oral health-related topics and issues can be introduced in subjects such as science, chemistry, biology, language, arithmetic, social studies, arts and music.

Other general health promotion activities also have oral health significance such as healthy eating. School policies and practices that promote good nutrition, healthy behaviours and self-esteem, and discourage smoking, tobacco use, alcohol consumption and substance abuse are also relevant to oral health. Undoubtedly, the co-operation from schools and teachers is crucial to the development of an effective oral health promotion effort.

Oral Health Promotion in Schools

Schools are microcosms of the larger community. With existing structures and systems in place, schools provide excellent opportunities for integrating oral health into the curriculum that is acceptable, appropriate and effective. Children are receptive to guidance and they are familiar with the learning environment and culture in school. Schools can effectively inform and influence students' oral health knowledge, beliefs, attitudes and behaviour.

It is important to target children, particularly at kindergartens and primary schools. Pupils need to acquire knowledge and skills that facilitate a healthy lifestyle and help them cope with social and peer pressure. Children are empowered to take control over their own health early in their lives and are encouraged to develop positive attitudes toward preventive measures. This is particularly crucial when they reach adolescence when they are challenged and exposed to risk factors such as tobacco and alcohol use and poor dietary practices. They become more mobile and travel independently in motor vehicles and bicycles, and engage more in sports and other high-risk activities that are more prone to craniofacial injuries. They may begin to experiment with sexual practices during this period, potentially subjecting themselves to infections that predispose to general and oral health problems.

School policies and physical environment are also imperative in the attainment of optimal health. Policies on diet, particularly in relation to sugars and carbonated drinks, are necessary to enable the canteen and tuck shops to promote healthy eating and sensible sugar intake. Many schools in Asia have implemented a daily supervised tooth brushing drill at lunchtime policy, according to a recent report. A safe physical environment in schools, particularly in play areas, helps reduce craniofacial injuries.

With appropriate dental trauma policies in place, timely actions can be taken in case of emergency to minimise permanent damage. Policies on bullying and violence between students, supported by education and empowerment, also help prevent intentional injuries. The provision of safe water and sanitation, together with pollution free environments, is a prerequisite for health. While access to safe water and sanitation facilities is a human right, about 1.1 billion people in the world have no access to safe drinking water and 2.4 billion lack basic sanitation facilities, most notably in Asian and African countries.

Without such facilities, health education and promotion are futile. More importantly, the school environment may be hazardous to children's health and well being. In contrast, by providing these facilities, schools are able to promote effective learning, to reinforce health messages and, particularly for oral health, to undertake health promotion activities. Schools, a well-established system, have the potential to reach a large group of people efficiently. Schools are more widely distributed even in rural areas of developing countries than health centres and clinics. This is particularly relevant to community-based preventive programmes for dental decay such as milk and water fluoridation schemes.

On the other hand, special attention can be given to students who are more susceptible to, or at a higher risk of, oral disease. Working collaboratively with the health services; dental treatment and preventive oral health measures can be made available in the school, a cost-effective approach with minimum disruption to learning and school activities. Children are encouraged to develop a good relationship with the dental team and a positive attitude towards regular dental attendance. The school dental clinic also provides important physical facilities for baseline assessment, monitoring, research and evaluation.

Furthermore, schools are often seen as a place for oral health knowledge and information by parents and the local community. This lay referral system for obtaining information is common in many countries and teachers play an important role in this process. It is therefore imperative that teachers and school staff are equipped with adequate oral health knowledge and skills. Schools form the heart of the community, a means for social networking for parents through local events and meetings. The schools can capitalise this school-home-community interaction to address common concerns, to form a united force to lobby for water fluoridation and healthy environments in the community where they live, work and learn.

School environments have a significant impact on sustainable healthy behaviours, a key success factor for

Health-Promoting Schools. Initiatives that target improving environments in schools for children are largely cost-effective. However, without supportive environments, optimal oral health for children cannot be realised. A review of Health-Promoting Schools supports the claim that a well designed and implemented programme which links the curriculum with other health promotion in school and the community is likely to produce health gains.

Provided that the intervention is substantial, over several years, and relevant to children's development, school health promotion is effective in improving knowledge, developing skills and promoting healthy behaviours. With supportive environment and adequate capacity building for staff, the programme is likely to be sustainable. The findings are in line with those reported by a WHO Expert Committee and other studies. There is considerable evidence to support the effectiveness of well-conducted school-based oral health promotion interventions worldwide.

In the region of the Americas, the US Surgeon General Report documents that most school-based or community-wide oral health preventive interventions are beneficial and cost-effective. Most school-based or school-linked fluoride and fissure sealant programmes are effective, particularly for children with high risk of dental decay. Tobacco use prevention and control programmes, as part of the school curriculum, are highly effective in influencing behaviour change. Along with the community-based and media based activities, school-based programmes are effective in preventing or delaying smoking onset in 20% to 40% of adolescents. Similar findings have been reported in other countries in the PAHO-AMRO region, where school-based preventive programmes are effective in improving oral healthy knowledge and behaviour.

Schools that adopt and implement the principles of a Health-Promoting School ('supportive schools') have a lower proportion of children with tooth decay (64%) and dental trauma (11%), compared with 'non-supportive schools' (66% and 17% respectively); the more comprehensive the curriculum, the better the oral health outcomes and less inequalities in oral health within the school.

In the European region, a comprehensive school-based oral health promotion programme has been in place for decades in some countries. Working closely with schools, the Danish Municipal Dental Health Service provides comprehensive oral health care to children and adolescents in school, with strong emphasis on prevention and health education to students, school staff and parents. Long-term epidemiological data show that dental knowledge, attitudes and behaviour have improved over time, as has children's oral health status. With improved dental knowledge and attitudes, parents are more involved in caring for their children's oral health. The findings agree with an earlier curriculum-based oral health education programme in England.

There are a number of school-based oral health promotion initiatives undertaken in Ireland, including the *Mighty Mouth* programme, Den TV and, while not exclusively about oral health, the Nutrition Education At Primary School and Social Personal and Health Education programmes. The programmes adopt the ethos of a Health-Promoting School and show promise. Children's oral health related knowledge, attitudes and behaviour, most notably healthy food choices, have improved.

In Central and Eastern Europe, school oral health programmes were established but brought to a halt during health systems transition. The effect of a school-based oral health promotion programme is more apparent in Hungary. A nation-wide programme was introduced in 1986 but ceased to exist in the mid-1990s during the health care reform. The oral health of children has improved after the introduction of the programme but deteriorated since the programme has stopped, according to national studies carried out in 1985, 1991 and 1996.

In the Western Pacific region, an oral health education programme has been undertaken in Wuhan, China, based on the concept of Health-Promoting Schools with a special emphasis on healthy environments and capacity building. The curriculum involves a regular classroom teaching programme on general health as well as oral health, with a daily tooth brushing exercise supervised by teachers. At the end of three years, oral health knowledge, attitudes and behaviour of children have improved, as has gingival health. Impact on teachers and parents is evident.

A study in Indonesia investigates the long-term effect of a school-based oral health education programme. While there is a significantly better oral health knowledge in the test group, tooth brushing behaviour, oral hygiene status and other oral health behaviours are found to be similar to those of the control group.

An oral health promotion effectiveness review in Australia shows that the use of a settings approach in promoting oral health can potentially lead to oral health benefits, with Health-Promoting Schools being most promising. The importance of supportive school environments is emphasised. A number of studies with this approach have proved to be effective. Evidence suggests that interventions that are incorporated into school curricula, part of other health promotion activities and needs-driven are most successful.

Programmes targeting parents, preschool children, schoolchildren and adolescents have made an impact on knowledge, healthy behaviour and, in some cases, health gains. Similar findings have been reported in New Zealand. Well-designed school-based initiatives that aim at improving knowledge and social competence are generally effective. In addition, the school dental service is a valuable means of promoting health and equity.

In Cambodia, oral health promotion activities form part of the school curriculum, including general and oral health education, daily tooth brushing drills and a weekly fluoride rinse programme. Some activities are led by student leaders, supervised by teachers. As a result of the programme, significant improvements in oral health knowledge and good practices among children have been reported, particularly in those schools that are more co-operative.

Similar findings have been reported in the South-east Asia region. In India, oral health education has been integrated into the school curriculum, aiming to provide dental knowledge and to empower children to take control over their own health. Oral health is featured in other subjects, including language, arts, arithmetic, sciences, social studies and music. Compared with the control groups, the test groups showed a significant improvement in knowledge and oral hygiene.

In the African region, oral Health Promoting Schools have been implemented in Madagascar. The initiative has been shown to be effective in improving dental health status and in influencing oral health knowledge and behaviour, compared with the control group. Parents are very supportive of the programme. Consequently, the levels of family support in oral care have also increased. However, training and professional development for staff, compounded by staff shortage, remain the key constraints. In South Africa, a 7-year school-based preventive programme results in a significantly lower prevalence (37%) and experience (DMFS 1.94) of tooth decay, compared with those who did not receive the programme (prevalence 62%; DMFS 6.12).

Similarly, in the region of the Eastern Mediterranean, a 9-year school-based oral health programme in Kuwait also shows an improvement in oral health in children. The programme includes bi-weekly supervised tooth brushing with fluoridated toothpaste and regular fluoride mouthrinse, fissure sealant and restorative dental treatment provided in schools, oral health education delivered by teachers and regularly oral health education programmes for parents and teachers.

Interventions that adopt the Health-Promoting School approach are generally successful. Effectiveness of school health education is associated with the amount of classroom or curricular time devoted to the programme, the extent to which the programme is supported and the commitment of teachers and students. However, the concept and application of a Health promotion School, or even health promotion, may not be well understood by dental service providers. In order to fully integrate oral health promotion activities in the school curriculum, training and professional development for teachers are imperative.

A comprehensive programme of professional development for teachers improves their skills in, and commitment to, sustaining oral health promotion innovations. Strategies that fit in with wider school and community initiatives are more sustainable. Working in partnership with parents and the local community enhances health gain and the impact of the programmes. While not all school-based programmes have encompassed all the components of a Health-Promoting School, it is encouraging that some schools have already made a sterling effort in incorporating oral health promotion activities in the school curriculum. It is necessary to build on the good work and achievements, broadening the efforts to maximise the full potential of a Health-Promoting School.

The cost-effectiveness of school-based programmes in enhancing the health and development of school-age children has been well established. The cost-effectiveness ratios are likely to improve when employing an integrated approach that addresses a number of health and educational problems. While the true benefits of school-based health promotion interventions may be difficult to ascertain in money terms, they have significant potential for cost savings. In general, the cost per capita of community preventive programmes is lower than that of treatment services.

A multifaceted school oral health programme, complemented by water fluoridation, has led to a significant improvement in dental health, with a substantial cost savings. The proportion of children with no experience of dental decay has increased from 0% to 34%. In countries without fluoridated water, school-based oral health programmes, combined with the use of fluoridated toothpaste, are also cost-effective. The findings are supported by a more recent report in Vietnam. Since the implementation of the nationwide school oral health programme, the oral hygiene and oral health of schoolchildren have improved, leading to a significant saving of 3.5 million US dollars.

Oral health promotion can trigger the installation of safe water supply and sanitation facilities in schools; this in turn may lead to a demand for similar facilities from the community. Parents and community members who are involved in the Health-Promoting School Initiative are aware of the important benefits of these facilities. The training and experience gained in working with others and in gathering resources can prove invaluable in lobbying for better environments at home and in the community. The school, parents and community members can support each other in the process.

Children have an important role to play in oral health promotion. Health-Promoting Schools empower children to take control over their health and become an active and responsible citizen in society. They are encouraged to impart their knowledge to benefit other members of the family and society. This 'spread of effect' of oral health promotion has been documented. Children may have a strong influence on their family and community.

Oral Health Promotion

Oral health can be an effective entry point for building a school's capacity to plan and implement a wide range of strategies and interventions in health promotion. It is important that oral health is considered a priority for both education and health. Once oral health is recognised as a key area, the next step is to plan the interventions, identifying the strategies that have the most influence on oral and general health, education and development. In order to maximise the impact, it is necessary to integrate the oral health interventions with other health promotion activities.

Interventions should empower students, parents, teachers and community members to make healthy decisions, practise healthy behaviours and create conditions and school environments conductive to health. Some important elements to planning oral health promotion are:

- Establishing or involving a School Health Team and a Community Advisory Committee;
- Conducting a situational analysis;

- Obtaining political, parental and community commitments;
- Establishing supportive school health policies;
- Setting goals and objectives.

Health-Promoting Schools involve members of the school and community in planning programmes that respond to their needs and that can be maintained and sustained with available resources and commitments. It is essential to work with the Parent/Teacher Association (PTA), where appropriate. However, experiences worldwide have shown that two important groups may be very helpful in creating a Health-Promoting School, namely a School Health Team and Community Advisory Committee.

A School Health Team is a designated group of people who are committed to work together to promote the health of all people who are working and learning at school. Depending on local circumstances, it should comprise a balance of representatives, including students, parents, school governors, teachers and school staff, members of teachers' representative organisations, PTA representatives, administrators, food service providers and health care providers.

Ideally, the School Health Team should have between 8 and 14 members. While it may not be possible to recruit all representatives in some schools, it is recommended that the Team should always include the school principal, at least one teacher and one parent, a health care provider and students. The Team is responsible for the management, co-ordination and monitoring of health promotion policies and action plans and for establishing links with district education personnel, local health officials and provincial or national network or ministry-level staff.

It also provides leadership, communication and support to school staff and community members and arranges training where necessary. If a school does not have a School Health Team, oral health promotion can provide a useful impetus for its formation, a model on which other health promoting activities may be based. Given that schools should implement programmes that are responsive to local needs, it is important that students, parents, school governors and school staff including teachers and management are consulted from the outset. Active participation provides a sense of ownership, a vital element of successful programmes. Each member has a valuable contribution to make.

The School Health Team should be given time, resources, authority and support to lead and oversee health promotion activities in school. Each member or a sub-group of members, while working with the whole of the School Health Team, can have designated special responsibility for a given task. For example, an Oral Health Sub-Committee may be formed to address oral health and related issues.

The Community Advisory Committee consists of members or leaders in the wider community who are best able to advise and provide support to the school. They understand the key oral health related issues affecting the community and school, have access to resources that can contribute to health promotion and have a significant influence on creating a supportive environment for oral health. Committee members foster good relationships between the school and the community at large, strengthening the impact of oral health promotion interventions. Working closely with the School Health Team, the Community Advisory Committee can help:

- advocate the development of a Health-Promoting School with leaders, staff and members of their own organisations and agencies;

- outreach to all parts of the community, lobbying for support; encourage other community groups to become involved in oral health issues and interventions, strengthening community participation;
- identify and obtain resources for projects and activities;
- help assess oral health problems and opportunities that affect the community.

The Community Advisory Committee should include men and women with a wide range of expertise and skills who are:

- interested in, and committed to, oral health and health promotion in general;
- knowledgeable about the community;
- influential in the community or district;
- capable of mobilising support and connections;
- representative of the local community in terms of geographical, social, economic, cultural and religious composition.

Potential partners include families, youth, health service providers and representatives of trade unions, women's groups, early childhood education, local government, arts and crafts societies, banking, sanitation/public works, law enforcement, local businesses, transportation, NGOs, charities and development organisations. The ideal size of the committee is between 10 and 15 members. Certainly, it is beneficial to work with existing groups and organisations that are already established.

If such a committee already exists, it is essential to find out whether oral health issues have been addressed adequately and to identify ways to work with the committee more effectively to promote oral health. If such a committee does not exist, oral health promotion provides a good opportunity to establish one. In some communities, it may not be possible to form two separate groups for the School Health Team and Community Advisory Committee. A single group comprising the School Health Team and selected community representatives may be considered.

Supportive School Policies

Supportive school policies are essential components of a Health-Promoting School. Policies should be brief and simple documents that provide a supportive framework, detailing the rationale, objectives and guidelines for the development, implementation and evaluation of oral health promotion activities in schools, made available. If preferred, a single policy document that covers all elements, areas and activities of a Health-Promoting School can be developed. Alternatively, a number of specific or individual policies can be generated, for example in relation to the school environment, behaviour/lifestyle and curriculum.

Nonetheless, they should take into account local factors and resources and, more importantly, incorporate input from students, parents, teachers, administrators and all relevant members of the school community. They should also consider the key oral health issues and concerns, reflecting the needs, priorities and cultural preferences of the school and local community. Collaboration and coordination between health, education and food and agricultural departments of the government and between the school and the community are crucial in planning policy.

Coherent policies and legislation across sectors are needed to avoid contradictory and unacceptable policies. They should be reviewed and evaluated regularly, ensuring that all components of a Health-Promoting

School are addressed. Policies regarding a Health-Promoting School environment, health education and training for teachers are particularly important for oral health promotion. For example, school policies should make healthy eating the easier choice and ensure that sanitation and safe water are adequately provided in school.

Teachers and school staff play a fundamental role in carrying out day-to-day oral health promotion activities and interventions. It is important to engage them early in the design and planning stages. A staff meeting is a useful forum for stimulating their interest.

Incentives should be given to teachers and school staff to encourage participation. Examples of these include time release, continued professional development points, qualifications and free materials.

Parents influence their children's oral health directly by providing a home environment that is conducive to oral health. Through primary socialisation, they convey norms and serve as role models. Their input in monitoring children's oral hygiene practices and dietary behaviours at home is paramount. Given that parents play a key role in promoting sustainable healthy oral health behaviours at home, their involvement and commitment are essential.

Parents and other significant family members should be educated about the importance of oral health, consequences of oral diseases and preventive oral health practices. They should be encouraged to take an active role in their children's oral health, reinforcing and complementing school efforts to promote good oral health behaviours and conditions that reduce the risk of oral diseases. Parental support can be mobilised through PTA, school governors and, if necessary, special meetings at school.

Goals and Objectives

Based on the information gathered in the situation analysis, an action plan should be developed. Goals and objectives are critical to the action plan, guiding the direction, monitoring the development and evaluating achievements of oral health promotion interventions. The School Health Team, in collaboration with the Community Advisory Committee, is primarily responsible for this task.

The goals provide a focus for action and should describe, in broad terms, what the programme will achieve. The goals of oral health promotion in a Health-Promoting School should include, but not be limited to, the following aims:

- To provide a physical, organisational and psychosocial school environment that is conducive to oral health of students, teachers and school staff, as well as families and the community;
- To reduce the risk factors associated with oral health;
- To improve oral health knowledge and attitudes;
- To develop skills and behaviours for good oral health.

The goals are then broken into specific outcome and process objectives so that it is clear what needs to be done, when and why. Objectives are explicit targets to be met in order to achieve the goals. They should be specific, measurable, achievable and appropriate but challenging, realistic and be set within a specified and reasonable time frame. It may be useful to divide the objectives into short-term, intermediate and long-term objectives, depending on local circumstances and the nature of the problems.

Outcomes aim to define in tangible and measurable terms what is to be achieved through the interventions. They help evaluate the impact and achievements of a

Health-Promoting School. Children's health status, learning achievements, health-related behaviours, quality of the school environment and school health programme implementation are useful indicators, as are beliefs, attitudes and the impact on quality of life and on society. Hence, the outcomes of an oral health orientated Health-Promoting School can include improvement in oral health status, knowledge, beliefs, attitudes, behaviours and conditions that are related to health and oral health. They can be divided into interim and ultimate outcomes.

It is crucial to gain insight into the processes involved in programme implementation and the social and environmental context. The processes describe what will be changed or implemented to achieve the desired outcomes.

Integration of Oral Health Promotion

A Health-Promoting School strives to use the school's full organisational capacity to improve the health of students, school staff, families and community members. Such a school offers many opportunities to promote oral health as an integral part of health and well being. Oral health promotion interventions can be used as an entry point for the development and enhancement of policies, planning groups and various components that serve as a framework for Health-Promoting Schools. Comprehensive school programmes should include:

- Healthy school environment;
- School health education;
- School health services;
- Nutrition and food services;
- Physical education and sport;
- Mental health and well being;
- Health promotion for school staff;

– School and community relationships and collaboration.

The effectiveness of interventions integrated into each of the components is determined by how they are supported by people, policies and trained staff. The effectiveness is also influenced by the extent to which interventions in each of these components integrate and complement with other health promotion efforts. Not all schools will have the resources to incorporate oral health into all components at the same time. Each school has to establish its own priorities.

A Health-Promoting School enables all parties concerned–students, parents, teachers and school staff, and community members -to work together to set the priorities and to decide how and the extent to which the components should be addressed. It may be more important, if not more feasible technically and financially, to start with small changes than to address all components simultaneously. Each school needs to assess what is realistically achievable, progressively building on strategies that work to maximise the full potential of a Health-Promoting School.

School Environment

School environment determines the effectiveness and sustainability of oral health promotion interventions. Supportive school environment enables students and school staff to develop their physical, mental and social potential, enhancing the relationships between members of the school community. Supportive environment encourages healthy lifestyles and behaviours that are conducive to oral health, making healthier choice the easier choice. In a Health-Promoting School, much emphasis is placed on the supportive school environment, both physical and psychosocial. The physical and psychosocial school environments should be coherent with, and supportive of, each other.

Physical environment

The physical environment includes the location and surroundings of the school, school grounds, buildings, classrooms, eating facilities and other structural features. The condition of the physical environment and policies regarding its use can have a significant impact on oral health directly as well as indirectly through lifestyles and oral health behaviours. The school should be located in a safe environment, away from busy roads, dangerous industrial sites and polluted areas.

The cleanliness of the premises, sufficient provision of rubbish disposal, safe water, hygienic sanitary facilities and structurally safe and well designed school buildings and playgrounds are only the basics, but without which other developments cannot be progressed. The physical environment of the local community in which the school is situated may also form part of the school environment. The following examples of oral health-related aspects of a healthy physical environment, supported by appropriate healthy policies, can be considered.

- *Safe water and sanitation*: The provision of clean and safe water, sufficient sanitary facilities and adequate waste collection and disposal is essential to good health and well being. These facilities are also fundamental to good oral health. They are essential to oral health promotion activities such as toothbrushing drills at lunchtime. Good sanitation and waste disposal facilities reduce the risk of infection. In some developing countries, many households may not have safe and clean water supply and sanitation; the school may be the only place where children can clean their teeth. If the school has not already been equipped with these basic facilities, oral health promotion can be used as an impetus for the school to install them.

- *Healthy dietary practices*: A healthy environment supports the adoption of healthy lifestyles. With the canteens, tuck shops and vending machines providing healthy foods and drinks, supported by healthy policies, the practice of healthy oral health behaviours is more sustainable. Promoting good dietary behaviours also reinforces other health messages in school, such as healthy nutrition, healthy heart and cancer prevention.
- *Health supportive environment*: A pleasant school environment with spacious and comfortable surroundings enhances physical, mental and social health and promotes healthy behaviours. Apart from policies governing vending machines, tuck shops and canteens, a no smoking or smokeless tobacco policy is critical to good oral health, most notably for periodontal health and oral cancer prevention. Creating a tobacco-free school requires the full support and commitment from everyone concerned. Safe school interior structures, buildings and playgrounds reduce the risk of dental trauma. With appropriate dental first aid and trauma policies, vital actions can be taken to avoid permanent tooth loss, if accidents occur.
- *Outside vendors*: Surroundings outside the school premises also need to be conducive to health, in order to avoid sending conflicting messages to students. It may be necessary to educate, if not impose restrictions on, food vendors and kiosk traders in or near the school premises to offer nutritious foods and drinks that are conducive to oral health. The sale of sweets, soft drinks and tobacco containing products to students in the vicinity of school should be prohibited.

School Health Education

Children's social, personal and life experiences and interaction at home, in school and the society have a significant impact on their oral health and health development in general. The primary goals of school oral health education are to help children develop personal lifelong skills, raise health consciousness, improve understanding and healthy attitudes, to promote healthy behaviours, and thereby to reduce risks of oral disease. School health education can be provided in school as a specific subject or as an integral part of other subjects.

It can also be included in extracurricular activities. Ideally, it encompasses a series of planned sequential courses of instruction from primary through secondary school levels, addressing the underlying physical, psychological, cultural and social determinants of oral health, in the context of good general health and well being. School health education focuses on:

- important behaviours and conditions that promote oral health or that reduce risk of oral disease;
- skills needed to negotiate and practise those behaviours or to address those conditions both personally and collectively;
- knowledge, attitudes, beliefs and values related to those behaviours and conditions
- learning experiences that allow students to model and practise skills;
- personal development;
- responsibility at home and in the society.
- In a Health-Promoting School, depending on socio-cultural conditions and resources, oral health promotion should target:
- maintaining good oral hygiene with daily toothbrushing drills supervised by teachers; the use

of fluoride, including affordable fluoride toothpaste and fluoride rinsing programmes;

- promoting good nutrition;
- reducing the consumption and frequency of sugary snacks and drinks;
- promoting the consumption of fruit and vegetables;
- promoting water or milk fluoridation;
- promoting regular dental check-ups and care;
- preventing or reducing tobacco use, alcohol consumption and substance abuse;
- preventing accidents, violence and anti-social behaviours;
- taking a wider responsibility at home and in the society.

In a Health-Promoting School, oral health education should be regularly reinforced at home and further developed in school at key educational stages throughout the children's school career. Oral health education should be combined with efforts addressing other health issues, such as tobacco use, violence and bullying, healthy nutrition, reproductive health, heart disease and obesity, enabling learning experiences to be strengthened. Similarly, oral health education can be complemented in curricular areas other than health.

Different countries may incorporate oral health in different subjects according to varying systems and circumstances. Some of the activities may produce useful data that can be used for monitoring and evaluation purposes and for the development of further interventions. However, each school must consider the local conditions, social and economic circumstances. Curricula for oral health and other health-related issues may be available through governmental and nongovernmental agencies and organisations, universities or teachers' unions. However, teachers and students are encouraged to produce culturally acceptable and socially appropriate materials that are specific to the local situation.

A good educational programme utilises a variety of learning and teaching methods, including lectures, seminars, practical experiments, discussions, group work, problem-solving exercises, debates and role-play with appropriate and stimulating visual aids. Self-directed learning encourages students to take responsibility for their learning. A diversity of instructional strategies is essential to effective curricular development. However, the learning and teaching strategies and materials employed must be appropriate and acceptable to the target students, taking into account the learning objectives and resources available. They should also aim to promote active involvement and reinforcement.

While some methods are more suitable for conveying knowledge, others are designed to promote skills and attitudes. For example, lectures are more efficient in providing knowledge to large number of students but they are less effective in teaching skills or in influencing beliefs or attitudes. Discussions, debates and problem-solving exercises may be more useful in challenging perceptions and myths. Practical sessions, such as laboratory experiments and toothbrushing exercises, are more effective in building skills. Many countries have developed toothbrushing exercises, supervised and instructed by teachers or school health staff.

While teachers are crucial to the implementation of school oral health education, they do not necessarily possess adequate knowledge and skills to enable them to deliver the programmes effectively. With adequate training, they can significantly improve the development and implementation of the programme. In addition to various learning and teaching strategies, teachers should also be trained in the use of health curriculum as well as in oral health and health promotion. Learning how to work with health professionals collaboratively facilitates a smooth running of the programme.

Training can be provided at the pre-service teacher training colleges and, more importantly, as part of the on-going in-service/on-the-job training and professional development. Project or school-based training should also be given. Effective teacher training builds commitment, understanding, skills and attitudes that enable a teacher to develop and deliver curricula competently and confidently. A complete training programme should encompass four broad goals:

– to develop positive attitudes toward, and commitment to, a comprehensive approach to school health;
– to increase the understanding of principles of behaviour change that are essential to health education;
– to improve teaching skills using a variety of learning and teaching methods;
– to equip teachers with skills to deal with sensitive issues and students with special needs.

Successful teaching training:

– addresses key issues identified by teachers themselves;
– takes place as close as possible to the teacher's own working environment; covers theories, demonstration, practice, feedback and peer-review in the classroom;
– has support of both colleagues and the school;
– provides participants with a sense of ownership;

– draws on adult learning theories;
– takes place over a sufficient period of time;
– provides opportunities for reflection and feedback;
– involves a conscious commitment on the part of the teacher;
– builds skills;
– involves groups of teachers rather than individuals.

In a Health-Promoting School, oral health education should be an important part of school health education and incorporated across a number of curricular areas, as relevant. Teachers in all disciplines should be encouraged to include oral health in their teaching programmes and activities. They should be inspired to make the curriculum exciting and stimulating for students to acquire good oral health knowledge and behaviours and to make healthy decisions. When teaching a practical skill such as toothbrushing technique, it is necessary for the teachers to learn, and be competent on brushing their own teeth effectively first. This is particularly important as teachers are often considered as role models by students. Guidelines for teachers in monitoring and supervising toothbrushing drills should be developed.

Given the competing demands in an already fully packed curriculum, some teachers may be too inundated with other curricular activities. In order to promote oral health education in the curriculum, it is imperative for the government and health professionals to provide sustainable support, in terms of technical assistance, funding and/or learning materials. Such a support makes it easier for teachers to consider oral health education in their teaching programmes.

Importance of Nutrition

Diet, nutrition and oral health are intricately linked.

Micronutrient deficiency, a condition that is common among school-age children in developing countries, and poor dietary practices increase the risk of oral disease. Healthy nutrition interventions with supportive policies are therefore an integral part of a Health-Promoting School that aims to promote oral health. As part of oral health promotion, schools can enforce healthy snacks or no sugar policies to support healthy eating behaviours, provide nutritious meals and, where necessary, micronutrient supplements.

Oral health activities can be included in the assessment and monitoring of nutritional status such as a school height census. While school food services are often managed by the public or private sectors through the ministry of education, it is important for schools, teachers, students and school oral health services to collaborate closely with them to support healthy eating initiatives in schools.

Exercise and Leisure Activities

Physical exercise, sport and leisure activities help maintain physical and mental fitness, a fundamental prerequisite to health and well being. Evidence suggests that physical and mental wellness improves academic performance. Exercise and leisure activities are an important part of stress management. However, there are oral health implications. Sports and physical activities inflate the risk of head and face injuries. Studies have shown that some sport drinks with high acidity that are popular among adolescents can lead to dental erosion. The use of mouth guards should be encouraged in high-risk contact sports to protect teeth.

Mental Health

A Health-Promoting School also promotes the mental health and well being of students and school staff, enabling them to fulfil their physical, social and psychological potential. Poor facial and/or dental appearance may have a negative impact on mental health and well being. Stress, bullying and violence can lead to the consumption of sugary snacks and alcohol, smoking and violent behaviours, which have serious oral health implications. These issues should be addressed by health promotion, with supportive policies. Students and school staff should be equipped with knowledge and skills that help them prevent and, if unavoidable, deal with interpersonal conflicts; cope with stress, peer pressure and other social forces; and develop self-esteem and confidence. Counselling and support services for students and staff should be available.

Health Promotion for School Staff

A Health-Promoting School places a special emphasis on staff welfare and working conditions, applying the principles and strategies of health promotion to the workplace. Employees and their families along with the organisational, managerial and environmental characteristics of the school are considered. Healthy working conditions and good management and organisational structure can help reduce the stress levels experienced by staff members.

Well-designed and health-orientated classrooms, offices, staff rooms, cooking and dining facilities can be a starting point. Health promoting facilities including those designed for exercise and relaxation are imperative. Staff morale and workload must be carefully monitored to avoid the risk of burnout. Oral health education materials together with other health messages should be prominent throughout the school including staff rooms.

A tobacco-free school, if feasible and supported by staff, is one of the most effective strategies for providing smoke-free working environment. However, support services that help the staff members deal with stress, give up smoking or tobacco use or lose weight should be available. As part of in-service training, a tailored-made oral health promotion programme that aims at providing knowledge and influencing attitudes and behaviours should be available regularly, helping staff members acquire and sustain healthy lifestyles. Teachers and school staff are encouraged to identify essential policies and practices and to work with the School Health Team, parents and the local community collaboratively to promote oral health and general well being in school and the community.

Role of a Community

The community is a critical component of a Health-Promoting School. Community members should feel that the school is approachable and receptive to their contribution and, more importantly, that they are valued. A Health-Promoting School provides a valuable link between the school, parents and the community, promoting joint working to support the development and implementation of oral health promotion initiatives. Family and community members can be involved in the following ways:

- Taking part in the planning and decision making process, such as taking part in the School Health Team and Community Advisory Committee;
- Participating in school-led oral health activities at school and in the community, such as Oral Health Day, exhibitions and health fairs;
- Providing support and resources, in terms of skills, expertise, materials and funding;
- Advocating oral health including lobbying for healthy environment and water fluoridation.

A Health-Promoting School collaborates with parents and families to ensure oral health promotion efforts are reinforced at home. Parents are important role models that help shape children's development and influence their lifestyles. Parents are responsible for providing pack lunches and, in many developing countries, toothbrushes for their children to use in schools. It is important that these foods, drinks and oral hygiene aids are conducive to oral and general health. Schools can serve as a focal point, providing essential training and health education materials for parents and families.

Parents are educated about their own oral health as well as caring for other members of the family. Educational programmes are most effective when parents and families meet together and support each other at regular meetings in schools. Good communication between school oral health services and parents is of paramount importance. Equally, students are encouraged to impart the knowledge and skills that are beneficial to other family members. For those who do not attend schools, outreach programmes that involve using parents and family members as facilitators can help promote oral health to these families and entice them to be part of the school community.

Community collaboration can strengthen interventions to promote better oral health. Successful partnership builds on trust, respect, effective communication, shared mission and resource coordination. The school and community partners can benefit from each other. There may be a wide range of organisations and local businesses with which collaboration can be fostered.

Role of mass media

The mass media can be used effectively to promote oral health. Information can be distributed efficiently through mass media. For example, a television programme that involves using popular icons or idols can be employed to promote oral health messages. Undoubtedly, such a high profile campaign can raise awareness. However, these campaigns can be costly and supplementary activities are needed to promote awareness, knowledge gain and behaviour change. Nonetheless, the media may be educated and encouraged to stop targeting children and adolescents in advertising products that may increase the risk of oral disease, e.g. smoking and smokeless tobacco, sugary foods and drinks.

Sun Protection Education

During the first 18 years of life, when much of one's lifetime UV exposure is received, a significant proportion of time is spent at school or participating in school based activities, such as camps or school sports. Students attend school for most of the year, and school hours generally incorporate peak UV periods. Some school events, such as sporting carnivals, can require students, staff, and spectators to be outdoors for the entire school day. Outdoor activities and break times, particularly lunch, frequently occur at times when UV levels are at their maximum.

Thus, the school environment and the manner in which a school operates can have a significant impact on children's UV exposure at the period in their lives when they are most vulnerable to its effects. Structural and organisational strategies that provide sun protection for students and staff while they are at school are simple to adopt and can also be used to compensate to some extent for the reluctance of adolescents to adopt personal sun protection measures.

Providing attractive shaded areas that are likely to be used by adolescents for passive recreation during breaks can reduce the need for use of protective clothing at these times. Implementation of such strategies also provides a practical demonstration of how such measures can be adopted beyond the school environment. For example, ensuring that sun protection strategies are an integral component of all outdoor activities, including school breaks and sports lessons, illustrates to students and parents how sun protection can be incorporated into other family and community activities.

It is important to target children's attitudes and behaviour at a young age, particularly in primary school, when children tend to be most receptive to the need for sun protection-during adolescence, influences of peers and fashion are more likely to take precedence. School programmes can not only help to reduce UV exposure at school, but also to facilitate the development of habits and attitudes that can have an impact on sun exposure at other times. Because children of school age have more leisure time, much of which tends to be spent outdoors, good habits carried over from the school setting can further contribute to reductions in total UV exposure.

Role modelling of appropriate sun behaviour by staff is a vital element in educating students and parents as well as protecting staff from excessive UV exposure, but the school can also become a role model for families and other community organisations, such as sporting clubs or kindergartens. Having to plan for sun protection at school can make it easier for parents and students to plan for sun protection during activities that occur outside the school environment.

Personal sun protection equipment is simple and readily portable-a hat, a shirt, and sunscreen can be carried from one venue to another in a small bag. Curriculum programmes focusing on or incorporating sun protection education can be used to develop communication and life skills. These are ideally part of a comprehensive approach that aims to develop positive attitudes toward preventive measures and to promote responsible decision making, all of which are essential for general health and well-being. Because reducing UV exposure is a more specific objective than, for example, "healthy eating", and personal sun protection strategies are quite easy to implement, sun protection education can be used as a starting point prior to tackling some of the broader, more complex issues.

UV exposure causes sunburn, accelerates skin ageing, and is the major risk factor for the development of skin cancer. It also contributes to eye damage and suppresses immune function. Hence, reducing exposure to UV radiation is an issue of global concern. It has been estimated that more than 2 million non-melanoma skin cancers and 200,000 malignant melanomas occur globally each year-one in every three cancers diagnosed is skin cancer. Given levels of ozone depletion and current trends, it is predicted that this will increase by as much as 300,000 nonmelanoma skin cancers and 4,500 melanomas each year.

However, appropriate sun exposure behaviour could prevent as many as four out of five cases of skin cancer. High levels of skin cancer in Australia, Europe, and the United States have resulted in campaigns designed specifically to reduce UV exposure. In Australia, where skin cancer is the most common form of cancer, there is evidence that public health campaigns conducted over the past 20 years to reduce sun exposure may be having a beneficial effect on skin cancer rates. It has also been estimated that up to 20 percent of the 12 to 15 million cases of blindness due to cataracts can be at least partially attributed to UV exposure, particularly in countries located near the equator.

Consequently, 3 million people's sight may be saved each year through the use of appropriate eye protection.

Moreover, a 10 percent decrease in total ozone levels is predicted to result in between 1.6 and 1.75 million additional cases of cataracts per year worldwide. The growing evidence that UV exposure can also result in reduced effectiveness of the immune system has serious implications for the efficacy of immunisation programmes and the spread of infection, particularly for many Asian, African, and South American countries. Strategies to reduce UV exposure at critical times may be essential to ensure that immunisation programmes are not compromised.

Sun protection strategies are relatively easy to adopt and incorporate into a daily routine, to the extent that they become habits. If these behaviours are regularly reinforced and role modelled, they are more likely to continue into adulthood, particularly as children's capacity to understand the reasons for such habits increases. Knowing how to prevent a recurrence of sunburn can provide children with a sense of control over their own health and well-being.

Most children are capable of putting on hats as they go outside and, with guidance and practice, can learn to correctly apply sunscreen. These simple strategies can quickly become part of the daily routine. Another helpful factor is that, unlike other preventive measures, where the effects may not become evident for several years, the symptoms of sunburn are more immediate, thus enabling children to relate the behaviour to the outcome (sunburn).

The influence of peer pressure and fashion becomes more powerful during adolescence, and good habits tend to be replaced by sun seeking behaviours. This is often based on the belief that a tan is healthy and attractive; it is also at least partially due to the fact that, with the possible exception of sunglasses, sun protective clothing is seldom considered fashionable by young people. Even when adolescents are aware of the long term implications, they tend to be reluctant to protect themselves, just as they are more likely to indulge in other forms of risk taking behaviour, such as tobacco use or unprotected sex.

It is important to address these issues through programmes that develop life skills, promote healthy decision making, and give young people the self-esteem to address these pressures. Such programmes may also help to change the group norms that are a factor in the rejection of personal sun protection. Surveys of Australian secondary school students suggest that the proportion seeking a dark tan had decreased, and those seeking a light tan increased between 1990 and 1996. This suggests that awareness of the need for sun protection can positively influence attitudes and behaviour, even in this age group. Although the majority of young people still indicate that they do seek a tan, it is a step in the right direction.

In the short term, excessive exposure to UV radiation causes sunburn. The symptoms, although painful, seldom last more than a few days, except in severe cases. However, childhood UV exposure is a major factor in the development of skin cancer later in life. Children must therefore be a key target group for prevention programmes. Non-melanoma skin cancers tend to develop around age 40, and melanoma can affect people in their late teens and early 20s.

In Australia, melanoma is the most common cancer in the 15-44 years age group. Since those who have been diagnosed with skin cancer are considered to be at greater risk of developing it again, the disease can potentially affect a person's health for a significant proportion of his or her lifetime. Sun exposure also causes other skin damage, including wrinkling, pigmentation changes, and other nonmalignant lesions. These can become apparent from a relatively early age.

Reducing childhood exposure should reduce the incidence of such problems during adulthood and, if good habits are maintained for much of the lifetime, should improve the health of older individuals. Similarly, use of eye protection is likely to delay the onset of cataracts and to reduce the incidence of blindness from cataracts. This has obvious implications for the health and well-being of adults, not the least of which is the preservation of their independence, something that is extremely important to older people.

Ozone Depletion

It has been predicted that depletion of the ozone layer, due to the release of substances such as chlorofluorocarbons (CFCs), will result in an increase in the amounts of UV radiation reaching the earth's surface. There are also seasonal holes in the ozone layer over the Antarctic and the Arctic, which contribute to higher UV levels at particular times of the year. While there is considerable uncertainty about the implications for human health, an increase in UV related problems such as skin and eye damage is a potential consequence, particularly in the Northern Hemisphere, where the "hole" is more likely to extend over heavily populated areas.

The Montreal Protocol, an agreement limiting the use of chemicals that destroy the ozone, should result in a reduction in the rate at which this damage occurs, provided that there is full compliance. However, even if compliance is complete, it is expected that the ozone layer will not recover until at least the middle of the 21st century. During 2000, the ozone hole over the Antarctic extended over such populated areas as Chile, where residents were warned that they could get sunburned in less than seven minutes due to increased UV levels. Furthermore, it is now believed that ozone damage may be exacerbated by the greenhouse effect, despite reductions in levels of ozone depleting chemicals in the atmosphere.

Given the uncertainties relating to the possible health consequences of ozone depletion, it is clear that taking action to reduce UV exposure is essential. The only way to protect people against the possible risks associated with ozone damage is to encourage them to protect themselves. In view of the sensitivity of children's skin, it is even more critical that action is taken to reduce childhood exposure to UV.

Effectiveness of Sun Protection Interventions

There is evidence that school based interventions are effective in improving levels of sun protection for children in younger grade levels. The key elements of effective sun protection interventions in schools are considered to be the following:

- Development of a comprehensive sun protection policy that clearly documents strategies: Involving parents and students in the policy development process is important to secure their support and improve their understanding of the strategies.
- A range of strategies relating to behaviour, the school environment, and curriculum programmes, appropriate to the local climate and the school community: Essential elements relate to clothing, particularly hats and sunglasses; scheduling of outdoor activities; shade provision and use; sunscreen; and curriculum programmes.
- A regular review process: The review should both evaluate the effectiveness of policy implementation,

and suggest changes in response to perceived areas of weakness or to the recommendations of relevant health authorities.

Effective school sun protection involves a holistic approach that employs strategies that address behaviour, the curriculum, and the environment. For example, the Health-Promoting Schools model provides an ideal framework within which to implement a comprehensive approach to sun protection.

Interventions to improve sun protection are relatively simple to implement and, in most cases, inexpensive. Changes to school uniforms or dress codes can be phased in over a period of time and incorporate clothing (including sunglasses) that can be worn outside the school environment. Sunscreen can be purchased in bulk by schools to reduce the cost to students, but, as awareness and understanding increases, this may be an item that parents are willing to purchase for their children anyway, for use not just at school but also at other times.

While shade development is often costly, it can be incorporated in a broader environmental programme. For example, tree planting can be promoted not just as a means of improving shade, but also of enhancing air and soil quality. Shade, whether provided by trees or structures, also has other obvious benefits in improving the overall school environment. Shade development can also be a process that fosters more active parental participation through, for example, fund-raising activities. Active involvement of children in the process can provide them with practical experience in setting and working toward shared goals, and perhaps even become the foundation for participation in similar activities at the community level.

Such participation can enhance students' sense of ownership of the outcome and help to develop their confidence and communication skills. Changes to scheduling of outdoor activities can be achieved relatively cheaply or at no cost. For example, extending the morning break and having it at a time when UV levels are lower, and shortening the lunch break, which usually occurs at the peak UV time, is cost neutral. There can even be benefits; for example, beginning sporting carnivals in the late afternoon may increase parental participation.

Simple, low cost activities can be used to educate children and their families about UV radiation and sun protection. In fact, children can gradually take on the task of educating other members of their family and the wider community. This can give them pride in their knowledge, as well as a sense of control over their own health and that of others close to them. Apart from reducing sun exposure of students while they are at school, these interventions serve to educate staff and parents and can readily be applied to situations beyond the school environment. For example, hats and shirts with collars can be incorporated into uniforms for community sporting clubs, and a tree planting programme could be introduced for a local sports ground.

Education for Girls

Improving the health and education of girls is likely to improve that of their children, because girls or women generally have most of the responsibility for supervision, education, and care of other members of their households. Teaching girls why and how to minimise UV exposure not only reduces their own risk of harmful effects on the skin, eye, and immune system, but also provides them with simple strategies to protect other members of their families and, in particular, their own children. Almost equally important is the enhancement of their own self-esteem and confidence as a result of their greater ability to control factors affecting their health and that of others.

Planning Programmes

Establishing a school health team and a community advisory committee are important steps in the planning process.

School health team

The school health team is responsible for the coordination and monitoring of health promotion policies and activities. It is essential that parents, students, and staff, including management, are involved in the planning process from the outset. If such a team does not exist, the introduction of sun protection interventions can be the stimulus for its formation and provide a model on which other health interventions may be based. Student involvement is essential in order to develop strategies that are relevant to student needs and concerns and will enlist their support.

Effective sun protection relies to a significant extent on student cooperation, which is most likely to be achieved if students actively participate in the decision making process and feel a sense of ownership. Parental input is also critical to ensure that strategies are feasible; i.e., parents must be willing and able to support the purchase of hats, sunglasses, and sunscreen and possibly to assist in shade development. As school staff are primarily responsible for implementation, their input is essential in order to ensure that strategies are practical within the context of the school environment, organisation, and available resources.

The school health team should include a balance of young people and adults with an interest in and commitment to the well-being of the school community, for example, students, teachers, administrators, and parents. This team must be given the time, resources, and authority to enable it to lead and oversee health promotion activities in the school. A sun protection working group that is a sub committee of this team would have responsibility for the planning and implementation of sun protection interventions.

Situation Analysis

Policy and decision makers and other interested groups should consider conducting a situation analysis, which involves the collection and analysis of relevant national, district, and local data. This data can be used to justify resource allocation and to plan, implement, and evaluate health promotion interventions. The school health team and the community advisory committee can begin planning sun protection interventions by conducting such an analysis at the local level.

Carrying out a situation analysis will help people better understand the needs, resources, and conditions relevant to planning interventions.

A range of qualitative and quantitative data is required for planning health promotion and sun protection interventions and to establish a baseline for evaluation. Qualitative data includes descriptions of feelings and beliefs, while quantitative data is numerical information. The following information can help to determine local needs and priorities in relation to sun protection:

- Levels of UV radiation, skin cancer incidence, and mortality at the national, regional, and local levels, and, if available, data relating to frequency of sunburn and use of sun protection strategies.

- Knowledge, attitudes, beliefs, values, behaviours, and conditions relating to sun protection and skin cancer. For example, people may believe that dark or olive skin protects them from the harmful effects of UV exposure and that there is therefore no need to adopt sun protection strategies; they may not understand the relationship between sun exposure and skin cancer; or they may adhere to traditional forms of dress that make it difficult to wear appropriate hats. Because values, beliefs, and attitudes have a major effect on health behaviours, this kind of information is essential in order to develop effective health promotion strategies. Interventions that do not take into account the potential barriers and make the best possible use of factors likely to facilitate implementation will be wasteful of resources and unlikely to achieve the desired health outcomes.
- Resources, including personnel and financial resources and services, that are available in the school and the community.
- Existing programmes. These should be evaluated to determine whether and how they may facilitate health promotion in relation to sun protection. For example, activities relating to peer pressure and tanning behaviour could be incorporated into existing programmes that focus on selfesteem and decision making for adolescents; education about the causes and nature of skin cancer could be integrated into science programmes on the nature of cells and cell division.

Commitment and Policies

To be effective, sun protection interventions require commitment and action from a wide range of individuals and groups. It is also important to obtain the support of relevant government departments, health and education authorities, community and business leaders, educators, parents, students, and the community.

Political commitment

Sun protection interventions in schools are greatly facilitated by support at various levels of government and from the ministries of health and education. Political commitment and support may take a variety of forms:

- Public endorsement by government representatives of the need for health promotion and sun protection interventions in schools
- Collaboration with health authorities in the development of guidelines or recommendations for schools in relation to sun protection interventions such as clothing guidelines and incorporation of shade in new school buildings.
- Assistance with the planning, conduct, and evaluation of interventions, possibly through the appointment, by their office, of an influential representative of the relevant level of government.
- Financial support for school health promotion and sun protection intervention.
- Provision or subsidisation of training and materials to assist schools in developing and implementing health promotion and sun protection interventions.

Community commitment

Efforts to achieve effective sun protection interventions in the context of a Health-Promoting School also rely on community understanding and support. It is essential that parents and community members participate in the design, content, delivery, and evaluation of interventions. This should occur from the outset to ensure that families and the community have the opportunity to raise any concerns and to participate in the planning process.

Such involvement is also important to create a sense of community ownership and to enable resources, facilities, and expertise to be shared effectively. It can be achieved through community group meetings, formal presentations, individual meetings with relevant groups and individuals use of school publications, and even local media.

Integration of Sun Protection Education

A Health-Promoting School strives to use the school's full organisational capacity to improve the health of students, school personnel, families, and community members. Such a school offers many opportunities to promote sun protection as an essential element for the attainment of health. Sun protection interventions can serve as an entry point for the development or enhancement of policies, planning groups, and various components, which serve as a framework for a Health-Promoting School. These components include, but are not limited to:

- skills based health education
- a healthy school environment
- school safety
- school health services
- physical exercise, recreation, and sports
- community and family involvement and outreach
- counselling and social support health
- promotion for school staff

The effectiveness of the interventions integrated into each of the above components is influenced by the extent to which they are supported by a variety of people, policies and trained staff. Their effectiveness is also influenced by the extent to which interventions in each of these components combine with other health promotion efforts to complement and reinforce one another. Not all schools will have the resources to integrate sun protection interventions into all of the components at one time.

Therefore, each school has to establish its own priorities, in collaboration with all parties concerned, and decide the extent to which the components should be addressed. A Health-Promoting School enables students, parents, teachers, and community members to work together to make such decisions. It is more important to start with small changes that are possible than to wait until resources become available to address all components simultaneously.

School health education should help individuals avoid health risks and create an environment that is conducive to health for all. Thus, behaviours and conditions that are to be influenced must be clearly defined.

Close collaboration between education and health officials, the School Health Team, the Community Advisory Committee, and other school and community members is necessary to identify the particular behaviours and conditions relevant to health in each community.

In a Health-Promoting School, sun protection education is designed to help students acquire the knowledge, attitudes, beliefs, and skills they need to make informed decisions, practice healthy behaviours and create conditions conducive to health. In a Health-Promoting School, skills based health education about sun protection addresses the nature of UV radiation and its beneficial and harmful effects on health and well-being. It also provides strategies to minimise of UV exposure in the context of a healthy lifestyle, which necessarily includes outdoor activities.

Sun protection education should be part of the school health curriculum and should be integrated into a range of subject areas. The most obvious of these is science, where, for example, the nature of UV radiation can be explored; students can investigate the structure and function of the skin, the eye, and the immune system, and the effects of UV radiation on each. However, it can also be part of a number of other subject areas. Sun protection education should also be incorporated into the school's extracurricular activities, particularly outdoor events, and integrated into other school health components, such as physical activity and staff health.

Appropriate scheduling of sun protection education, taking into consideration factors such as latitude, climate, lifestyle and cultural factors, enhances its relevance for students. Children's understanding of sun protection messages is enhanced and reinforced by experience of warm, sunny weather and the practice of taking care in the sun. Often, spring will be the best time of year to incorporate sun protection education, however it may also be relevant prior to the skiing season or a holiday period.

Sun protection education should be combined with efforts addressing other health issues, as appropriate. For example, a primary school programme on safety could include such topics as road safety, hygiene, and safe behaviour in the sun. A secondary school programme on healthy decision making could incorporate critical discussion of images of good health and attractiveness relating to body shape, tanning, and tobacco use. A variety of issues can be addressed simultaneously, with specific issues explored in greater depth to make a particular point.

Alternatively, by coordinating or linking the presentation of related topics in different classes, the issues can be linked, and learning experiences can reinforce and complement one another. Linking of sun protection issues with other relevant topics can also be enhanced by co-teaching, sharing teaching resources, referring students to related lessons, and involving students from different classes in different activities. Curriculum resources for sun protection education may be available through governmental and nongovernmental agencies and organisations, universities, or teacher's unions. Supplementary materials relevant to the local situation can also be generated by teachers and students themselves or adapted from resources obtained from other countries.

Use of a variety of educational methods, including lectures, discussions, debates, role plays, and audiovisual aids, is essential for effective health education. Methods should be selected and lessons prepared in such a way as to increase knowledge, build positive attitudes and values, dispel myths, increase skills, and provide support for a healthy lifestyle. Choice of methods should be made on the basis of lesson objectives; for example, a lecture may enhance knowledge but is less effective in influencing beliefs and building skills.

Discussions, debates, and practical activities or demonstrations may be effective in exposing and dispelling local myths. In selecting essential knowledge for students in relation to UV radiation and sun protection, information that will enable students to make and act on sensible decisions regarding sun protection, rather than technical information in relation to the nature of UV radiation or sun protection methods, should be emphasized. For example, students being able to apply sunscreen effectively is more important than their ability to explain how the SPF for sunscreen is determined.

Objectives and activities should have a practical focus and be relevant to the students' own experiences. There should be opportunities to develop skills and knowledge that can be applied at school, at home, and in the community. For example, students can actively participate in the design of school uniforms or the development of a sun safe school dress code, and they can develop a plan to reduce UV exposure for participants in a favourite leisure activity.

Training is an essential prerequisite for school personnel involved in the development, implementation, and delivery of school health education programmes. Ideally, training should be ongoing and incorporate time for personnel to receive accurate information, discuss issues, share ideas and resources, and evaluate programmes. Opportunities should be available for teachers to develop their own skills in the kinds of teaching strategies necessary to influence attitudes and beliefs and develop skills, rather than simply focusing on knowledge.

Teachers need to be both competent and confident in using such strategies as discussions, debates, role plays, practical activities, and community education projects. Such strategies are sometimes avoided by teachers because they can be more time consuming and difficult to manage than conventional methods; they must also be well planned and executed if they are to achieve their objectives. Therefore, it is important that teachers are given the opportunity to develop and practice these necessary skills.

In a Health-Promoting School, health education may be integrated across several curriculum areas, and thus teachers in all curriculum areas should be encouraged to incorporate health issues into their programmes. Furthermore, all personnel have a responsibility to act as role models for students by demonstrating appropriate sun protection behaviours; in doing so, they will be seen by students as supportive of sun protection interventions and therefore understand the rationale underlying the strategies the school implements.

Finally, school personnel should understand why sun protection is necessary and how to protect themselves for their own health and well-being. Their duties often require them to participate in activities that increase their exposure to UV radiation, and it is important that they understand both the risks and how to minimise them. Additional components relating to, for example, the importance of early detection of skin cancer should also be incorporated, as appropriate.

In Northern latitude countries, the potential for excessive sun exposure poses a health risk for only a relatively short period of each year. As a consequence, health risks of UV radiation exposure are often not perceived as important or relevant in the school context. With an already packed curriculum many teachers may decide to concentrate their limited time and resources on key curricular activities. However, they are usually happy to promote the message if ready made lesson plans are provided as a sustainable resource and these are linked to key curricular areas. The following simple guidelines may help to motivate teachers to be committed to integrating sun protection in their teaching:

Healthy School Environment

For sustainable improvements in levels of sun protection, the Health-Promoting School must create an environment that supports interventions through changes, not just to the physical environment, but also through policies and practices.

School policies are brief documents that clearly state what a school will do and how it will do it. Policies guide the planning, implementation, and evaluation of efforts to improve health and reduce UV exposure..

The physical environment is made up of the school buildings, classrooms, and school grounds, including areas used for passive and active recreation. The condition of the physical environment can have a significant impact on the UV exposure levels of members of the school community. Signs or prompts can help to encourage sun safety.

Psychosocial environment

The psychosocial environment relates to the social and mental conditions that affect education and health. The ambience of a Health-Promoting School is one that respects the individual and fosters confidence in healthy lifestyles. The following aspects of a healthy psychosocial environment should be integrated into a Health-Promoting School:

- *Teacher role models*: Teachers play an important role as adult role models and mentors. Teachers can encourage students to protect themselves from the sun by wearing protective clothing and sunscreen and seeking shade. This applies particularly to physical education/sports teachers who are often key role models for popular students and student leaders. If student leaders are positively influenced, they can in turn influence others.
- *Peer reinforcement*: Students can provide positive reinforcement to their peers by showing that sun seeking behaviour is not a requirement for peer acceptance. Schools therefore need to provide time and opportunities to enable students to socialise in environments where UV exposure is avoided or minimised.

Health Services

School health services help foster health and well-being as well as prevent, reduce, monitor, and treat important health problems or conditions. In Health-Promoting Schools, health services and are provided to students, school personnel, families, and community members, and are coordinated with other sun protection services and activities in the school and community.

Models for providing school health services vary tremendously, not only from developed to developing countries, but also among and within nations themselves, and not all schools can provide access to school health services. Where they exist, school health services may consist of, for example, one teacher designated to be responsible for first aid, a trained school nurse, or a school health team. One role of a school health service may be the provision of sunscreen, which should be available for all school activities.

A further role for school health services is in the treatment of sunburn and, if necessary, referral to other agencies. Health services providers are also in an ideal position to compile sunburn related data, which can be used to assess whether current programmes are effective and to better target interventions. For example, if cases of sunburn are related to particular school or community activities, such as sports days, strategies can be modified accordingly.

Where particular individuals or groups are affected more frequently, appropriate action can be taken respond to their specific needs. Health service providers know the health effects of excessive UV exposure and often have firsthand experience in dealing with the consequences. Their expertise can be valuable in communicating the need for sun protection and appropriate strategies on an individual basis, in a classroom setting, and to the wider school community.

Role of Family and Community

A Health-Promoting School addresses health promotion

and sun protection by engaging students, school personnel, families, and community members in collaborative and integrated efforts to improve health in the school and through school/community projects and outreach. Community members and parents should believe that their school is open and receptive to their ideas and participation. Family and community members can be involved in Health-Promoting Schools in various ways:

- *Taking part in planning and decision making*: For instance, by participating in the school health team or community advisory committee.
- *Participating in activities and services offered through schools*: For instance, attending projects to gain specific knowledge and skills relating to sun protection, such as exhibitions, performances, or health fairs.
- *Providing support or resources*: For instance, supplying material or financial donations, identifying or acting as guest speakers, or providing specialist services related to sun protection. Community health workers can assess current sun protection practices, and local suppliers can offer sun protective items, including clothing, sunscreen, and sunglasses.
- *Advocating for health*: For instance, knowledge and skills acquired in a school/community project can be used by community and family members to take communal actions that will result in sustainable sun protection interventions.

The family and community also provide a setting for students to understand, practice, and share what they learn about health and sun protection in the classroom. For example, a homework activity could involve comparisons of adults' (and even, if available, a baby's) skin with the students' to identify signs of UV exposure.

Older students could also be asked to explain the signs of sun damage to older family members. This enables students to take pride in their knowledge and ability to help others.

Healthy practices in relation to UV exposure are more likely to take place if there is consistent information and support from the family and community. If this is to occur, parents and community need to be well informed, which can be achieved if schools are willing to act as leaders through role modelling and community education programmes. Outreach also provides opportunities to facilitate healthy decision making and enhance health outcomes for those who are not reached by schools directly, particularly in areas where a high proportion of young people do not attend school.

It is essential that parents understand the objectives of sun protection interventions and the underlying rationale, and that they have the knowledge and skills to allow them to reinforce the appropriate health messages at home. This increases the likelihood that parental attitudes and behaviours will be consistent with those of the school, and that parents will provide the things their children need to protect themselves, such as clothing, sunscreen, and sunglasses.

Tapping in to the concern that parents feel for their children's health is also one means of persuading them to be more proactive about their own health and that of other family members. While improving parents' sun protection behaviour may be one way of promoting sun protection for their children, the reverse may also be true: The messages children take home can encourage parents to adopt more sun protective behaviours themselves.

Although this is not an objective of school based interventions, given that, with the exception of sunburn, most of the effects of UV exposure are long term, greater parental awareness of the risks of UV exposure may also facilitate community interventions focusing on secondary prevention. If parents are aware of the signs of UV damage, they may be more likely to seek further information and early treatment, which will generally improve health outcomes.

Sun protection interventions can be a means of involving the broader community in school based activities. Health services can deliver health education programmes that provide knowledge about the consequences of UV exposure and how to reduce the risk of damage, or provide advice about content and presentation. Resources can be developed jointly and shared between the school and the community.

Community members who have themselves experienced health problems relating to UV exposure are often willing to provide firsthand accounts to others. The value of this type of participation is enhanced if those providing the information are respected by students, for example, successful sports people. In return, these people often appreciate the opportunity to "give something back" by encouraging young people to take preventive measures. Cooperation with local businesses can guarantee the availability and promotion of sun protection items.

Any promotion of sun protection strategies within the community will serve to further spread and reinforce the message beyond those with direct links to the school. In turn, the school can demonstrate leadership by incorporating sun protection interventions into all of its activities and thus acting as a role model for the community. Sports days and school fairs are all ideal opportunities for the school to showcase its sun protection strategies.

Role of media

The media, including television, radio, signboards, posters, calendars, newspapers, magazines, and leaflets, can be used to raise awareness and to encourage more sensible sun exposure. This can occur on any scale, from local to national, and is an effective means of communicating simple messages that can be further developed through more comprehensive education programmes. Securing the cooperation of media that appeal particularly to young people can help to ensure that messages consistent with sensible sun behaviour are promoted. For example, information on the ageing effects of sun exposure can be included in articles on skin care in magazines targeting young girls.

Recruitment of successful sports people or celebrities with whom students can identify through the media is one way to influence young people's behaviour. If such people are seen to behave sensibly in relation to sun exposure and protection, there is a greater likelihood that young people will do the same. While schools themselves seldom have the resources to secure the services of such people, developing partnerships with other agencies that do-for example, government and nongovernmental organisations, business, and national sporting bodies can-is one way of gaining access to them.

Critical discussion of the images provided through mass media is another useful way of developing students' analytical skills both in relation to health messages and in a broader context. Techniques used in the media are often subtle and pervasive; for example, use of darkly tanned models in skimpy clothing may be used to promote a range of goods intended for young people, reinforcing the view that the behaviour and appearance thus portrayed is necessary for acceptance. It is not always possible to present images to counteract those presented in the media, but it is important that students understand how they are being influenced.

Importance of Staffs' Health Promotion

Health promotion and training in relation to UV exposure and sun protection for school staff is essential for a number of reasons:

- Staff need to understand that health promotion and education is not just the responsibility of some staff members, like, health teachers, but part of the role of all staff.
- If they are to effectively communicate sensible sun related behaviour to students, staff must have the requisite knowledge and skills.
- Complete staff support is essential for the effective implementation of interventions.
- Staff should be able to assess their own sun related behaviour and to protect their own health.
- Staff are obviously well placed to identify measures that can be incorporated into their practices to improve levels of sun protection for themselves and their students.

Health promotion for staff should be ongoing to ensure that all staff, including those new to the school, are kept up to date. Promotions should incorporate a critical evaluation of current policies and practices to ensure that those not conducive to health are identified and modified

7

Sports Exercise

Most top athletes and coaches believe that psychological factors play as crucial a role as physical attributes and learned skills in the make-up of champions. When physical skills are evenly matched-as they tend to be in competitive sport—the competitor with greater control over his or her mind will usually emerge as the victor. Mental strength is not going to compensate for lack of skill, but in close contests it can make the difference between winning and losing.

A key question for sport and exercise psychologists is whether champions have simply inherited the dominant psychological traits necessary for success or whether mental toughness can be acquired through training and experience. Recent research has attempted to explore the concept of mental toughness in sport more thoroughly, and it appears that, while some people are naturally more tough-minded than others, people can be 'toughened-up' with the correct approach to training.

Mental toughness is probably easiest to define in terms of how it affects behaviour and performance. A mentally tough athlete is likely to:

- achieve relatively consistent performances regardless of situational factors;

- retain a confident, positive, optimistic outlook, even when things are not going well, and not 'choke' under pressure;
- deal with distractions without letting them interfere with optimal focus;
- tolerate pain and discomfort;
- remain persistent when the 'going gets tough';
- have the resilience to bounce back from disappointments.

Influence of Personality

These characteristics are obviously related to success in most life situations. But it seems that some of us may be tougher than others because of personality traits and learned ways of coping. Personality research has always stirred up controversy- usually because researchers have not been able to agree on the correct approach to studying it. Some have taken what is known as the 'trait' approach, which views personality as stable and enduring, based on individual characteristics. However, others see personality as shaped by environmental influences, while 'interactionists' view individual traits and the environment as codeterminants of behaviour.

In recent times, this latter position has tended to predominate, based on the view that personality structure involves both a stable core of attitudes, values and beliefs about self, that remains relatively unchanged after early childhood, and more changeable, dynamic behaviours that are influenced by our environment.

Research on the relationship between stress and illness has revealed that some people have characteristics that act as buffers against stressors, making them less likely to succumb to ill health in difficult times. The leading researcher Suzanne Kobasa showed in one study that a personality characteristic known as 'hardiness' was a key factor in whether or not highly-stressed executives succumbed to illness. The hardy executives, who avoided illness, tended to perceive stressors as 'challenges' rather than threats, so maintaining a sense of control over events.

Until recently, few studies had attempted to transfer the concept of hardiness to sport and exercise settings, but it seems very similar to the idea of mental toughness outlined earlier. One study on the relationship between hardiness and performance in basketball showed that seven out of eight season-long performance indicators were significantly correlated with a total hardiness score. This finding needs to be interpreted with caution, however, since correlations do not necessarily reflect causation.

A key development has been the development of a questionnaire to assess mental toughness that can be used to assess its influence in experimental studies. The Hull researchers carried out two studies to show how mental toughness was related to performance and cognitive appraisal. In the first study, 23 volunteers performed 30-minute static cycling trials at three different intensities of 30, 50 and 70% of their maximum oxygen uptake, rating the physical demands of the trials at five-minute intervals.

Participants were classified as having either high or low mental toughness based on their responses to the above-mentioned questionnaire and, as predicted, those with higher levels of mental toughness reported significantly lower perceived exertion at 70% of maximum. No significant differences were noted at lower levels of exertion which, as the researchers acknowledged, is consistent with the cliché that 'when the going gets tough, the tough get going'. The observed differences at higher levels of exertion could reflect a tendency of the more tough-minded to somehow act on the incoming stimuli before it reaches the level of perception, to reduce the perception of strain. Mentally tough exercisers might perceive themselves as having greater control during such conditions, or interpret the higher intensity as a challenge rather than a threat.

The second study, on 79 participants, considered the influence of mental toughness on resilience in adverse situations. Participants were given either positive or negative feedback after completing a variety of motor tasks, and then asked to perform a planning task which was used as the objective performance measure. The key question for the researchers was how participants would respond to feedback that could alter their confidence. As predicted, mentally tough participants performed better on the planning task, delivering relatively consistent performances whether their feedback had been negative or positive. However, those with lower levels of mental toughness performed significantly worse after negative feedback, confirming the greater resilience of those with high levels of mental toughness.

A few years ago, a close-up shot of former world motor racing champion Damon Hill in his Formula One car as his head swayed from side to side. There was nothing new about TV producers wanting to get closer to the action, but the odd thing about this shot was that Hill was sitting in a stationary car, waiting to exit the garage in an attempt to qualify for the race. In fact there was a simple explanation for Hill's behaviour: like many other top sports people, he was using the time leading up to a performance to mentally rehearse and (in his case no doubt) imagine steering the correct racing line through each corner.

On top of the time spent honing skills and developing physical readiness, studies of top performers have shown that the élite from a variety of different sports complete many laps of the track, lengths of the pool or throws of the javelin in their minds before major competitions.

Once learned, imagery can be applied in many different ways to aid sports performers, and is one of the most regularly used tools of the sport psychologist. However, recent research evidence suggests that to achieve maximum benefits athletes and coaches should select the content of their images very carefully.

Scientists have now turned their attention from the question of whether imagery works – given the strong evidence that it does – to the question of how it works. On this issue opinion remains divided and a healthy debate continues. Some experts believe that small neuromuscular 'firings' that have been demonstrated in some research studies provide sufficient feedback from imagined stimuli to allow for changes in performance.

The evidence suggests that imagery may work more indirectly – facilitating changes in someone's psychological state by building confidence, promoting motivation and reducing performance anxiety. At present, the exact mechanisms by which imagery works remain unclear, although recent work using brain imaging techniques has advanced our knowledge by confirming that the right hemisphere of the brain is the primary imagery centre.

If you watch children playing, you can rapidly appreciate how creative and imaginative they are. As children play with dolls and toys they create their own inner worlds, thereby engaging the right hemispheres of their brains. Unfortunately, much systematic education focuses on logical and analytical processes, which use the left hemisphere and tend to be more highly valued by adults.

The trouble is that without constant practice the brain's imagery centre reacts in much the same way as your muscles do if you stop training—ie it atrophies. Again using a body analogy, when you return to using this part of your brain after a long lay-off, it's like doing that first exercise session all over again. However, as with physical exercise, the more you train, the faster you adapt and the easier it gets.

Although imagery can be applied in very dynamic situations, it is best to learn how to do it in quiet, relaxed, non-competitive settings. You need to start by relaxing—closing your eyes and focusing on deep rhythmical breaths. You cannot afford to be half-hearted, so commit yourself to the process and try to decide beforehand what you are going to imagine. Some people might even decide to record a series of instructions onto a cassette tape to help direct their images.

Sport psychologist Rainer Martens suggested that, in developing a systematic approach to using imagery, people should first work on increasing overall sensory awareness. A fundamental point that must be made at this juncture is that visualisation and imagery are not one and the same; imagery should involve far more than visualisation, including the feelings of movements, sounds, emotions and, in some cases, even smells.

A cricket batsman, for example, might attempt to become more aware of sensory process by recalling the important visual environmental features, as well as the sound of the bowler running-in and the noise the ball made through the air. He may recall the feel of swinging the bat and making contact with the ball. The subsequent sounds of bat on ball and the call of his partner to run may also be considered. The sense of control as the ball reached the boundary, a feeling of determination and the smell of freshly mown grass may help to stimulate all the senses. So Martens proposes a first stage dedicated to appreciating things that the individual may have come to take for granted.

The next step is to develop vividness. It is true that some people are able to recall or create very clear and vivid images, while others may struggle to get an image at all. With practice, though, most people are able to sharpen their images so that recognisable sensory experiences are evident. This is the stage to be creative and experiment by using scenes and experiences that are very familiar to you. These exercises do not need to be sport-specific at first, as the general idea is to promote overall clarity. You might like to try exercise 1, above, to help develop vividness.

The final stage of your development plan involves control. If you are mentally rehearsing what you are going to do, it is important to have control over your images. That is because imagery can be destructive as well as helpful. If, for example, a golfer is imagining the path of the ball on the green but continually sees herself missing the putt, this is hardly likely to help. The great thing about imagery is that, even if the golfer has missed putts in reality, imagery provides an opportunity to correct errors.

This stage is more sport specific and should incorporate your desired outcome. You should feel the movement and see a positive result, such as the golf ball following the correct path and entering the hole. If you do start imagining negative outcomes, try to recall a previous success—or even watch another person successfully complete the skill and try to replicate this in your mind, with yourself in the role of successful performer.

Although the most obvious application of imagery is in the learning and performing of sport skills, there are many other ways to use the technique. For example, imagery can also be used to practise strategies, manipulate levels of arousal, manage stress, build confidence, deal with pain and periods of injury and develop an appropriate focus.

Recently researchers have suggested that, for maximum effect, athletes should match the content or type of imagery with the desired outcome. Towards this end, you should think carefully about the components of your imagined experiences and ask yourself what you want to gain. Do you seek to facilitate learning and performance of skills and strategies, or are you attempting to build confidence or even psych yourself up?

The five main categories of imagery have been identified as follows:

- *Motivational-specific (MS)*—This involves seeing yourself winning an event, receiving a trophy or medal and being congratulated by other athletes. MS imagery may boost motivation and effort during training and facilitate goal-setting, but is unlikely on its own to lead directly to performance benefits;
- *Motivational general-mastery (MG-M)*—This is based on seeing yourself coping in difficult circumstances and mastering challenging situations. It might include maintaining a positive focus while behind, and then coming back to win. MG-M imagery appears to be important in developing expectations of success and self-confidence;
- *Motivational general-arousal (MG-A)*—This is imagery that reflects feelings of relaxation, stress, anxiety or arousal in relation to sports competitions. There is good evidence to suggest that MG-A imagery can

influence heart rate—one index of arousal—and can be employed as a 'psych-up' strategy;

- *Cognitive specific (CS)*—This involves seeing yourself perform specific skills, such as a tennis serve, golf putt or triple-toe-loop in figure skating. If learning and performance are the desired outcomes, evidence suggests that CS imagery will be the most effective choice;
- *Cognitive general (CG)*—This involves images of strategy and game plans related to a competitive event. Examples could include employing a serve-and-volley strategy in tennis or a quick-break play in basketball. Case studies support the use of this type of imagery, although controlled experimental evidence is still needed.

Clearly there is potential for these types of imagery to overlap if, for example, you imagine specific sports skills, such as a golf putt (CS), with the accompanying positive outcome and tournament-clinching result (MS). However, research suggests that if you choose the wrong type of imagery, you may not achieve any benefits. For example, one study showed that CS imagery significantly improved sit-up performance, while MG-M imagery was ineffective. Conversely, other studies have shown MG-M imagery to be more effective than CS imagery for boosting self-confidence. The trick is to decide what it is you want to achieve, then make the imagery content match your goals.

In designing imagery training programmes, FITT principle, which has often been associated with physical training.

F is for Frequency. Aim to incorporate imagery into every day of your training schedule. For busy people, just before you sleep could be a good time, and it helps if you are in a relaxed and tranquil state;

I is for Intensity. Try to create an all-sensory experience that is as vivid and clear as possible. Initially, practising in a quiet environment can help to minimise distractions and facilitate clear images;

T is for Time. Imagery should make big demands on your attention, so short (5-10 minutes) frequent quality sessions are preferable to long ones;

T is for Type. Remember to decide on your desired outcome and select the type of imagery to match it.

Mental Fitness

Mental toughness is what makes Michael Jordan and Pete Sampras so special. These athletes know their real battle is not so much on the court, but inside their heads. You absolutely must manage your mental side if you want to be the best. If you are one of those athletes who spends all your training time on technique and fitness while paying no attention to your mental side, you are doing yourself a serious disservice. We know from countless studies that mental skills are acquirable and you can, with practice, learn to perform mentally. You can improve your confidence, concentration, motivation and anxiety levels if you chose to.

Feelings affect your performance. Whether you are aware of them or not, how you feel affects how you perform. Feelings are based on what you imagine or interpret from an event and not from the event itself. Two players appearing in the Wimbledon final for the first time will imagine different things about the match. One might imagine she will be unable to play well in such a big final. This player is likely to feel nervous and uncertain and her performance will be poor. The other might imagine it as the experience of a lifetime for her to go out and enjoy - she might feel liberated and relaxed and her play is likely to reflect these emotions. The same event evokes two different responses which result in two very different performances. The message here is very simple - learn how to change your interpretations and you learn how to manage your emotions. When you can manage your emotions you can perform at your best.

The mind and the body are inextricable linked - how you feel physically affects how you feel emotionally. This means that we can improve our mental performance using physical interventions (relaxation exercises) and vice versa. You operate within a system - your performance is just a symptom or outcome of how your system operates. The parts of your system are all interrelated. A cricket player's confidence may be affected by his technique, which may be affected by his fitness, which may be affected by his lifestyle which may be affected by his time management. It is always more potent to look to remedy the underlying causes of a problem than the symptom itself.

If Alan Shearer is not scoring goals, the problem might lie not with him but with the midfield who are not creating chances for him (a moot point in this case). In situations where your performance was greatly influenced by your relationship with another person. As humanistic psychologists, we believe that under the right circumstances you will want to reach your potential. Our focus is not just on your performance but also on your welfare. Often the two are linked. You can divide mental skills training into two approaches: individual work and group work. A standard programme for both may last for a minimum of six weeks with sessions of 60-90 minutes.

Psychological or psychometric testing has been used for decades by big business to screen prospective employees, it's only really taken off in the last few years. Psychometric testing remains highly controversial. People are afraid that it will reveal their dark side: it still has the reputation of being a voodoo science. These included two of five British candidates applying to the Giants who ruled themselves out of the running by refusing the tests.

Pressure of Competition

What causes skilled and experienced athletes to 'choke' under the many pressures of competition? This question, highly relevant in the wake of Paula Radcliffe's dramatic and high profile collapse during the recent Olympic marathon, has been investigated by a team of Australian researchers, who set out to examine the role of self-consciousness and trait (or dispositional) anxiety as predictors of choking in sport.

Choking has been defined as 'performance decrements under pressure circumstances' and is thought to occur when a performer focuses in a conscious way on skills that have become automatic, with a detrimental effect on performance.

In the Australian study, 66 student basketball players completed questionnaires designed to measure self-consciousness and sport anxiety before completing 20 free throws under two different conditions: 1. Low pressure - observed only by a research assistant with no consequences attached to performance; 2. High pressure (about one hour later) - videotaped, observed by an audience and with a performance-contingent financial incentive.

The hypothesis was that performance would decline under pressure and that performers displaying high self-consciousness and/or trait anxiety would be most susceptible to choking. In fact there was an overall decline in performance from the low pressure to the high pressure condition, with a mean score (successful shots out of 20) of 13.56 under low pressure, falling to 12.53 under high pressure. Of the 66 participants, 35 had a lower score under pressure, seven scored the same and 24 scored better. When analysing the relationship of selfconsciousness and sport anxiety ratings and free throw scores, the researchers made the following findings:

- As expected (but contrary to some previous research) high self-conscious participants were more likely to choke than their low self-conscious counterparts;
- This tendency was particularly evident for the private self-consciousness sub-scale (where attention is directed inwards, to private thoughts and feelings, as opposed to public selfconsciousness, where attention is directed to the self as the object of others' awareness);
- In terms of trait anxiety, only somatic trait anxiety (measuring physical feelings, eg jitteriness) was a significant predictor of choking.

Because a significant minority of the participants actually improved their performance under pressure, the researchers believe that a good deal could be learned by studying athletes who are 'choking-resistant'.

A friend was in a cancer ward and his treatment involved going without food and water for eight weeks. He survived on a drip and lost three stone in weight. Around him other patients frequently died. It was a depressing period. Nearly 40 years ago the great Australian runner Ron Clarke broke world records for two miles, three miles and six miles, and 3000 and 5000m, as well as the distance run in one hour. The 10,000m world record, however, had eluded him many times, and on one of his training runs by the sea, he was pondering why this was so when, in the distance, he heard much squealing and splashing coming from a rocky alcove.

The word 'recreation' literally means recreating our mind and body. Because we can, we should. If we enjoy sport we will enjoy it more if we get better at it.

Improving involves the allocation of time. Our lives revolve around the three eights - eight hours work, eight hours sleep, eight hours free time. Some of the free time is required for taking meals and for travelling to and from work. At the very least we can find one hour a day to practise our sport. When we choose that hour is our prerogative.

The world's first sub-four-minute miler, Roger Bannister, was a medical student at St Mary's Hospital, Paddington. He chose to use his lunch hour for a 10-minute jog to Paddington track. There he ran 10 x 440yds in about 60secs with two minutes rest, then he ran back to work. The whole procedure took exactly 48 minutes, leaving him time for lunch. If you want to train for sport you can always fit it in somehow.

We are at our physical peak in sport for about five years, although we may compete in one way or another for 25 years. This means that you should regard every training session - like every day - as a precious piece of your time. Regard it as an investment which will pay dividends in the future.

Mental stress can hurt your performances in a variety of different ways. It can raise heart rate and oxygen consumption, harming your exercise efficiency and causing particular workout and race speeds to feel tougher than they actually should. It can increase muscle tension, reducing stride lengths (if you are a runner) and making your legs and arms considerably less 'springy' and powerful. On a cognitive level, stress prevents you from 'mentally managing' your tough workouts and races; instead of relaxing and focusing on the task at hand, you are preoccupied with stressful thoughts and emotions, so the quality of your performance decreases.

If you feel stressed-out before and during your competitions or hard training sessions, what can you do to control the stress, and thus increase your chances of performing at your highest-possible level? Sport psychologists have proposed a number of different stress-managing techniques over the years, but one of the most successful has been something called 'stress-inoculation training'. Developed in the late 1970s and early 1980s by Donald Meichenbaum, a psychologist at the University of Waterloo in Canada, stress-inoculation training takes its name from the fact that it exposes individuals to stress in manageable but gradually increasing amounts, thereby enhancing 'immunity' to stress for the persons practising the technique.

The key, however, to stress inoculation is not simply that stress levels are increased in a governable way during training; athletes also learn skills for coping with psychological stress and enhancing performance, including the development of productive thoughts and self-statements and the utilisation of centring strategies. There are usually three stages in the overall stress-inoculation process:

1) A conceptualisation phase, in which an athlete becomes more aware of how positive and negative thoughts, self-talk, and imagery influence performance,
2) a rehearsal period, during which an athlete learns to use centring, positive self-statements, and other coping skills, and
3) an application phase, in which the athlete actually practises his/her skills, first in low-stress situations and then in settings in which stress levels are gradually increased .

Avoiding unsuitable 'Headwork'

Stress-inoculation training was originally developed for the public-at-large, but psychologists quickly realised that it could be applied to sports settings. They knew that many athletes unwittingly respond to stress with maladaptive thoughts and images which greatly hinder performance. Once such athletes understand how their unsuitable 'headwork' is keeping them from reaching their potentials, they begin to eagerly construct new self-statements and images which can have a profoundly positive impact on their performances.

Scientific studies concerning the effects of stress-inoculation training on exercise capacity have generally been positive: In one study, two sessions of stress-inoculation training per week for 5.5 weeks improved the running economy of eight male collegiate cross-country runners. Stress-inoculation training has also been linked with improved performance during abseiling (descending mountain faces) and lower stress levels during squash competitions, and it has been particularly effective at boosting the performances of gymnasts.

Not too surprisingly, a number of sport psychologists have examined the effects of stress-inoculation training on basketball players, particularly with regard to free-throw shooting, which is often a high-stress activity within the game. One study found that stress inoculation improved both free-throw and field-goal shooting, and a second investigation (carried out with just three players, however) determined that free-throw shooting accuracy increased from 50 to 88 per cent and self-statements changed from 86-per cent negative to 71-per cent positive after just 10 hours of stress-inoculation training.

In addition, the self-statement, although temporarily relieving in a small way, is neither truthful nor realistic. The truth is that the individual is a good runner who performs well in other races, so she can do well in the marathon, too. The reality is that the individual is not doomed to a late-race slowdown; she can train to overcome the plunge in velocity over the final miles. The transiently relieving self-statement gives the runner the temporary 'warm-fuzzies' but actually works to block better performance and smooths the pathway to failure. In spite of the modest relief it provides, it needs to be completely jettisoned in favour of a positive and realistic statement which can push the individual toward better running.

There are many similar, transiently stress-relieving but emotively negative self-statements which endurance athletes commonly make. 'I don't have good foot speed', 'I'm not much of a 40-K bike racer', and 'I have trouble with interval workouts' are just a few examples. In the conceptualisation stage of stress inoculation, it's important to become aware of how you talk to yourself about your training and racing. Try to gain an appreciation for the emotional content of your self-statements and understand how they might help or hinder your performances. Once you have gained a good understanding of how you have been talking to yourself and what your statements mean, you can move on to the next stage of stress management - rehearsal.

Physical Exercise

There are two basic relaxation techniques circle breathing and a progressive relaxation session. These skills are necessary to perform at an optimal level in athletics, and they are the same sort of skills that are taught in stress management classes for businesses, and can be used in any facet of your life. It's important to note that the days of pep talks to psych up your team are over. Rigid, tight-jawed determination is not the key, a sense of relaxation and letting go is. The athlete/team that is mentally and physically relaxed and has "quiet intensity" is the one that is going to come out on top.

Circle breathing is a great on-the-spot tool for athletes. Right before you throw a pitch, shoot a free throw, swing the bat, field a ball, kick a field goal all these tasks require great concentration and focus. The breathing will help you be better prepared and allow you to keep your poise in tough situations. You are better able to read your environment if you are calm and relaxed. Mental poise and emotional control are key to you performing well and being successful.

The center of your body is right behind your belly button, and this is where you want to start your breath from. Starting from there (the center of your body), draw air in slowly through your nose, all the way up to your chest for a count of 4, hold it for a count of 2, then slowly exhale through your mouth for a count of 4. Let go of all tension and old energy, and completely clear your mind. Focus only on your breathing. That is one deep breath. Approximately 5-10 of these in a row will help get you into a more relaxed state. Now, stop here and try to do a few deep breaths on your own before moving on. Go at your body's pace, it will tell you when to take another breath.

In the 1930s, Edmund Jacobson demonstrated that you can't be on opposite ends of the physiological and emotional spectrum. That is, an anxious mind cannot exist in a relaxed body; or, a quiet mind can not exist in a tense body. He introduced Progressive Muscle Relaxation. This entails tensing each muscle, holding it and then relaxing each muscle on the exhale. It's a loosening up and letting go mentality. The letting go lets you know what absence of tension feels like. This type of relaxation skill gives you a heightened awareness of when and how you experience tension, this can then serve as a cue that you should do something to relieve the tension. You need to be able to communicate with your body and understand what it is trying to tell you.

BREATHING TECHNIQUES IN RUNNING

Sports psychologists believe that the way you think, your ability to relax, the manner in which you regulate your state of arousal, and your confidence, concentration, and determination all help determine how well you can perform. On the other hand, sceptics contend that athletic activity is mainly a matter of muscle and heart and sometimes make jokes, such as, 'If the mind matters so much, Einstein would have been a 2:05 marathoner'.

Despite such doubts, scientific studies have often supported the idea that mental strategies can improve exercise capacity. Interestingly enough, one of the best-validated ideas has been the notion that a few skillful tweaks of the nervous system can improve muscular efficiency, lowering the energetic cause of specific exercise intensities and thereby permitting athletes to work at higher-than-usual levels.

How could a shift in mental status help you run, cycle, or swim more economically? One idea is that a change in arousal - a shift to a more relaxed and less uptight state - can ease muscle tension and allow the legs and arms to flow more smoothly and with less resistance as one trains and races. The contention is that having too-tight muscles is a bit like driving a car with the handbrake on. Just as the brake keeps the vehicle from rolling along with maximum speed, overly tight muscles waste energy and diminish muscular power. Of course, critics caution that one must somehow find a balance between tightness and looseness; if there is too much relaxation, an athlete might lose the determination to work at a high rate, actually lowering workout and race quality.

In addition to decreasing the resistance to motion, relaxation might work in another key way. Basically, the idea is that if you can tone down the excitement in your nervous system, there will be less nervous-system stimulation of the heart and respiratory muscles. This would lead to lower heart and breathing rates at particular exercise intensities, reducing both the oxygen and calorie cost of exerting oneself.

Critics contend that you might not be able to move along at your normal paces if your heart and breathing rates dropped off, but supporters of relaxation point out that the lungs could still oxygenate the blood effectively with more modest breathing rates - and that the heart may already be pumping 'surplus' blood because of over-stimulation by the nervous system.

Do mental-relaxation strategies really work? If they did, they could definitely benefit your performances. In the world of running, for example, just a 1-per cent amelioration of economy could shave 20 to 30 seconds from an average runner's 10-K time. With a 3- per cent gain, there would be a greater-than one-minute improvement, enough to push the 41-minute 10-K harrier down into the magical 'thirty-somethings.'

Awareness of relaxation techniques for athletes actually dates back to the 1970s, when a noted medical doctor named Herbert Benson started taking an avid interest in exercise. Benson, the author of the very popular book, *The Relaxation Response,* which showed large numbers of people how to use relaxation therapy to soothe their simmering blood-pressure readings, began interviewing successful long-distance runners and concluded that the use of mental strategies had a marked impact on their performances. He became fascinated by the idea that relaxation techniques could lower the oxygen cost of running, thereby upgrading economy and improving performances.

That wasn't a bad idea, since research had already shown that mental techniques could induce a 'hypometabolic state' in individuals who were at rest. In a unique study to determine the effects of relaxation on exercise, Benson first taught a group of four males and four females how to carry out the 'relaxation response'. This involved sitting quietly in a comfortable position, closing the eyes, and then deeply relaxing all the muscles, beginning at the toes and working up to the face. Subjects were instructed to breathe through their noses and become more aware of their breathing patterns, and with each exhalation, the word 'ONE' was stated silently. The focused breathing and muscle relaxation continued for a period of 20 minutes, after which the subjects sat quietly for several minutes, first with closed eyes and then with them open.

Relaxation beginners often have trouble 'getting into' such efforts, but Benson enhanced his students' abilities to relax by encouraging them to avoid worrying about how 'successful' they were at relaxing. Pupils simply maintained a passive attitude and permitted relaxation to occur at its own pace. Distracting thoughts popping into the mind during the technique were ignored or were pushed out of the brain with the rather relentless use of the word 'ONE'.

After the subjects had practised Benson's relaxation technique twice daily for a period of at least six months (!), they were ready for a bit of exertion. During the exercise test, all eight individuals pedalled an exercise bicycle at a constant intensity for 30 minutes, but only during the middle portion of the workout did the subjects attempt to use their learned relaxation responses. Their heart and oxygen-consumption rates from this middle portion of the workout were compared with those from the first and last 10-minute periods, when no special relaxation was attempted.

While the relaxation didn't have any effect at all on heart rate, it did decrease oxygen consumption by as much as 10 per cent in a couple of subjects and by 4 per cent overall, a statistically significant change. Although it appeared that Benson's technique actually worked, critics carped that the chosen exercise heart rate - a mere 100 beats per minute - was too low for the study to have much applicability to serious athletes. In addition, those interested in weight loss complained that they needed workouts that used more oxygen and burned more calories, not less. Those people wanted to tense up a bit, not relax, during their training sessions.

The athletes who were using displays of internal, usually unavailable physiological information in an attempt to regulate what was happening inside their bodies were utilising a technique called biofeedback. After practising heart-rate lowering during four different workouts, the athletes viewing heart-rate monitors were tested in a fifth training session at a work load which had previously elicited a heart rate of about 65-per cent max. Observation of their heart rates during this test did help the athletes slow down their cardiac centres rather impressively.

In fact, athletes viewing heart-rate displays exhibited a useful 22-per cent smaller increase in heart rate during exercise, compared to those pedalling along without such biofeedback. In addition, the individuals who looked at monitors used oxygen at approximately 6-per cent lower rates and reduced ventilation by around 14 per cent, even though actual exercise intensity had not been lowered.

Centreing is a relaxation and concentration exercise which emphasises abdominal breathing and the use of key words. As they engaged in centreing, the athletes were usually standing, with feet shoulder-width apart and hands resting on their abdomens. As part of the process, the runners focused on a point just behind their navels and were told to 'feel the relationship of their entire body' to this point. They also were attentive to the motions of their abdominal areas as they expanded and contracted during breathing. At all times, they attempted to breathe with their stomachs, not just with their chests. As they breathed in, the athletes repeated a cue word to themselves as a reminder to centre, usually either 'centre' or 'focus'. As they exhaled, they uttered another word reminding them to relax. After exhalation, and just before inhalation, they tried to focus on lowering oxygen consumption, heart rate, and ventilation.

Ten minutes after the end of each relaxation and/or centreing practice, the athletes began cruising along on treadmills at lactate-threshold running velocity. Each treadmill effort lasted for 10 minutes; for the first five minutes, runners received no biofeedback, but during the second five minutes heart, oxygen-consumption, and ventilation rates were displayed on a screen in front of them. During this second five-minute period, the runners tried to lower these rates using the relaxation and centreing techniques they had learned.

Did the combination of relaxation and centreing work? You bet it did! While employing the relaxation and centreing during the second five minutes of the treadmill rambles, the athletes were able to lower their ventilatory rates by over 9 per cent, oxygen consumption by greater than 7 per cent, and heart rates by almost 3 per cent. The 7-per cent amelioration of economy would have translated into approximately a four-minute improvement in 15-K time for someone normally completing the race in about 60 minutes. That's a tremendous bonus, especially when you realise that the improvement was not the result of any upswing in actual physical fitness.

Would the athletes have been able to move so economically without the displays? That's an important question, since most of us are unable to view representations of what's going on inside our bodies on video monitors as we train and race. Of course, the biofeedback is a help, since it provides immediate information about how well one's relaxation-and-centreing strategy is working. If nothing is happening on the screen, one can try harder or slightly change one's mental focus.

Again, that's where a heart monitor might come into play: while remaining at one's goal pace during a race, one could centre, relax, and use the feedback from the little device to determine how well the mental strategies were working. Note, however, that heart rate was much less responsive to the relaxation-and-centreing intervention than oxygen consumption and ventilation, dropping by just 2.54 per cent, versus 7 and 9 per cent, respectively. If your heart rate were 160 or so, that would be a downturn of just three or four beats, not much to look for, especially considering the fact that heart rate naturally tends to wander around, even when you're training at fixed velocities.

Endurance Exercise

Endurance exercise reduces the risk of cardiovascular disease and lowers blood pressure, and it also has positive psychological effects. Various scientific studies have shown that regular exercise reduces anxiety, improves self-esteem, and increases self-confidence.

Aerobic exercise, chocolate, and guided imagery produced similar reductions in anxiety levels. However, the fourth, 'control' group had little relief from tension and found it difficult to concentrate during the second mental test. Their performance on the second test was below-par compared to the first three groups, which performed equally well on the second challenge. So, exercise does a good job of calming people down when they feel anxious and helpless, but in many cases it's probably no better than using positive mental images or taking in one's minimum daily requirement of chocolate.

Fatigue during prolonged exercise is definitely associated with depletion of glycogen stored in the liver (causing hypoglycaemia - low blood sugar) or in the muscles. It is also known that reversal of hypoglycaemia by intravenous or oral administration of glucose allows exercise to continue. Finally, pre-exercise carbohydrate loading and/or carbohydrate ingestion during exercise delays the onset of fatigue and improves exercise performance.

The fact that reversal of hypoglycaemia alone allows exercise to continue proves conclusively that liver glycogen depletion can limit exercise performance under certain specific conditions. Indeed the rapidity with which the restoration of blood glucose levels restores performance suggests that a central 'governor' is activated by changes in blood glucose concentrations and acts to prevent activity that would further reduce the blood glucose concentration, posing the risk of brain damage.

However, since no technique has yet been devised that will instantly reverse glycogen depletion in the muscles, it is impossible to prove that muscle glycogen depletion alone limits prolonged exercise performance. Evidence against the energy depletion model comes from a study showing that athletes ingesting carbohydrate stopped exercising after four hours when their muscle glycogen concentrations and rates of carbohydrate oxidation were no lower than they had been one hour earlier, when they were not exhausted.

Another study showed that athletes who adapted to a high-fat diet were able to exercise to significantly lower muscle glycogen concentrations at exhaustion than when they were carbohydrate-adapted. And a trial of previously untrained subjects, who trained on a high-fat diet for seven weeks before switching to a high-carbohydrate diet for one week, found that although they increased their pre-exercise muscle glycogen concentrations by 44%, there was only a small further improvement in performance.

It is possible that the capacity to oxidise fat at high rates when body carbohydrate stores are depleted may delay fatigue and determine performance during exercise of moderately high intensity that lasts more than four hours and is typified by ultradistance running and triathlon events.

Exercise and Depression

There is evidence that vigorous exercise is good for one's health and can, if not too stressful, improve the immune system. It can also reduce the chances of heart disease and increase lifespan. But is that why we all do it? Now there is striking new evidence relating to the brain, depression and exercise. It has been found that contrary to the long-held view that no new neurones are generated in adults, it is now clear that there are stem cells in various regions of the adult brain that divide to give new neurones.

Stem cells are special cells which have the remarkable property that, when they divide, one of the two daughter cells remains a stem cell and can divide again while the other cell can become a specialised cell like a nerve cell. The first suggestion for this came from birds in which new nerve cells were generated in relation to song-learning.

Then came studies of the brains of patients who had died of cancer and who had previously given permission to be treated with a substance that labels dividing cells. These showed the formation of new nerve cells - a revolutionary discovery which has completely changed the way disease of the brain can be thought about and it opens up possibilities for quite new therapies.

The hippocampus is a region of the brain that is associated with memory, particularly the conversion of short-term memories into long-term memories, and is also involved in mood disorders. There is evidence that the hippocampus is smaller in the brains of depressed patients. In one study involving 10 depressed patients, the volume of the hippocampus was measured using magnetic resonance imaging, and was found to be about 10% smaller than those in controls of similar age, matched for height, education and evenhandedness. Other studies support this finding.

The reduction in the size of the hippocampus may be related to the effects of stress. Stress suffered over quite a long period due, for example to a significant loss, is a common trigger for depression. Stress causes an increase in certain hormones such as cortisol which can, in turn, cause both cell deterioration and cell death in the brain. The new research on generation of neurones has found that this occurs in the hippocampus. It also shows that stress can inhibit cell multiplication in the hippocampus in an animal model, resulting in fewer nerve cells being produced.

Antidepressants like Prozac can, by contrast, promote an increase in cell proliferation and this offers a totally new perspective on how antidepressants may act: it seems likely, though the evidence is at an early stage, that antidepressants work by increasing brain cell growth. Of particular significance is the effect of exercise. Mice which had access to a running wheel so that they ran nearly five kilometres a day for several months had twice as many multiplying cells in their brain compared to mice which took no exercise.

Beating Drugs for Depression

Aerobic exercise has been prescribed for a wide range of medical disorders (including heart disease, arthritis and diabetes) and tipped as a potential treatment for various psychiatric conditions, especially depression. Population studies have shown an inverse relationship between physical activity and depression, and there is evidence that active people who become inactive are more at risk of depression that those who remain active.

A more detailed analysis at 10 months of the 83 patients who had been assessed as being in remission after four months showed that those in the exercise group were more likely than those in either of the other groups to be considered either partially or fully recovered. Furthermore, only 8% of those in the exercise group had relapsed, compared with 38% in the medication group and 31% in the combination group.

During the six-month follow-up period the participants had been free to move between therapies, and it was interesting that just under half of those in the medication group took up exercise while around two thirds of those assigned to exercise in the original study remained active. As far as medication was concerned, 40% of those in the combination group took antidepressants during the follow-up period, compared with 26% in the medication group and 7% in the exercise group. Analysis taking account of these changes showed that patients who engaged in regular aerobic exercise during the six-month follow-up were less likely to be depressed at the end of that period, with each 50-minute increment in exercise per week associated with a 50% decrease in the odds of being classified as depressed.

There were major limitations to the study, including self-selection of the participants - who might have been biased in favour of exercise - and self-reporting of exercise during the follow-up period, introducing possible inaccuracies into the data. Nevertheless, conclude the researchers, 'the present findings suggest that a modest exercise programme (eg three times per week with 30 minutes at 70% of maximum heart rate reserve each time) is an effective, robust treatment for patients with major depression who are positively inclined to participate in it, and that clinical benefits are particularly likely to endure among patients who adopt exercise as a regular, ongoing life activity.'

8

Body Composition and Nutrition Analysis

A person can alter his or her body composition by losing fat mass and/or by gaining lean body mass. A good strength training programme and a well-constructed diet can allow a person to lose fat while preserving lean body mass, or build muscle mass while keeping fat gain to a minimum. If a person's clothes are fitting more loosely, or his body measurements are changing without his body weight changing, that person has altered his or her body composition. Individuals with poor body composition can sometimes be described as "skinny fat". This is when a person is not overweight, but because such a small proportion of their total body weight is made up of muscle, they appear flabby and weak.

Body composition (particularly body fat percentage) can be measured in several ways. The most common method is by using a set of measurement calipers to measure the thickness of subcutaneous fat in multiple places on the body. This includes the abdominal area, the subscapular region, arms, buttocks and thighs. These measurements are then used to estimate total body fat with a margin of error of approximately four percentage points.

- Another method is bioelectrical impedance analysis (BIA), which uses the resistance of electrical flow through the body to estimate body fat.
- A more accurate but less convenient method is using a large tank of water to measure body buoyancy. Increased body fat will result in greater buoyancy, while greater muscle mass will result in a tendency to sink.
- A technique for measuring body composition has been developed using the same principles as under water weighing. The technique uses air, as opposed to water, and is known as air displacement plethysmography (ADP). Subjects enter a sealed chamber that measures their body volume through the displacement of air in the chamber. Body volume is combined with body weight (mass) in order to determine body density. The technique then estimates the percentage of body fat and lean body mass (LBM) through known equations (for the density of fat and fat free mass).
- Body Composition is also estimated using cross-sectional imaging methods like magnetic resonance imaging (MRI) and computed tomography (CT). Since MRI and CT give the most precise body composition measures to-date, many pharmaceutical companies are very interested in this new procedure to estimate body composition measures before and after drug therapy especially in drugs that might change body composition.

Skinfold Measurements

This method is the most widely used body composition testing method for assessing percent body fat. Equipment used for this assessment includes a skinfold caliper. A Skinfold Caliper is designed specifically for simple accurate measurement of subcutaneous tissue. Either a 7 or 3 site skinfold may be assessed.

7 site skinfold:

- chest,
- triceps,
- subscapular,
- axilla,
- suprailiac,
- abdomen,
- thigh

3 site skinfold (Men):

- chest,
- abdomen,
- thigh

3 Site Skinfold (Women)

- tricep,
- suprailiac,
- thigh

Commonly used Calipers

- *Lange Skinfold Caliper*: This type of caliper is widely used in schools, colleges, and fitness centers. It is very popular among physical educators, coaches, and health and fitness professionals. The price range is $ 179.00–$220.00.
- *Harpenden Skinfold Caliper*: the standard caliper used in research. The majority of data involving body composition assessments dealing with the relationship of skinfold thickness to percent body fat in use today are based on studies using this caliper. It's accuracy is within ± 0.2 mm and can be read to

the nearest 0.1 mm. Harpenden Skinfold Caliper is popular among Exercise Scientists and or Health Science Researchers. The price range is $275.00–$400.00.

Underwater Weighing

This method uses Archimedes principle which states that when a body is submerged in water, there is a buoyant counter force equal to the weight of the water which is displaced. Because bone and muscle are more dense than water, a person with a larger percentage of fat free mass will weigh more in the water and have a lower percent body fat. Conversely, fat floats. Therefore, a large amount of fat mass will make the body lighter in the water and have a higher percent body fat.

If each test is performed correctly according to the recommended guidelines, there is a +/- 1.5% error. (Note: Accuracy depends on the client's ability to blow all the air out of their lungs both during a pretest screening with a spirometer, and during the test itself. Since air makes the body float, inability to perform either of these maneuvers will result in miscalculation of the percent body fat.)

Bioelectrical Impedence

By standing barefoot on metal foot plates, undetectably low voltage electric current is sent up one leg and down the other. Since fat is a very poor conductor of electricity, a lot of fat will impede the current more so than a lot of lean tissue. By measuring the resistance to the current, the machine estimates the percent body fat.

How accurate is it? BIA accuracy, if done correctly on properly operating equipment, is approximately +/- 3%. However, accuracy is dependant upon several client-based variables. It is recommended the following guidelines be followed:

– Abstain from eating and drinking within 4 hours of the test
– Avoid exercising within 12 hours of the test
– Void (urinate) completely prior to testing
– Do not drink alcohol within 48 hours of the test
– Avoid taking diuretics prior to testing unless instructed by your physician

Dual Energy X-Ray Absorptiometry (DEXA)

DEXA is a fairly new technology. It is based on the three component model of body composition. DEXA uses two X-ray energies to measure body fat, muscle, and bone mineral. When having the scan done, one must lay still in the supine position on what looks like an x-ray table. It takes approximately twelve minutes for the computer software to produce an image of the tissues. The results may be viewed as whole body estimates of body fat, muscle, and bone mineral as well as regional body estimates. DEXA takes bone mineral content into consideration when estimating body fat and muscle, therefore it is considered to be more accurate and valid than a two component model of body composition such as underwater weighing.

Near Infrared Interactance (NIR) Futrex 5000

This method of assessing body fat is based on the principles of light absorbtion , reflectance, and near infrared spectroscopy. To estimate body composition , a computerised spectrophotometer that has a scan and probe are used. The probe is placed onto a selected body site such as the biceps; it emitts an infrared light which passes through both fat and muscle and is reflected back to the probe. Subject data such as height, weight, sex, age, frame size and activity level are taken into consideration. Density measurements are obtained and incorporated into the manufacturer's prediction equations. A digital read out including percentage body fat and lean tissue are displayed. Futrex 5000 is an example of NIR. This method of assessing body fat is not the most accurate. In a study by Mclean et al, it was found that skinfolds more accurately predicted body fat than NIR when underwater weighing was used as the criterion measure. In their study, Futrex 5000 underestimated body fat by more than 4% in subjects greater than 30% fat and overestimated body fat by 4% in subjects less than 8% fat.

Nutrition

Carbohydrates

Carbohydrates (CHO) are the most efficient fuel for athletic performance. Because energy from carbohydrate sources can be released within exercising muscles up to three times faster than energy from fat, carbohydrate is the preferred fuel for working muscles. Carbohydrate is used for immediate energy by being converted to glucose, which is circulated in the blood. However only a limited amount of carbohydrate can be stored as glycogen in the liver and in muscles. Once used, glycogen must be replaced or the athlete will have less energy for endurance.

The body uses carbohydrate mainly to provide energy for muscles to do work. How much and what type of fuel (glycogen or fat) is used depends on how intense the activity and how long the period of exercise. Glucose converted from glycogen in the muscles is used for brief, intense exercise, such as sprinting or jumping, as well as for intermittent sports, such as basketball, football or volleyball. Endurance sports such as long-distance running or cycling use glycogen stores initially and then turn to body fat for energy. Exercise must be performed for 30-40 minutes before fatty acids are available for energy.

As the intensity of the exercise increases, working muscles have less oxygen available to them, and fat cannot be used as fuel. As the intensity decreases the body is able to use more fat stores for energy and spare the glycogen. Carbohydrate needs are also based on body weight and level of intensity of activity. Often counting carbohydrates is easier for athletes to understand than percentage of calories from carbohydrate, protein, and fat. Table 1 provides daily ranges for carbohydrate based on weight and level of intensity. In addition to knowing the optimal amount of carbohydrate intake to maintain or build glycogen stores, athletes should also be aware of the optimal timing of the high-carbohydrate meals and snacks.

Table 1. Daily Ranges for Carbohydrate Based on Weight and Level of Intensity

Intensity of Activity	*Carbohydrate (g/kg)*
None/light training	3-5 g/kg
Moderate/heavy training	5-8 g/kg
Pre-event (24-48 hours)	8-9 g/kg
Post-event (within 2-3 hours)	1.7 g/kg

Carbohydrate loading has been used by many athletes in the belief that it would improve endurance and performance. However, while carbohydrate loading is popular among adolescents, it has not been shown to be effective. True carbohydrate loading has an athlete deplete glycogen stores by eating a low carbohydrate diet and exercising at maximum capacity for about five days before competition. Then two to three days before competition, the athlete stops exercising and eats a very high carbohydrate diet.

In theory, this allows the muscles to readily accept carbohydrate and increase the muscle glycogen, but this routine raises many concerns. First, during the low CHO phase the athlete feels fatigued and is at risk for injury. Second, during the high CHO phase the athlete cannot exercise and this often causes anxiety in the athlete. Research has shown that if an athlete does not go through the low CHO phase and only increases the CHO for two to three days before an event, while continuing light training, the athlete will receive the same benefit without the negative aspects.

Fluids

Proper fluid balance is essential for peak athletic performance. Inadequate hydration not only hinders an athlete's ability to perform but can result in potentially life-threatening injuries such as heat stroke. A fluid loss of 1% of body mass can result in an increased heart rate, perception of effort, and premature fatigue. Proper hydration is important in all climates; studies have demonstrated that up to 2 liters of fluid can be lost with 90 minutes of vigorous of exercise, even in temperatures as low as 50°F. Exercise conducted in extremely low temperatures is also complicated by the body's increased urine production in response to cold stress.

Proper preexercise hydration can help minimise the potential for dehydration in numerous ways. Athletes should consume at least 400–600 ml of fluid 20–60 minutes before exercise. Preexercise fluid intake not only serves to maintain plasma volume but boosts gastric volume. Gastric emptying plays a crucial role in maintaining adequate fluid balance, and gastric emptying is higher when gastric volume is high. Because it is not uncommon for some elite level athletes to be chronically dehydrated, some athletes use hyperhydration as a strategy to boost athletic performance.

In elite soccer players, a systematic regimen of 4.5 L/ day of fluid 1 week before competition resulted in greater water reserves, improved thermoregulation, and increased body fluid by 1.1 liters. Additionally, hyperhydration with 500 ml of a carbohydrate drink 2 hours before competition for events where drinking is impractical or where the event is less than 1 hour (for example, in soccer or field hockey) may be useful.

Athletes typically do not hydrate themselves adequately *during exercise*. Numerous factors influence this, including coaching pressures, the nature of the sport, and ignorance. Thirst is a poor indicator of hydration status; in fact, most individuals are already dehydrated by the time they become thirsty.

Adequacy of rehydration is measured by body weight; athletes exhibiting excessive weight loss due to fluid loss should be excluded from competition. Numerous studies have shown that a solution high in sodium content improves fluid restoration. Postexercise hydration is particularly important to help avoid the chronic mild dehydration seen in many athletes. Additionally, athletes must generally consume at least 150% of weight lost to restore preexercise weight. For instance, if an athlete loses 5 kg during a training session, he or she needs to consume 7.5 kg of fluid to restore preexercise weight. Therefore, large volume coupled with high sodium (up to 2.9 g/L) are necessary for proper rehydration.

Most commercial sports drinks do not contain this large amount of sodium and therefore it may be necessary to couple a meal high in sodium content with fluid intake. The exact type of fluid required for hydration depends on many factors, including duration of event, type of event, and athlete's palate. A general recommendation is that the fluid contain some carbohydrate and some electrolyte; however, the exact quantities of each are debatable. Drinks with large amounts of carbohydrate, such as fruit juices and soft drinks, have been shown to cause some gastrointestinal upset in athletes during competition, and those with a lower concentration of carbohydrate may not be as beneficial for certain types of events.

However, there are some general guidelines to follow. For all exercise lasting 1 hour or longer, hydration should take place with fluids that contain between 5%–8% (1.3–2 g/oz) of carbohydrate. Additionally, adding some sodium (0.5-0.7 g/L) to any rehydration beverage appears to be beneficial.

Fuel Sources

There are essentially two sources of energy for exercise: glycogen and fat. During periods of low to moderate exercise, fats make up most of the fuel used for energy. During periods of high intensity exercise, fat cannot supply adenosine triphosphate (ATP) quickly enough to be used as a fuel source. Therefore, adequate carbohydrate stores become paramount for peak athletic performance.

During early stages of exercise, muscle glycogen is the major source of carbohydrate used for exercising muscle. As activity progresses from low to high intensity, the liver increases its release of glucose to fuel the muscle. Blood glucose can supply 30 percent of the total energy required by active muscle, but liver glycogen stores are reduced by half after 1 hour of strenuous activity and nearly gone within 2 hours. Trained muscle exhibits the ability to use less muscle glycogen and more fat during submaximal exercise. This "glycogen-sparing" effect increases endurance, beacuse the body generally has more fat stores than muscle glycogen.

Muscle glycogen also is used with low-to-moderate intensity exercise because it takes about 20 minutes for fat to be available as a fuel source. Fat can be used as a fuel source for 4 to 6 hours for low-to-moderate intensity exercise. Because most athletic events are high-intensity endeavors, muscle glycogen is the primary fuel for most sports. For athletes to maintain adequate muscle glycogen, they must have a diet that is high in carbohydrate. Without adequate carbohydrate intake, the muscle rapidly uses its available glycogen, and exercise intensity is decreased to the level allowed by the oxidation of fat. General dietary guidelines for athletes state that at least 7-8 g/kg should be taken on a daily basis. The exact amount of carbohydrate depends on the level and duration of training.

During a preexercise or precompetition meal, athletes should focus on obtaining adequate carbohydrate. A meal consumed 2 to 4 hours before competition should have 1–4 g/kg of carbohydrate to ensure adequate muscle and liver glycogen for those athletes involved in events lasting 1 hour or longer. Carbohydrate "loading" has some theoretic benefit for endurance events lasting longer than 90 minutes, such as long distance cycling and marathon running. A 6-day regimen consisting of tapered training and intake of 5 g/kg carbohydrate for the first 3 days, followed by 10 g/kg carbohydrate for the final 3 days, may boost performance. Potential adverse side effect of carbohydrate loading include excessive weight gain and stiffness.

For those events lasting longer than 1 hour, carbohydrate ingestion during the event has been shown to improve performance. For continuous events, such as a running race, the most practical way to obtain carbohydrate is with a sports drink containing 5%–8% carbohydrate. Consider high carbohydrate snacks or meals for events lasting significantly longer or in situations where several events are held on the same day.

Replacement of carbohydrate after exhaustive exercise or training can help minimise fatigue and may play a role in reducing the likelihood of "overtraining syndrome". Within 30 minutes after exhaustive exercise, 1.5 g/kg carbohydrate should be consumed to speed muscle glycogen resynthesis. High carbohydrate fluids, such as soft drinks and fruit juices, can be used for this purpose. An additional 1.5 g/kg of carbohydrate should then be consumed within 2 hours. It is also advisable that some protein be consumed with the carbohydrate because this can speed muscle glycogen recovery. Even with proper dietary intake, it takes at least 24 hours to replenish muscle glycogen after prolonged exercise. Most athletes typically require 1 to 2 days rest coupled with high-carbohydrate intake to replenish their muscle glycogen.

Fat

Although the average American consumes nearly 40% of total calories as fat, dietary fat should constitute no more than 30% of total calories. This is especially true for athletes who are dependent on carbohydrate as a main source for muscle glycogen. However, significant reductions in dietary fat can impair performance for endurance athletes. Fat is used as fuel by exercising muscle when carbohydrate stores are depleted. In addition, extremely low-fat diets may not be able to provide adequate calories or carbohydrate, especially during periods of intense training or in preparation for an endurance event.

Also, the fat-soluble vitamins A, D, E, and K are taken through diet, as are some essential fatty acids. Some studies have shown that on a diet consisting of less than 20% fat, the expected increase in testosterone levels seen after resistance training are blunted. Therefore, some dietary fat is needed to maintain hormone synthesis and to avoid vitamin deficiencies. During low-to-moderate intensity exercise, fat is used as a significant fuel source. Hormones such as norepinephrine and glucagon stimulate lipolysis and mobilisation of free fatty acids.

When exercise becomes intense, however, release of these free fatty acids does not keep up with the muscles' demand, and there is a shift to use of muscle glycogen as fuel. Regular aerobic exercise greatly increases the body's ability to use fat as a fuel source. Chronic exercise increases the proliferation of capillaries in trained muscle, increases the size and number of mitochondria, and facilitates the rate of lypolysis within fat cells. The fat stores themselves within endurance-trained muscle are also increased. Hormones such as norepinephrine and glucogon are released during exercise, which stimulates lipolysis.

Endurance athletes are able to exercise at a higher level of submaximal exercise due to this adaptive response. Despite this training adaptation, near-maximal sustained effort requires the presence of adequate muscle glycogen or circulating blood glucose. Higher-fat diets typically do not increase performance in endurance events for this reason.

Protein

Although the recommended daily allowance of protein for the general population is 0.8 g/kg/day, the average American diet provides far more than this (1.4 g/kg/day). A popular belief among athletes, especially those involved in static exercise such as weight training, is that a large amount of protein needs to be consumed to counteract the muscle "breakdown" resulting from training. In fact, a large market of dietary supplements has been developed on this basis. However, whereas the recommended daily allowance for athletes is, in fact, higher than for nonathletes (between 0.9 and 1.9 g/kg/day), the increased requirement is relatively minimal.

Studies based on strict nitrogen balance suggest that 1.2 g/kg/day is adequate for endurance athletes, for instance, whereas those athletes involved in resistance training, such as weightlifters and bodybuilders, may require up to 1.7 g/kg/day of protein. Physicians should make athletes aware that increasing protein intake beyond these levels does not result in additional increase in lean tissue, because there is a limit to the rate at which protein tissue can be accrued. Protein itself may be used as an energy source.

When carbohydrate stores are depleted, muscle protein may supply 5%–10% of the fuel used for energy. Therefore, physicians should advise those individuals who desire additional muscle mass that a well-balanced diet should be maintained; otherwise, protein may be used as an energy source during training, negating the effects of increased protein intake.

Vitamins and Minerals

Micronutrients play an important role in many metabolic pathways, such as protein and bone synthesis, hemoglobin synthesis, and immune function. Exercise may place a stress on these systems and therefore increase the demand for these micronutrients. This demand is generally small, and vitamin and mineral supplementation is typically not needed in well-nourished athletes. Athletes at risk for these nutrient deficiencies are those who restrict caloric intake in an effort to alter body habitus or compete at a certain weight. Additionally, those athletes who engage in "fad" diets may be at risk of micronutrient deficiencies.

B-complex vitamins have several functions related to exercise. Thiamin, riboflavin, vitamin B6, niacin, pantothenic acid, and biotin play a role as conenzymes in the catabolism of carbohydrate, protein, and fat. Additionally, vitamin B_{12} and folate are involved in the synthesis of hemoglobin and protein. Some data suggest that regular exercise may slightly increase the need for these nutrients, but these needs can generally be met with the increased dietary volume seen in most athletes. No studies suggest that supplemental B-complex vitamins improve athletic performance.

Vitamin D plays a role in calcium homeostasis. The main sources of vitamin D are fortified foods and the intrinsic production of the vitamin itself through exposure to ultraviolet light. Athletes at risk for vitamin D deficiencies are those who restrict dietary intake of fortified foods such as milk and those who lack exposure to UV radiation (for example, figure skaters). These athletes may benefit from vitamin D supplementation, not as a performance enhancer, but for overall health reasons.

Calcium is important for maintaining bone mineral density and blood calcium levels. Studies have shown that female athletes, in particular, are at risk for inadequate calcium intake. This is generally seen in sports where body habitus may be viewed as important (for example, figure skating and gymnastics). Because maximum bone density is not achieved until the age of 30 to 35, calcium supplementation should be considered for at risk athletes to assure that adequate bone mineral density is attained and maintained. The Nation Institutes of Health recommend that female athletes ingest between

1,000–1,500 mg of calcium per day, depending on menstrual status. Amenorrheic females should have more calcium in their diet than those who are not.

Iron deficiency is the most common type of nutrient deficiency seen in athletes. In theory, exercise may increase the demand for iron. Iron may be lost from sweat or from the loss of hemoglobin in urine as a result of intravascular hemolysis. Occult GI bleeding, sometimes seen in long-distance runners, may also cause iron loss. Additionally, improper diets that generally avoid meat, fish, and poultry greatly contribute to iron deficiencies. Vegetarian diets also place athletes at risk for iron deficiency because these diets have poor iron bioavailability. Early iron depletion generally does not effect athletic performance; however, if the condition is left untreated and progresses to iron deficiency anemia, performance will decrease dramatically.

Many athletes exhibit transient decreases in hemoglobin and hematocrit during the early stages of training. These changes generally are the result of increases in plasma volume and therefore represent a "dilutional" anemia. As training progresses, typically hemoglobin and hematocrit will return to baseline. Measuring serum ferritin concentrations is the best way to accurately measure iron stores. In mild iron deficiency, serum iron levels may be normal but the deficiency is evident by the low serum ferritin.

Studies have shown that in competitive skaters, serum ferritin concentrations may be reduced by one half. Decreases in circulating iron, as measured by serum iron concentration, typically signal significant iron deficiency. These deficiencies may take months to correct, and it is therefore better to begin nutritional intervention before actual deficiencies develop. Such interventions include, for example, education of at-risk athletes, such as those involved in endurance sports and in sports like gymnastics where "body image" may be an issue.

Overall, the frequency of iron deficiency in female athletes is no different than in the general female population. It is on this basis that iron supplements generally are not recommended for all athletes. Even with mild iron deficiency, supplementation may not improve performance. Additionally, the indiscriminate use of iron supplementation may cause iron levels to increase to toxic levels; this is especially true for the 1.5 million Americans who are genetically predisposed to hemochromatosis.

Zinc is another trace mineral needed for energy production. Regular exercise may increase the need for dietary zinc. Some studies have shown a significant loss of zinc in the urine after exercise. Some zinc also is lost in sweat. Athletes who avoid animal products may not have sufficient zinc in their diets, so these individuals should be counseled on the importance of alternative sources of zinc, such as whole grains or wheat germ.

Bibliography

Burgeson CR, Wechsler H, Brener ND, et al., "Physical education and activity: results from the school health policies and programs study 2000", *J Sch Health.* 2001.

Dwyer, T. et al., "Relation of Academic Performance to Physical Activity and Fitness in Children." *Pediatric Exercise Science,* 2001.

Fenton, Jennifer, Bryna Kopelow and Tammy Lawrence, "On the Move: Increasing the Participation of Girls and Young Women in Recreational Sport and Physical Activity", Ottawa, ON: Canadian Association for the Advancement of Women and Sport and Physical Activity, 2000.

Gortmaker SL, Peterson K, Wiecha J, et al. "Reducing obesity via a school-based interdisciplinary intervention among youth: Planet Health", *Arch Pediatr. Adolesc Med.* 1999.

Grunbaum JA, Kann L, Kinchen SA, et al., "Youth risk behavior surveillance - United States", 2001. *In Surveillance Summaries,* June 28, 2002. MMWR. 2002

Jaffee, Lynn and Peggy Wu, "After-School Activities and Self-Esteem in Adolescent Girls." *Melpomene Journal,* 1996.

Jamner MS, Spruijt-Metz D, Bassin S, et al, "A controlled evaluation of a school-based intervention to promote physical activity among sedentary adolescent females: project FAB", J Adol Health. 2004.

Keays, J., "The Effects of Regular (Moderate to Vigorous) Physical Activity in the Schools Setting on Student's Health, Fitness, Cognition, Psychological Development, Academic Performance and Classroom Behaviour", North York, ON: North York Community Health Promotion Research Unit, 1993.

Kerr, Gretchen A. "The Role of Sport in Preparing Youth for Adulthood." In Burt Galaway and Joe Hudson (eds.), Youth in Transition: Perspectives on Research and Policy, Toronto, ON: Thompson Educational Publishing Inc., 1996.

Lumpkin, Angela, "Physical Education and Sport: A Contemporary Introduction", 3rd edition. St. Louis: Mosby, 1994.

Neumark-Sztainer D, Martin SL, Story M., "School-based programs for obesity prevention: what do adolescents recommend?" *Am J Health Promot.* 2000.

________________ , Story M., "Recommendations from overweight youth regarding school-based weight control programs", *J Sch Health.* 1997.

Reid, Colleen, Lesley Dyck, Heather McKay and Wendy Frisby, "The Health Benefits of Physical Activity for Girls and Women", Vancouver, BC: British Columbia Centre of Excellence for Women's Health; 2000.

Shephard, Roy J. "Curricular Physical Activity and Academic Performance." *Pediatric Exercise Science,* 1997.

Index